LIFE
FORCE

Also by Jean Houston

THE SEARCH FOR THE BELOVED
THE POSSIBLE HUMAN
GODSEED
THE HERO AND THE GODDESS
A FEMININE MYTH OF CREATION
(with Diane Vandenberg)

Co-authored with Robert Masters

MIND GAMES
LISTENING TO THE BODY

LIFE FORCE

The Psycho-Historical Recovery of the Self

JEAN HOUSTON

*This publication made possible with
the assistance of the Kern Foundation*

QUEST BOOKS
The Theosophical Publishing House
Wheaton, Ill. U.S.A.
Madras, India/London, England

The Theosophical Publishing House
P.O. Box 270
Wheaton, IL 60189-0270

A publication of the Theosophical Publishing House,
a department of the Theosophical Society in America.

Library of Congress Cataloging-in-Publication Data

Houston, Jean
    Life Force : the psycho-historical recovery of the self /
Jean Houston
        p. cm.
    ISBN 0-8356-0687-2 (pbk.) : $14.00
    1. Self-actualization (Psychology)—Problems, exercises, etc.
2. Consciousness—Problems, exercises, etc.   3. Group relations
training.   4. Psychohistory.   I. Title.
BF637.S4H675   1993
158—dc20   92-50567
                                                                    CIP

Printed in the United States of America
by Versa Press

9 8 7 6 5 4 3 2 1 * 93 94 95 96 97 98 99

This edition is printed on acid-free paper that meets the
American National Standards Institute Z39.48 Standard

CONTENTS

CONTENTS

ACKNOWLEDGMENTS

The exercises and experiences described in this book were created and tested by me during the course of experimental research done at the Foundation for Mind Research and further tested in some of my workshops and seminars. However, a few of the exercises included were suggested by the work of Frederick Leboyer, Gay Gaer Luce, and Brugh Joy.

I would like to express my gratitude to the many participants of my Dromenon and New Ways of Being seminars who entered so fully into the psycho-historical journey and brought back the rich and detailed traveler's tales with which to further map the topography of consciousness.

Special thanks are due to Arthur and Prue Ceppos, the publishers of *The Five Ages of Man,* who first introduced me to Gerald Heard and his associate and collaborator Jay Michael Barrie.

Susan Graumann of the Foundation for Mind Research did yeoman service in assisting me to verbalize the psycho-historical process as well as in typing the manuscript.

Catherine Riley brought her remarkable literary skills as well as a profound understanding of the nature and potentials of consciousness research to the editing of the first edition of *Life Force.* I was similarly blessed for this second edition in the skilled guidance of my Quest editor, Brenda Rosen. Ms. Rosen is an editor that every author dreams of, for she has the transcendent ability to enter into the mind and thought of the writer, and guide them to fruition.

I am very grateful to John Cody for writing a wonderful portrait of the life and work of Gerald Heard for this edition. Mr. Cody understands the importance and depth of Heard's work better than anyone alive today and his insights add much to the themes and understandings of *Life Force*.

And then there is my husband, Robert Masters—who made me do it.

PREFACE TO THE NEW EDITION

It is with pleasure that I welcome the publication of the new Quest Books edition of *Life Force*. In the years since this book's initial publication in 1980, I have been able to experience and work with many cultures the world over, some of which still retain features which I describe in this book. Thus through the auspices of the Institute for Cultural Affairs, UNICEF, and other international agencies, I have studied and lived with aboriginal peoples in their native habitat, worked with cultures that have scarcely changed form since the time of Christ as well as with societies that are still "medieval" in style and content, and have given many seminars and trainings in human development and cultural growth in so-called "first and second world" societies. These experiences have taught me that we are truly in a time of harvest of the world's cultures and the planet's history. It is as if every kind of society that has ever existed can be seen today, from the few remaining examples of paleolithic stone-age people deeply attuned to the rhythms of nature and their own inner spirit, to high-tech societies that are themselves collapsing into inwardness.

With the entire spectrum of historical social development at hand and with the present move towards planetization described in the last chapter of this book now much more a reality than it was a decade ago, I discover that the world is set for a Whole-system transition. This transition is one in which all cultures, regardless of where they are socially or economically, have something of supreme value to offer to the whole. Indeed, it would be almost impossible to speak now of any one culture being "superior" to another or even "more developed" than another. For example, the stage of the historical present which I describe as that of the Full Individual and First Maturity, for all its technique and objective mastery, is sadly lacking in the depth of spiritual awareness and psychological relationship found in aboriginal societies belonging to the earlier stages of historical development. Further, some of these earlier societies that still endure have continued to develop over the millennia until now they are immensely brilliant and luminous versions of themselves, or were, before the tragic intervention of colonialism. As Johann Sebastian Bach took the old-fashioned music of the Baroque era and brought it to a genius and fulfillment never realized while it still ruled the musical world, so these ancient peoples have plumbed their own inner worlds, creating depths of symbol and meaning beyond our understanding, while maintaining an outer existence that looks much the same as it must have looked ten thousand years ago.

Thus I want to assure the reader that there are many modes of development, some of which have nothing to do with "progress" or linear stages of movement towards economic and technological mastery, but which are focused instead on the deepening of the processes of a particular culture and its reality over long periods of time. It is these cultures of depth which have much to teach us concerning different and more humane styles of learning, being, having, doing. If the genius of so many cultures could indeed be brought together, as I believe is now happening, then the crisis of present social breakdown and psychological and moral disorder can be transformed in the creative symbiosis of the coming world civilization, allowing the findings of each culture to seed the others, while preserving and enhancing its individual cultural style and difference. Then, for example, the unique knowings and wisdom of the aboriginal peoples across the world could raise the immigrant inhabitants of those lands beyond their present diminished consciousness, while the colonists could honor and empower the very people whom they tried to destroy and repress.

From these firsthand cross-cultural experiences, I find that although I still hold with much of the material in this book, I am uncomfortable with the emphasis placed on the masculine view of history, or, should I say, with history seen largely as the story of men through time. Since the original edition of this book used the term *man* generically, as do many of the theorists whose work is discussed, it appeared to exclude the woman's point of view. This, of course, is true of many historical studies, since it was men for the most part who have written the histories and have excluded women's perspective, relegating the story of women's contribution to the underside of history. The women's contribution was immeasurable but hidden from the formally written pages, the ethos and sensibility of the culture often being the woman's responsibility, as it continues to be today. Lately however, there is developing a more conscious awareness of this hidden history in what is coming to be known as *her*story in contradistinction to the male-oriented *his*tory.

In the years since this book was written, an upsurge of critical scholarship has suggested that the primal cultures with their matrilineal and matrifocal structure were not just agrarian-based neolithic societies but, indeed, were highly sophisticated cultures of partnership between men and women as well as partnership with spiritual powers. As the remarkable work of Marija Gimbutas and others has shown, the culture of old Europe from about 7000 to 3500 B.C., was essentially a neolithic agrarian economy centering around the rites and worship of the Mother Goddess.[1] Although I referred to these cultures in passing in the original edition of this book, I could not give them the emphasis they deserve and thus their place in the unfolding of historical stages because the research was not then available. Now that more is becoming available, I include in this new edition some of these recent findings to supplement the stages of historical development presented in my original discussion.

These gentle matrifocal civilizations perished under the marauding bands of Indo-Aryan invaders. (*Indo-Aryan* is a generic term for the waves of invaders that conquered many peoples during this period. Specifically, these invaders were the Aryans in India; Hittites and Mittani in the Fertile Crescent; Luwians in Anatolia; Kurgans in Eastern Europe; Achaeans and later Dorians in Greece and Crete.) Warrior nomads, they not only imposed their own rigid authoritarian rule, replacing matricentric values with patriarchal ones, but also, as I indicate in my chapter on the heroic stage, inflicted an ideology and a style of divided consciousness that shattered the finely wrought symbiosis between humans, nature, culture, and spiritual realities. We see a late version of this in *The Iliad*, when the holy communicant and prophetess Cassandra is ravaged. The altar of Athena is similarly defiled. As we see later in this book, whether in Greece, in India, or in the Fertile Crescent, the patriarchal hero invader, to keep up his separateness, dreads the caress. When he gets close, it is to subdue by duel or rape.

Not that these invaders didn't adopt many of the ways and skills of the more ancient partnership cultures, as for example the Achaeans adopted much of the Minoan culture. But they did so in such a way as to tear out the feminine threads in the cultural tapestry, leaving a ragged social fabric, missing many pieces, lacking many parts.

The patriarchal suppression of the rich and complex feminine characteristics of the goddess Athena is typical of this rending of culture and consciousness. Too powerful a spiritual force to remove, she is instead pre-empted by the Achaean patriarchy to become Daddy's girl, the spirit of Zeus, born from her father's head shrieking a harrowing cry that frightens even the gods. What was in this cry, one wonders? Was it perhaps the cry of outrage of one forced to live a lie, to inhabit a projection? This is hard enough for humans; one can only imagine how devastating it must be for a god. And so, caught in the long dark night of the heroic ages of Mycenean power and might, Athena is constrained as warrior goddess and protector of the citadels of power. But one can never contain an archetype for long, and certainly not one of such antiquity and complexity. Even raging through *The Iliad*, her deeper nature is there *in potentia*. In *The Odyssey* she is clearly in transition, as all her acts attest, thus her changes, her disguises, her transformings. Her transition is not only to grow beyond the heroic image thrust upon her and to acquire again the fuller dimensions which she had in earlier times, but to become something more, a goddess who exceeds both Minoan and Mycenean visions of her, a goddess of transformation, who partners the evolutionary journey of both individuals and culture. For Athena, it is as if what had been laid there *in potentia* in Minoan culture emerges again in *The Odyssey* (circa 720 B.C.), after eight hundred years of being kept literally in the dark. There she becomes a transpersonal and transformational goddess, no longer the patron of heroic adventures, but the guiding spirit for the refining and deepening of the culture of the home place.[2]

The present rise of women to full partnership with men in the whole domain of human affairs requires an Athena-like honoring and accessing of the fullness of human experience of earlier times, and with it, the reexamination of the historical record, the record of *herstory*. Like Athena, one recovers lost passages of the past in order to redeem the unread vision of the higher dream and thus grow more confidently into the future. Throughout this new edition, therefore, I have tried to indicate something of the highs and lows of *herstory* in the evolving psycho-historical recovery of the self. However, to give *herstory* its full telling would require a whole new book, which, someday, I perhaps shall write. In reading this book then, I recommend that one remember throughout that the women were always there, engendering the developing consciousness, forcing the issues of an emergent humanity. In earlier times, they were helping tribal cultures to grow into matrifocal cultures of immense complexity and beauty. These cultures may have reached a rarely seen balance and equanimity which the "heroic" patriarchal invaders feared and destroyed. Now that the destruction of the ultimate Mother Culture, the Earth Herself, seems a possible danger, the ancient voices of partnership are once again heard, but this time in a harmonic that speaks to the emergence of a planetary culture and a partnership with the whole Earth.

Notes

1. Marija Gimbutas, *The Goddesses and Gods of Old Europe, 7000-3500 B.C.* (Berkeley and Los Angeles: University of California Press, 1982). See too the findings of James Mellaart in his work *Catal Huyuk* (New York: McGraw-Hill, 1967).
2. A fuller discussion of the pre-empting of the Goddess Athena by the patriarchy is to be found in Jean Houston, *The Hero and the Goddess: The Odyssey as Mystery and Initiation* (New York: Ballantine, 1992).

PREFACE TO THE FIRST EDITION

When I was twenty-three years old, I was asked to review a manuscript by a man of seventy-three who had spent much of his life considering issues of history, psyche, and human transformation. The man's name was Gerald Heard, and the book, *The Five Ages of Man,*[1] was the culmination of his life's work. With a palette of great subtlety and erudition, Heard joined the principles of phylogeny and ontogeny to the social and personal history of man, so effecting a psychological interpretation of history, in which history is seen as a reflection cast by the evolving consciousness of humanity. In this work Heard joined the latest scientific and psychological data to the boldest historical speculations, creating a therapeutic dialogue between inner archetypal realms and outer worlds of record.

As an added thesis, Heard proposed that man's consciousness has evolved historically in five stages, and in such a way that in each stage, consciousness became more and more divided as it progressed from a stage of pre-individual co-consciousness to total individuality and then, finally, to post-individuality. At each stage man was beset by a specific crisis—ordeal—under which he either broke down or devised a psychophysical method of transition or initiation that could enable him to go on to his next stage of consciousness. Heard even ventured to suggest therapies of initiation along the lines of the ancient mystery traditions, which he believed would help individuals in their personal ordeals of passage from one stage of their lives to another.

PREFACE TO THE FIRST EDITION

As I read the book, I felt it was a document of ideas that could have extraordinary importance in the future; but I knew that in the setting of 1963, it would be ignored by the critics (which it was) and read by only a few (which it has been). Its theses were too dramatic, too daring, too original; some of its scientific documentation was open to many alternative interpretations and could be dismissed as out of context and the product of an eccentric if ingenious mind. The psycho-technology that Heard advised as providing the impetus for an initiation of movement from one stage of life to the next was sometimes outrageous and often surreal (LSD, electrical stimulation, walking on fire). But the book as a whole had a core of truth that would not go away, and it haunted me through all the following years of my research into the nature, extension, and application of human capacities. In a curious way, Heard had brought together the speculations of the theologians, philosophers, poets, historians, and psychologists of the past who had dealt with this mighty theme. He had suggested ways in which theory could become practice and the trauma of the stages of man's cultural and personal evolution could be transmuted in present time to provide the basis for a new humanity.

When I knew him, Gerald Heard was a beautiful old gentleman of boundless curiosity, elegant playfulness, and a passion for discovery. We would walk down New York City's Madison Avenue together, and his long, poetic hands would carve ideas out of the air in front of him, his bushy eyebrows would dance arcs of questions, and he would laugh as a child might laugh when some inquiry met with a response that brought our worlds of interests together. He seemed to want to know more about the things I was studying and led me to discourse on Thucydides and Euripides and the more arcane aspects of my doctoral work in ways that illumined my mind as it had not been by my graduate school professors. I later learned that he had done the same for Aldous Huxley and Christopher Isherwood, as well as for many other innovative minds of the twentieth century. He tried to show what Gregory Bateson calls the Pattern That Connects; and, in his vision of what humanity could be, he provided the seedings of what subsequently led to the development of the best in the human potential movement as well as the psychospiritual and psychophysical growth movements of the next decades. There is little doubt in my mind that Gerald Heard was a key figure in the genesis of these movements and deserves far more attention and appreciation than he has received.

As the years went by, I became a professor of philosophy and of religion, with specialties in process philosophy and the philosophy of history. Later I pursued a doctorate in psychology and taught in that area also. Early in my graduate school years, a remarkable opportunity came my way. I was asked to join a project studying the effects of LSD on human personality. The chief investigators were physicians who thought that my education in the humanities would be helpful in identifying and guiding the mythic, archaic, cross-cultural, and symbolic themes that seemed to recur with subjects under the effects of LSD. Guiding several hundred subjects over the next few years, I was able to observe an extraordinary range of human processes. What had been abstract and elusive in my philosophical and historical studies became extremely concrete in my LSD work. In the process of taking depth-soundings of the psyche, it was as if a lifetime of witness to the spectrum of human behavior and possibilities was condensed in the experience of a few years.[2]

The research ended too quickly, in the wake of the irresponsible deportment of several researchers and the public Roman spectacle that followed. The drug was withdrawn from investigative use by the embarrassed Swiss pharmaceutical firm that manufactured it. Still, what had been glimpsed of the vast terrain of human potential could not be easily abandoned; and so in 1965, Robert Masters and I formed the Foundation for Mind Research to continue a nondrug exploration of these areas. Seeking clues to human latency in many fields—history, literature, anthropology, physiology, and brain and mind research—we began to develop many methods of evoking the enormous latent potentials of the body-mind, which too often culture and education have distorted, inhibited, or altogether blocked. As I did this research, my historical sensibilities were constantly ruffled as I realized that most people were being crippled and repressed by the prescribed potentials of nine-teenth- or early twentieth-century society. This grew into a chilling awareness of what could happen in a world in which a nineteenth-century psychology was guiding the affairs of a twentieth-century technology. Herein atavism could lead to apocalypse.

Working with hundreds of research subjects since 1965, we investigated methods with which the body can be psycho-physically rehabilitated and a physical functioning that more closely approaches the optimal can be achieved. We explored the experiential and pragmatic value of altered and expanded states of consciousness, alternative cognitive modes, new styles of learning, thinking in images, thinking kinesthetically, time distortion, and the evocation of the creative process. This work has been fertilized by a variety of techniques ancient and modern: the programming of dreams, the voluntary control of involuntary physiological states assisted by biofeedback and autogenic training, the many varieties of neurological reeduca-tion, and even the induction of religious and other peak ex-periences, as well as many other varieties of innate mental and physical capacities—all available to, but rarely used by, most human beings. Some of this work is described in detail in Chapter Five.

From these experiments emerged the evidence that "or-

PREFACE TO THE FIRST EDITION

dinary people''—given the opportunity, given education—have
the means to develop their body-minds and innate capacities
to levels of use and understanding abundantly able to deal
with the challenges of the time. They can learn to think, feel,
and know in extended and enhanced ways, gain supple and
well-coordinated bodies, become more creative, and aspire
within realistic limits to a multidimensional awareness. Once
we understand the generally unrecognized limits we impose
on ourselves by a myriad of false concepts, atavistic mind-sets,
shrunken aspirations, and irrational taboos, we become able
to achieve a larger freedom to think, to dream, to experience,
and to reinvent ourselves, so that we open up possibilities for
authentically new ways of being.

Over a dozen books, many articles, and a quarterly journal came out of this research; and, as our work became more
widely known, we were asked to create programs applying
our findings to many areas of social and institutional
change.[3] These ranged from helping to create model schools
and redesigning curriculum to teaching ''nonlearners,'' helping elderly people get back failing capacities and acquire new
ones, rehabilitating ex-prisoners, and even to creating confer-
ence-seminars in which public administrators and bureaucrats
could experience the possible human within themselves and,
from this, begin to envision what the possible society could be.

In 1975 I formed the Dromenon Center, which was named
after ancient Greek rites of growth and transformation, in
Pomona, New York, to offer workshops in this material as well
as specific training to professionals in education and the helping professions.[4] I continue to teach these; but since 1977 we
have expanded, to reach larger numbers of people through
seminar programs which have now been held in many countries of Europe, Africa, and Asia, as well as North and South
America. Several three-year programs in human capacities and
a yearly ''Mystery'' school—a ten-year-old program of spiritual

study and sacred psychology—have also grown out of this work. To date, over half a million seminar participants have joined these programs.

These institutes began as rather formal attempts to bring our scientific findings to the general public; but in the process, the spirit of the ancient Dromenon must have moved in, for now they are dancing, pulsing, often wildly funny journeys. During the day, participants go to lectures and experiential workshops designed to expand the breadth of knowledge about human capacities. But at night, celebrations of learning are raised to Dromenons, and knowledge is deepened to mythic levels. Indeed, an emphasis on myth and story began to be essential to my work since about 1980. I discovered that one could go further and deeper with human capacities development work if it was encoded in myth. This is because the Great Story inherent in many myths provides the template for transformation. However ancient, myths carry the coded matrices of the next steps in human development and evolution.

When actively engaged, a myth's Great Story leads you from the frustrations of the personal-particular to the fulfillment of the personal-universal with its broadening contexts and more inclusive formulations. You "become" Isis and Osiris; with Percival you take on the quest for the Grail; you adventure with Odysseus; you assume the passion and the pathos of Psyche; with Jesus you discover the Godseed within; you search for the Beloved of the soul with Rumi. As you engage these mythic and symbolic dramas, you take the journey of transformation by identifying with a mythic character who enlarges some aspect of yourself. Symbolic happenings then appear in undisguised relevance to your personal story, and you soon discover that these stories are your own stories. They bear the amplified pattern of certain rhythms and cadences in your own life, showing you ways of understanding

PREFACE TO THE FIRST EDITION

and deepening your life as, following the larger story in the myth, you discover ways to go beyond your previous limitation.[5] Although a mythic treatment is not as explicit in *Life Force* as it is in my later books, the reader will discover that history is treated in a mythic and imaginative way, as are the stages of human development. One becomes Everyman and Everywoman in the course of experiencing the stages described, living out a symbolic drama as vast and potent as any mythic epic in story or literature.

Also, as mentioned in the preface to the new edition, I now work with development agencies in many countries, helping them to preserve and deepen their cultures and rediscover the genius and coded power of their great myths for both personal and social transformation. And of course, in all of this work, the inevitable thing happened: I started out to teach others, but I soon found that the direction was being reversed, and more and more, the individuals and cultures I worked with began to teach me—about how human potentials, once broadened and deepened, can be put to use in improving the daily life of the planet. Physicians and psychiatrists have discovered ways to help their patients on deeper levels. Teachers and school superintendents have begun to reseed their curricula with multimodal ways of knowing. Gerontologists and community workers are developing the most sensitive and evocative methods of enhancing the lives of the elderly. Artists and writers are exploring new depths of myth and creativity. Most important of all, teaching-learning communities based on this work have sprung up not only in many parts of the Americas but throughout the world. These problem-solving, mutually empowering communities are establishing networks through which the members share experiences of deepening, encouragement, growth, and transformation, for themselves, their communities, and—eventually—their planet.

PREFACE TO THE FIRST EDITION

Notes

1. Gerald Heard, *The Five Ages of Man* (New York: Julian Press, 1963).
2. Here, for example, is a partial listing of the phenomena my husband Robert Masters and I observed during the course of this research. It is drawn from our book *The Varieties of Psychedelic Experience* (New York: Holt, Rinehart and Winston, 1966; paperback edition, New York: Delta, 1967):

   Changes in visual, auditory, tactile, olfactory, gustatory, and kinesthetic perception; changes in experiencing time and space; changes in the rate and content of thought; body image changes; hallucinations; vivid images—eidetic images—seen with the eyes closed; greatly heightened awareness of color; abrupt and frequent mood and affect changes; heightened suggestibility; enhanced recall or memory; depersonalization and ego dissolution; dual, multiple, and fragmentized consciousness; seeming awareness of internal organs and processes of the body; upsurge of unconscious materials; enhanced awareness of linguistic nuances; increased sensitivity to nonverbal cues; sense of capacity to communicate much better by nonverbal means, sometimes including the telepathic; feelings of empathy; regression and "primitivization"; apparently heightened capacity for concentration; magnification of character traits and psychodynamic processes; an apparent nakedness of psychodynamic process that makes evident the interaction of ideation, emotion, and perception with one another and with inferred unconscious processes; concern with philosophical, cosmological, and religious questions; and, in general, apprehension of a world that has slipped the chains of normal categorical ordering, leading to an intensified interest in self and world and also to a range of responses moving from extremes of anxiety to extremes of pleasure.

   Gerald Heard was also extremely interested in the effects of LSD and guided many sessions, among them, a number with Aldous Huxley. These experiences and others led Huxley to write his famous works on psychedelic sensibility, *The Doors of Perception* and *Heaven and Hell*.
3. See, for example, Masters and Houston, *Mind Games* (New York: Delta, 1973) and *Listening to the Body* (New York: Delacorte, 1978). See also my book, *The Possible Human* (Los Angeles: J. P. Tarcher, Inc., 1982).
4. Again, I owe a considerable debt to Gerald Heard, for it was under the name of H. F. Heard that he published a remarkable fictional story "Dromenon," the inspiration of which provided me with the naming of my own first center. In the story an archaeologist encounters a therapy in stone, a mystical transformation of body, mind, and spirit,

by following the pathways (dromena) inscribed on the floors and walls of a medieval English cathedral. The story can be found in H. F. Heard, *The Great Fog: Weird Tales of Terror and Detection* (New York: Vanguard Press, 1944). An example of a dromenon is found on p. 1. This is the famous dromenon found on the floor of Chartres Cathedral. I often use it in my seminars by inscribing it on the floor and having the participants walk its pathways, always to great effect.

5. My work on myth is to be found in my books *The Search for the Beloved: Journeys in Sacred Psychology* (Los Angeles: J. P. Tarcher, Inc., 1987); *Godseed: The Journey of Christ* (Wheaton, Illinois: Quest Books, 1992); and *The Hero And the Goddess: The Odyssey as Mystery and Initiation* (New York: Ballantine Books, 1992).

HOW TO USE THIS BOOK

This book is intended to enable groups of people to create shared experiences as co-voyagers in the psycho-historical journey. Together you will embark on five mysteries, here called Dromenons, and the Dromenon group that meets together to experience these must devote careful attention to the preparation and conducting of these sessions. Included also are recommendations for those who will be journeying alone. The notes that follow are offered as guidelines for these Dromenon sessions. They are similar to preparatory notes that I offer in some of my other books dealing with transformational journeys.

The Nature of the Group

As the import of these experiences can be trivial or profound, it is necessary that the intention of the group and of its members be clear from the beginning. The group should consist only of those who freely choose to participate and who feel well motivated to do so. The community that composes the members of the group may take any form: family, friends, colleagues, students, clients, parishioners, and so forth. In general, the experiences should be undertaken by intelligent, resourceful people who are mature enough to have had sufficient life experience to appreciate the historical and psychological scope of the human drama they will be required to go through. Children or young teenagers will usually not have the needed maturity and understanding to make an adequate response to the experiences, though they can participate in some of the exercises (like *The Castle of Constraints* or *Mea Machina, Mea Mandala*)—but preferably in situations apart from the actual Dromenon journey. (Most of the exercises, for that matter, can be performed separately by individuals or groups and will be found to have their own efficacy. They will not, however, have the cumulative developmental effect of the journey described in these pages.)

Working in groups helps to eradicate one of the worst tyrannies that afflicts Homo sapiens—the tyranny of the dominant perception. This perception is reflected in such smug statements as "If it's good enough for me, it's good enough for you" and "Why can't you respond like everyone else does?"

The participants in the Dromenon journey stimulate, support, and evoke each other. In their diverse reactions, they prime a diversity of responses within and between themselves. While consensus and commonalities are important, differences are equally enriching. "Thank God," we say to ourselves, "I need not be limited to my own experience but may share in yours." As we recognize the enormous variation and richness of experience in others, we drop simplistic judgments and projections and stand in awe before the wild abundance of human variation.

By pursuing the Dromenon adventure as part of a group, we also bypass one of the most insidious of human failings—the potential for sloth. Self-discipline and good intentions have a way of evaporating without some consistent external commitment. The practices and procedures in this book challenge deeply entrenched patterns of mind, body, and psyche; for this reason, we need allies to steady us up the slope of thought and to help us climb to new ways of being. Resistance to change is natural, sometimes even healthy. One of the few ways to overcome it when necessary, however, is through regular participation in the mutually helpful, empowering, and celebrating company of co-journeyers. This is why those who are voyaging alone need to tell at least one person close to them of their undertaking.

The group of co-voyagers should probably number not less than five nor more than twenty-five, although I have conducted groups of over one hundred and fifty for the entire process. There should also be an odd number of participants, since some of the experiences are performed by couples, while one member of the group is acting as Guide.

At its initial meeting the group should assign members to take responsibility for obtaining and preparing the setting or settings (indoors or out-) for each of the Dromenons. This includes providing appropriate music and record, tape, or CD players, art supplies, musical instruments, paper, drawing and other art materials, as well as bringing food for closing celebrations after each Dromenon. Special attention must be taken that during the sessions there be no intruders—wandering dogs, curious children, ringing telephones. The setting is to be treated as sacred space.

As the group meetings are built around a particular stage of the psycho-historical experience, it is necessary that prior to each meeting, every member of the group read the relevant material from this book. The text should be read in such a way that the reader dialogues with it, taking note of images and ideas that emerge so that these may feed the group discussion. The group discussion of this material should in most cases be the subject of the first part of the meeting, so as to explore the meaning of its content in the lives and understanding of the members. The purpose of the text is only to evoke a depth sensibility of historical and personal patterns, not to describe and dissect times past. Another part of the discussion session (which can be led by a member of the group or by the Guide) might be devoted to a sharing of reflections concerning the changing patterns of viewpoint and awareness that members have observed in themselves since the last meeting. Many have found it extremely valuable to keep a journal of their journey, often decorating the cover of their journals with images or drawings that evokes both the spirit and content of their journey.

After the discussion has ended, there should be a break of at least fifteen minutes before the group comes back together to share the Dromenon experiences of the particular stage of the journey that they have reached. A good way to do this is to leave the space in which the discussion was held and reenter it after a while as sacred space—silently, with full awareness of a commitment to making the journey meaningful. Each member of the group will spend some time centering herself and bringing her consciousness to an awareness of the experiences she is about to undertake. Each should make a kind of internal commitment to take responsibility for herself, and at the same time, be respectful to the needs of others and of the group as a whole.

The Guide

Ideally the Guide is a person who has already made the psycho-historical journey with another group, though this need not be the case. At the initial preparatory meeting the group will decide on who the Guide or Guides will be and how they will function. The Guide can be the same for all sessions, or the role can rotate. Dromenon groups must avoid the error: Guide equals Leader. The role of the Guide is to be understood by everyone as that of one who assists, one who enables. As enabler, the Guide serves the needs of the Dromenon voyage and of the co-voyagers.

The person who is to be Guide will prepare for the session by reading the historical and psychological material with great care and, wherever possible, will do extra reading (some of which is described in the bibliography). Also, prior to each Dromenon the Guide will ready herself for the task by a period of relaxation, deep breathing, and meditation. This meditation should be used by the Guide especially to become conscious of, and to eliminate, ego hungers and power drives, as well as any other improper attitudes or tendencies that would be exploitive or manipulative of the Dromenon voyagers. Each Guide will determine his or her own needs, and prepare the meditations accordingly. It must be remembered that the role of the Guide is a most ancient one, which found one of its most accomplished forms in the hierophants of the ancient Greek mysteries. In this tradition the Guide is the midwife of souls, the evocateur of growth and transformation. In becoming Guide, then, one knows oneself to be part of a continuity stretching across millennia. It is a role of the greatest challenge and responsibility, and therefore one invests it with High Self.

The Guide needs to have the capacity to be at once part of the experience and observer of the voyage of the travelers. She, or he, must be able to judge sensitively the amount of time needed for each part of the journey and to use the experiences flexibly. The experiences described are not cast in stone and would probably gain much from the suggestions and additions of the group and the Guide.

The Guide will have read the Dromenon materials aloud several times to herself before the group meeting, sensing as she does so the nature of the journey and allowing her voice and timing to reflect that experience. The voice must not be intrusive, lugubrious, or overly dramatic but must remain clear and in relation to the experience. Wherever music is part of the experience, the Guide must rehearse her part, so as to carefully integrate the timing of the reading and the music. (This is especially true in *The Castle of Constraints.*)

The Guide will always have one or more ''soul catchers'' present. These are members of the group selected because of their ability to be sensitive to the needs of others. Thus, even while going through the experience themselves, they will have a part of their consciousness available to help others should this be required. It must be stated, however, that part of helping others may be in knowing when to let someone alone and not intrude unnecessarily on his or her experience. The soul catcher will also have the task of guiding the Guide through the experience shortly after the group journey has ended, if the Guide so desires.

Time and Space and the Places in Between

The entire Dromenon with its five stages can be performed over different time periods—even over the period of a very long day, or a weekend, although some have found this too compacted and intense. Others, however, have found this condensed sequence extremely powerful for the immediate continuity it provides for all stages in the psycho-historical process.

A better procedure is probably meeting once a week for seven weeks. The first meeting is devoted, as I have described, to preparation—assigning responsibilities and choosing the Guide or Guides. This is followed by the five weeks of the Dromenon journey. And in a seventh meeting the co-voyagers reflect together on the journey as a whole and on the understandings they have gained. This pattern of seven meetings can also be held over seven consecutive days.

It is extremely important that each member of the group make a firm commitment to the other members to be on time and to see the entire journey through to its completion. To leave it suddenly at the stage of adolescence or at the era of human development circa 1000 B.C. is to open oneself to further fissures and frustrations in the ecology of the self. Completed, however, the process has proved to be a most potent and revealing *therapy*, providing the orchestral dynamics with which to integrate the structures of one's being with the energy and genius of the human past. What emerges is the possible human as a living reality, ready and willing to enter into the next spiral of human development.

If You Are Journeying Alone

If you are taking the Dromenon journey by yourself, you need to make a serious commitment to engage and complete all of the stages of this psycho-historical recovery of the self. Then, perform whatever are your most effective modes or rituals of preparation. Buy a new notebook for journaling. Make sure you have art materials for drawing, pens and pencils for writing. Create a very special sacred space where you will work; it is best if this space has a boundary of some kind, so that you cross a threshold to enter it. This prevents the energies of everyday life from bleeding through and diverting your attention.

Make sure there is music available for you there—your favorites as well as some of the kinds of music suggested throughout this book. The musical selections listed at the end of the book are meant only as suggestions for the types of music you might want to use.

You may wish to decorate the front of your journal with appropriate images. If it seems helpful, you might even decorate your space and create some kind of costume or robe to wear for your sessions.

Set specific times for doing this work. As journeying solo

can be more challenging than journeying with a group, it is probably not advisable to attempt to complete the stages of this journey during the course of a long day or even a weekend (although some have been known to have done this successfully). If you decide to do this work on a weekly basis, make an agreement with yourself about times; try not to let more than a week go by between sessions. Dedicate the interval between sessions to complete immersion within the psychohistorical stage through which you are journeying.

Write out a contract with yourself to embark upon this journey through history and human development and to complete it. Set the time span that you allow yourself for the entire journey. Sign and date the contract. You might even wish to set a forfeit should you not comply with the terms of the contract. This could be giving up for a time special foods or entertainments that you enjoy. Or, more constructively, giving a service to friends or community.

Tell someone who cares about you and will support your inner work that you're making a transformational journey of the soul. Ask if you may call upon this person occasionally for assistance, for a second opinion, or for a shoulder to lean on. Have this friend witness and sign the contract you have made.

In my experience it has proven to be good practice to work with at least one other person in making this journey. Another voice, another life story, a companion for the road helps train us in that most valuable of human skills—working and playing and growing together with mutual and equal honor. I also realize that, for many people, this is not easy or practicable. But, as least, tell someone what you're doing and invite her or him to participate in the process, to see that you keep your side of the bargain and assume fully the psycho-historical recovery of the self.

The most important thing that you have to do in voyaging

solo is to pre-record the scripts for the Guide on tape. This will give you greater freedom and spontaneity in doing the exercises. A cautionary note here. Please do not use an overly dramatic or peculiar voice when you make the tapes, or you'll end up not trusting the person on the tape! Also, be sure to leave yourself pauses of sufficient length wherever they're called for so that you have enough time to do the exercises properly. If you prefer not to make your own tapes, I have made a set of tapes of the exercises and processes in this book, which are available from the publisher at a moderate cost.

Where processes require working with other people, there are suggestions at appropriate places in the text for solo journeyers. But, as a general rule, using your imagination is key. Wherever a partner or partners are needed, you can always imagine or visualize them being present and then enact the interaction and/or dialogue with them by writing in your journal. In fact, try to create an ongoing process of dialogue, interchange, and persuasion by devising new ways of working with your journal. It is a marvelous thing to experience yourself as all the stages in history and human development. Record the images and feelings that will inevitably come of this journey. If you can, create art with your learning and your feelings. Most especially, write poetry. But also draw and paint, work in clay and other materials. It makes no difference whether you think you have no special gift for writing or for painting—just let your imagination loose. Free your hand to move as it wants, directed by your inner knowing and seeing. You may be surprised and pleased with the results.

Let Us Begin the Journey

Thus warned and primed, let us begin. We are about to take a depth experiential look at a field theory of human psychosocial development. This will be an exploration in pro-lepsis: To gain the future, one casts back into and recovers the past.

In ancient days the gods of the spring Dromenon called us forth from our slumbers. Now it is something deeper and wider, more mysterious and transformative. The present Dromenon is evolution entering into time, calling us to awaken to a citizenship in a universe larger than our aspirations and richer and more complex than all our dreams. It is the call of the larger cycle, the dance of the larger life—or, as Christopher Fry put it in *A Sleep of Prisoners:*

> The human heart can go to the lengths of God.
> Dark and cold we may be, but this
> Is no winter now. The frozen misery
> Of centuries breaks, cracks, begins to move,
> The thunder is the thunder of the floes,
> The thaw, the flood, the upstart Spring.
> Thank God our time is now when wrong
> Comes up to face us everywhere,
> Never to leave us till we take
> The longest stride of soul men ever took.
> Affairs are now soul size
> The enterprise
> Is exploration into God.
> What are you making for? It takes
> So many thousand years to wake,
> But will you wake for pity's sake?[1]

Notes

1. Christopher Fry, *A Sleep of Prisoners* (New York: Oxford University Press, 1951).

INTRODUCTION:
THE NEW DROMENON

So, what is a Dromenon?

It is a rhythm of awakening, a root pulse that carries with it the codings of all our becomings. It is a yeasting in the searching soul. It is the bell that tolls in the back of our minds, calling us to remembrance of where we came from. It is evolution entering into time. It is the insistence that bursts up from the mud. It is the dance in which one is danced, the song in which one is sung. It is the doing of the Done.

Sometimes it looks like this:

The Labyrinth pattern of the floorstones of Chartres.

INTRODUCTION: THE NEW DROMENON

Or this:

Pima Indian basket.

Or even this:

Whirlpool galaxy.

INTRODUCTION: THE NEW DROMENON

Again, what is a Dromenon? What are its historical roots?
Jane Harrison in *Ancient Art and Ritual* suggests that it is
"a pattern of dynamic expression in which the performers express something larger than themselves, beyond their powers
of speech to express, and a therapeutic rhythm in which they
find release and fulfillment."[1] In her masterly work *Themis*,
a study of the social origins of religion and ritual in ancient
Greece, Harrison stresses the seasonal activity of the Dromenon, especially the spring Dromenon in which there occurred
a performance by the *Kouretes* (young male initiates) of a magical dance that had the effect of commemorating and induc-
ing a new birth of the land, the social order, and the psyche.
It was also an initiation, a second birth into a larger order,
wherein one was relieved of the tyranny of the personal and,
in the ecstasy of the dance, one's heart became congrega-
tionalized. For the ancients the enactment of the Dromenon
extended the boundaries of the self so that it became part of
the larger social order. In the modern Dromenon, one becomes
part of an even larger eco-system, a larger ecology of Being.
Ancient or modern, the Dromenon is a movement into a larger
reality, an initiation that leads to a union or continuity with
powers and principalities beyond one's little local self.

At the heart of the ancient Dromenon is the principle of
conflict, the conflict that comes of the dying of the old year
and the old self and the birth of the new year and the new
self. From the spring Dromenon, with its intent of magically
evoking the new year, there arose two of the main forms of
Greek life and civilization, each of which had conflict or contest at its core: the *agon* or athletic contest, and that other contest significantly bearing the same name, the *agon* of the drama,
in which we find a tragic split that can be resolved only by
a new order of reality. Today the dramatic agon is played out
against the necessity of a new spring and a new vision of what
it means to be human. Millennia-old constructs of society,

belief, and behavior are eroding. The usual formulas yield stop-gap solutions which inevitably create more problems. Older sureties are forgotten as humankind, ripped by urban sprawl and technological prostheses from its biorhythmic roots in nature, loses those primordial moorings which tied it to the moral flow of the universe. If humanity is to survive, I believe it must undergo the agony of the Dromenon—the dancing, stretching, dying, and re-membering of itself beyond its conditioned social and cultural limitations.

Whereas the ancient Greek Dromenon played out a yearly cycle of the eternal return of god, nature, community, and psyche, the present Dromenon belongs to a larger cycle in which we find ourselves in one of those rare pivotal points in human history, leaping beyond the old Adam into a new arena of humanness and awareness. Perhaps a similar moment occurred when our ancestors ceased to depend on the nomadic meanderings of the hunt for sustenance and settled into village agriculture, preparing the way for the coming of civilization.

The present Dromenon begins, as did the earlier one, in a state of conflict and defeat. It is not just the old year that is dying; it is the old time. For we are all living (as of this writing) in the closing time of the twentieth century, with the end of the millennium approaching as a major construct in our lives. And the end of the millennium warrants far more serious concern and challenge than do the fears and fancies that accrue around the fin de siecle.

The age in which we live is shivering amidst the tremors of ontological breakdown. It's all shifting: the moral mandates; the structural givens; the standard-brand governments, religions, economics; the very consensual reality is breaking down, that underlying fabric of life and process by which we organized our reality and thought we knew who and why and where we were. The world by which we understood ourselves—a

4

world that began in its essential mandates several thousand years ago with certain premises about humanity, God, reality, and the moral and metaphysical order, and which in terms of our existential lives, began about three hundred years ago with the scientific revolution—is a world that no longer works. It is a world whose lease has run out, whose paradigms are eroding, and which no longer provides us with the means and reference points by which we can understand ourselves. We are not unlike the cartoon cat who runs off the cliff and keeps on running, treading air over the abyss before he discovers his predicament and says, "Oops!"

There is a lag between the end of an age and the discovery of that end. We are the children of the lag, the people of the time of parenthesis—and there is no juicier time to be alive. For the future is open in a time of parenthesis—the new age is being seeded; the new myths are beginning to appear; the new Dromenon is waiting to be danced.

A science-fiction movie script I once read deals with the discovery by the Mount Palomar astronomer of the Quasar, described in the story as the original pulse, the first Big Bang. In it was coded much of the evolution of humanity and the universe. To see it through the telescope and hear it on the radio astronomy band was to encounter and resonate to the next stages of the evolutionary program and to enter into an accelerated evolutionary process. First the astronomers, then the children, and then everybody else began to undergo transformation. Madness came to some; illumination to others. Latent humanity emerged. Mystic perspectives became commonplace realities as body, mind, and spirit worked in concert and humankind listened to the pulse of its distant coding and grew into what it really was.

I mention this story because it is typical of a new genre of myth that is emerging in our time: myths of evocation and potentiation, myths of new ways of being. We must recall the importance and power of the myth for psyche and civilization, for the myth is something that never was but is always happening—the coded DNA of the human psyche calling us to reflesh the dream that has been pushed so far away.

Be it the myth of Gilgamesh or that of the Grail, of the many god-men who have died only to rise again or even of the divine comedy of Don Quixote de la Mancha, the myth is always the stimulus, the alarm clock, the lure of becoming. It quickens the heart to its potential and prepares the ground for society's transformation.

It follows, then, that to discern the emerging new forms of culture and consciousness in this age of parenthesis, one should look to the myths and symbolic images that have begun to flower in the cultural mindscape of the past few years. What are these new archetypes that fascinate, these new myths that bypass ordinary critical consciousness and call to the deeps that lie within? What are the images of the more- or the less-than-human that rise unbeckoned in the dreams of modern men and women or their waking fantasies? What or who makes the hair stand up on the head, the toes curl, and the breath quicken? Think about it.

In ancient Greece, on the occasion of the great dramatic festivals that grew out of the rituals of the Dromenon, the cosmic probings and lofty yearnings of the mythic tragedies were more often than not preceded by Dionysian satyr plays, grotesque and ribald revels, the pop myths and lowlife liturgies dealing out images of vulgarized sex and rascally violence. These lesser and more profane myths served to prepare the heart by degrees for the powerful and soul-charging tragic myths to come.

The same may be true today. A look into present-day consciousness reveals a veritable cornucopia of satyrs, Dionysiacs, grotesques—the whole peculiar crew that serves the lesser mysteries. Some of their names? Dracula, Frankenstein's monter, Batman, the Hulk; Unidentified Flying Objects, *Star Wars*, the Starship *Enterprise*, Atlantis rising, California falling into the sea; the year 2000; the astrologers, witches, soothsayers, and swamis-of-the-month coming at you from out of the national woodwork; the entire city of Los Angeles.

On the next wave there come those musicians whose music serves not to amuse but to mythologize. The Beatles were among the first and probably the best, and after them the deluge: the Grateful Dead, Metallica, Guns and Roses, the Motley Crue, Madonna, Nirvana—many sporting primeval bearded faces and costumes fit for shamans. Lately—and right on schedule, too—the androgyne appears, still a creature of indeterminate sex, but this time electrified and amplified, a shrieking, frenetic acoustical terror, gifted with some strange Dionysian alchemy to evoke the freak in all hearers, turning ballads into orgies and concerts into celebrations of Walpurgisnacht.

Outrageous and vulgar as all these may or may not be, they serve their purpose. As in the ancient Greek theater, they profane and make less awesome the sacred way leading to the depths where lie the great and potent sacred myths that may be about to be born again to bring new life to consciousness and culture.

What are these sacred emergent myths? I do not think we know as yet, but we do have some powerful thematic clues that lie close to the heart, if not at the core itself. I, for one, see these clues in three contemporary proto-myths that came out of the 1960's, an era of heightened mythic mentality, that subsequently have profoundly moved a multitude of people with a kind of shock of recognition. Using the words of Joseph Campbell, we could say that these three proto-myths and symbols "touch and exhilarate centers of life beyond the reach of vocabularies of reason and coercion."[2] Each carries the intimation of things to come, the emotive thrust toward actualiza-

7

tion. They are found in the figure of the Yaqui Indian sorcerer Don Juan as he is described in Carlos Castaneda's books; in the story of Michael Valentine Smith, the hero of Robert Heinlein's remarkable work of psychological science fiction, *Stranger in a Strange Land*; and finally, in the image of the star child, the cosmic fetus that looms over the Earth in the final moments of the film *2001*.

All three of these images share many of the same themes. Most important, they all tell of a mutation or change of consciousness. The reality felt and known by each of these figures is not the everyday garden-variety reality that most of us know. Whereas many of us spend most of our days after childhood ends looking out on a world circumscribed and severely restricted by psychological and sensory horse-blinders, these figures see reality as a dynamic flux, a flowing infinity of worlds within worlds within worlds. Two of the characters, Don Juan and Michael Smith, are adept at altering consciousness at will to perceive people and places with more profound understanding. Each has honed his senses to such acuity that colors, smells, sounds, and tastes become a revelation in themselves, intimations of immortality, and not just some fleeting sensory binge. Nor are these figures limited to a paltry five senses. Their senses crisscross in an orchestral play of synesthesias (cross-sensing), so that they hear color and see sound, touch light and taste God. With their extended perceptions and heightened sensitivity to all subliminal cues, it is not surprising that telepathy and clairvoyance, too, are natural and ordinary faculties, common ways of knowing in the uncommon reality in which they live.

The two critical constructs of time and space are likewise perceived as fluid and creative. Each has the capacity to see infinity in a grain of sand and eternity in an hour. Neither is enslaved to the circadian shackles of clock time, but both can experience subjective realities in which months occur in moments and moments in months. Having conquered the Euclidian geometric tyranny of clock time, they have the freedom of space to wander in their bodies or their minds through a wilderness of worlds, whether in the aroma of a desert flower or ten parsecs past Andromeda. All three of the figures have traveled over the horizon and then over that horizon to the land of someplace else. Michael Smith was born on Mars and then returned to Earth as an adult, albeit one with a Martian psychology; the cosmic fetus was once a spaceman who journeyed to Jupiter and came back transformed; and Don Juan is a modern Odysseus of inner space. I might add that in the emergent *mythos*, "out there" and "in here" are analogues for each other.

What I have been suggesting is that each of these myths may, as myths do, prefigure a reality to come. As such they are myths of the emerging Dromenon and of new ways of being. They tell of humans gaining potentials and capacities once thought of as belonging to the gods. They tell with a stirring poignancy of people, for the first time in human history, becoming fully human. Not that this planet has not seen many thousands of richly actualized human beings. Obviously it has, but only with the random individual—never, so far as we know, with the great numbers of humankind. What these myths portend is the activation and democratization of the potentials of the human psyche, the opening up of the ecology of inner space to humanity at large. One notes, for example, that Don Juan does not pass on his secrets to another budding shaman. He tells all to an anthropologist from the University of California, who then broadcasts it in many best-sellers and a doctoral dissertation. For most of the past forty thousand years, characters like Don Juan and his acolyte Castaneda would have been spoken of only in whispers by the very few who had some dim inkling as to the nature and significance of their activities. In our age they become the subjects of a cover story in *Time*. *Stranger in a Strange Land* has also been very widely read, by college students especially; and the image of the *2001* cosmic fetus wrapped in a luminous placenta has been imprinted on the minds of millions.

Most powerfully of all, these myths support and stimulate the emergence of a new image of humankind and of what it means to be human. Until very recently the dominant image governing human self-identity had been that of *Homo laborans:* man the worker, man who defines and discovers himself in terms of what he does to put some food in his mouth and a roof over his head. Man and woman in search of subsistence therefore became proficient at using only those potentials that enabled them to subsist. And so we see the consequent narrowing of human vision, its dissociation from the body of nature and from the human body itself. So, too, we see the continued maintenance since prehistoric times of a psychology of manipulation. Since the time when he lived in a cave, *Homo laborans* has looked outside himself for the fulfillment of his needs. Today we persist in much the same attitudinal stance we took toward the world ages ago. Sophisticated technology is in many ways an extension of the axe, the stone, and the spear. It involves the same primitive materialism that has discouraged human beings for so long from discovering and exploring their own innate powers. And in the discovery of prosthetic extensions for human hands, feet, and eyes, material crutches were given priority over more difficult-to-find inner resources. Technological improvements and their widespread deployment have resulted in the speeding-up of the process of plundering the planet. The logic of *Homo laborans* and of his stepchild, the dominant economic and technological paradigm, leads to his prosthetic ravaging of the environment and to eventual ecological holocaust.

But now many thoughtful students of culture and consciousness are suggesting that we may be in the early stages of a qualitative and quantitative departure from the dominant paradigm. Whether you chalk it up to Aquarius or to necessity, there are many signs (of which the new myths are one) that we are finally moving out of the reign of quantity, out of the objectifying, manipulating philosophy and psychology of power that has reigned too long.

It is significant that the current crisis in consciousness, the loss of a sense of reality felt by so many, the rising tides of alienation, occur concomitantly with the ecological destruction of the planet by technological means. We are forced into the awareness that we are not encapsulated bags of skin dragging around a dreary ego. Rather, a human being is an organism-environment, symbiotic with many fields of life.

This fact brings us to the momentous point in human history where, if we are to survive, we have no choice but to reverse the ecological and technological plunder; and that will mean discovering or rediscovering forms of consciousness and fulfillment, forms of human energy apart from those of consumption, control, aggrandizement, and manipulation. It is time to take off the human shelf all those potentials lying dormant there that were not immediately necessary to man in his role as *Homo laborans* or as Promethean man-over-nature.

The ecological crisis is both external and internal, for it has to do not only with an overuse of our external environments, but also with a gross underuse of our interior environments. And this crisis is doing what no other crisis in history has ever done—it is challenging us to a realization of a new humanity and a new way of dealing with our world. For surely, it is becoming all too evident that we cannot have a greening of the Earth unless we have a greening of the mind. Again, I refer you to the myths and scenarios of the new becoming. They suggest human beings coming to involve themselves in what I have been calling the larger Dromenon, which calls us to a deeper awareness of and participation in the surrounding reality, a wider and more sensitive utilization of the environment at hand, and a joining in fuller consciousness to a larger universe, a more complex knowing, a richer sensibility.

It would seem that the human race is about to take some major growth steps. We have evolved physically and culturally to have a remarkably fine psychosocial instrument. Now the time has come for the instrument to work, explore, and create with levels and capacities of existence that have previously remained in the realm of mythic promise. The necessary darkness of our time is indicative of the growth period about to begin. In that respect, to use Dr. John Perry's interesting image, we are not unlike deciduous trees, with periods of leafing and flowering alternating with periods of recession and resorption.

The human psyche, both personal and universal, is a tale of death and resurrection, with rhythms of awakening alternating with rhythms of forgetting and even sleep. While in darkness we grow and change and prepare for reawakening to new life forms. The present winter of our discontent, with its ontological breakdown of most of the structural givens of the social, moral, political, and psychological orders, is also the cocoon of a different way of being human and a different way of living on this Earth.

In my home and at our foundation, the arts and artifacts of millennia are to be seen everywhere. Statues of the gods of Greece and Egypt sit in solemn witness to the most advanced biofeedback equipment. A mummy case overlooks the conference area, while a wildly colored nine-foot carving of the Garuda bird-god of Indonesia shares quarters with a Xerox machine. Sekhmet and Ptah, Athena, Thoth, and Aphrodite are the daily companions of our research subjects. To get to the electroencephalograph equipment, one has to pass an old Spanish suit of armor, a marble mask of tragedy from a second-century Roman sepulchre, a leonine table leg reputed to have belonged to the emperor Nero, a Balinese angel flying from the ceiling, and a very sinister-looking drum and trumpet used in fifteenth-century Tibetan exorcism rites. In the room where the psychophysical research is done, the mother-daughter team of Demeter and Persephone and the devine couple Isis and Osiris watch with archaic smiles as you attempt to integrate your body with your body image.

Why this museum? It is not just that I've been a collector since childhood, or that archaeology is my avocation. It is rather that we have found these ancient forms more evocative of the depths and potentials of consciousness than all of our sophisticated equipment and psychotechnologies. Very deep is the well of the psyche, to paraphrase Thomas Mann. And to encounter those images that have quickened and sustained the cultures of the past is to charge that psyche with a remembrance that is at once an energizing and an unfolding of levels of existence that belong to once and future times. One feels a continuity that is, at the same time, a momentum to further growth and knows one's essential ubiquity with the cultures and consciousness of ages past. The icons of old are the codings of tomorrow, and tomorrow holds the promise of recovery of forgotten wisdom.

In the culture of the psyche there is apparently no time line. History is present in all its parts and is there to be recovered and drawn upon as a vast and inexhaustible resource. The status of present scholarship only enhances this extraordinary opportunity. For here we are, unique in human history, in that we are the first of the generations to have reclaimed the spectrums of human history, the first to be able to consciously reflect on the nature of our happenings. The revealing of humanity's historic past over the last two centuries may well prove a more important and, indeed, more critical contribution to our survival than all our scientific knowledge. This recovery of our historical patterns can involve the absorbing into conscious awareness of a perspective on chaos and failure of nerve that, if unidentified and unrecognized, will continue to thwart and even to destroy us. Joined to this, the fact that our personal and cultural development is marked by interruptions, but our psyches have within them the wherewithal to complete and deepen the interrupted journeys leads us to the conclusion that we have reached a point in awareness and ability where we can choose to become the co-trustees of the evolutionary process and begin to put together what Nature in her wisdom left asunder, so joining Nature in the cocreation of ourselves.

The putting-together involves the joining of history and psyche, the marriage of what we have been with what we eternally are. But first we must agree to dance with history and treat it more as Dromenon than as didactic drama. For contemporary historical research has suffered from the excess of its own successes and now bears the burden of its own inundations. This has led to accumulations, dissections, analyses, and the parceling out of specialized disciplines until history, leeched of meaning, wears only the bare bones of its former vitality.

How do we restore to history its heart and viscera? How do we make it full of juice and redolent of the wine of its own fermenting? How do we make it speak to the psyche with the kind of shock of recognition that occurs when one views the ancient artifacts? And above all, how do we see it whole and wholly allow it to lead us to the Pattern That Connects? These are the questions that inform the unusual journey we are about to begin.

I propose that, instead of regarding history horizontally and factually, we look at it vertically and mythically. We view it not as empirical data to be plotted and graphed but as something to be done and danced and encountered in our depths—a living metaphor that gives us both the music and the clues to play the great game of Lost and Found in the maze of time and meaning. The reward will be the classical one of Coming Home Free, becoming perhaps "great rooted blossomers," free to expand our humanity in all directions now that we have recovered the roots of our personal and cultural pasts.

The reader is gently warned not to become too preoccupied with issues concerning the details of historical exactitude, as that is not what the Dromenon journey is about. Some students of history will agree with the perspectives offered here; others will not. The metaphoric mode demands a symbolic use of the historical material, and when history is treated mythically, it gains in usefulness and creative energy what it may lose in provable facts.

The Ages of Humanity

All the world's a stage,
And all the men and women merely players:
They have their exits and their entrances;
And one man in his time plays many parts,
His acts being seven ages. At first the infant,
Mewling and puking in the nurse's arms.
And then the whining schoolboy, with his satchel,
And shining morning face, creeping like snail
Unwillingly to school. And then the lover,
Sighing like furnace, with a woeful ballad
Made to his mistress' eyebrow. Then a soldier,
Full of strange oaths, and bearded like the pard,
Jealous in honour, sudden and quick in quarrel,
Seeking the bubble reputation
Even in the cannon's mouth. And then the justice,
In fair round belly with good capon lin'd,
With eyes severe, and beard of formal cut,

INTRODUCTION: THE NEW DROMENON

> Full of wise saws and modern instances;
> And so he plays his part. The sixth age shifts
> Into the lean and slipper'd pantaloon,
> With spectacles on nose and pouch on side,
> His youthful hose well sav'd a world too wide
> For his shrunk shank; and his big manly voice,
> Turning again towards childish treble, pipes
> And whistles in his sound. Last scene of all,
> That ends this strange eventful history,
> Is second childishness, and mere oblivion,
> Sans teeth, sans eyes, sans taste, sans everything.
>
> Shakespeare, *As You Like It*

Human beings have always been fascinated by the Ages of Man. Traditions, both literary and cultural, ascribe to the human drama some three ages, or more often five, occasionally six, rarely more than eight. Frequently these ages are found to have their complement in the development of the human being from infancy to old age as in Jaques' speech from *As You Like It* above. The adherents of a rigid historicism have often dismissed this correlation as both foolish and fantastical; but the tradition continues, strong and persistent, leaving its detractors to immolate themselves in archival dust.

Celebrants of the psycho-historical point of view are among those who have led in the quickening of the human spirit and the humane sensibility: Hesiod, Plato, Aristotle, Polybius, St. Augustine, Joachim of Floris, Vico, Hegel, Marx, Comte, Sorokin, Toynbee, Teilhard de Chardin.

As early as the eighth century B.C., Hesiod enumerated five ages of man on the order of a continuous devolution from an age of gold, to one of silver, then to copper, to a heroic age, and descending finally to a dreadful age of iron. The people of each era had characters to match and had little to do with the age that followed theirs, this being the responsibil-

ity of the gods. The five ages are cyclically recurrent and therefore reminiscent of the *kalpas* of India with their cycles of four
ages.

Plato and other thinkers of the classical world correlated
the waxing and waning of political and social forms with the
rotation of the heavenly spheres and with organic patterns of
growth, maturation, and decay.

In seeing history as eternal return, ancient classical thought
had as its psychological counterpart the rule of metempsychosis
wherein one returned with the recurring cycle, there to live
exactly the same life one had lived before. This view drove
St. Augustine to acerbic fury against the doctrine of the inevitability of the repetitious:

> Far be it from the true faith that we should believe that
> there are cycles in which similar revolutions of times and
> of temporal things are repeated so that, as one might say,
> just as in this age the philosopher Plato sat in the city of
> Athens and in a school called the Academy teaching his
> pupils, so also through countless ages of the past . . . the
> same Plato and the same city and the same school and the
> same pupils have been repeated as they are destined to
> be repeated through countless ages of the future. God for-
> bid that we should accept such nonsense! Christ died, once
> and for all, for our sins.[3]

The Christian linearism of St. Augustine is a fascinating
early prototype of certain critical themes in the psycho-historical journey. Augustine sees history as the place of mystery
and adventure initiated by God but vested in man, who has
been given awesome freedom and responsibility to redeem
or destroy both self and history.

The wide-ranging scholarship of the Neopolitan Giambattista Vico offered in the early eighteenth century the first ex-

plicit analysis of the history and development of consciousness as it realizes itself in cultural institutions. Gathering evidence from language, literature, custom, law, and religion, Vico described a view of history as an ascending spiral in which cycles or stages *(corsi)* of Primitive, Heroic, and Humanic ages are repeated on higher levels *(recorsi)*, so that gradually a more refined and complex humanity emerges. For me the most complete and exciting statement about the co-evolution of culture and consciousness was that of Georg Friedrich Hegel. In *The Phenomenology of Mind,* one of the most multi-dimensional, mysterious, baffling, and important books ever written, Hegel presents a phenomenology of the states through which human consciousness must pass in order to reach the stage of the Absolute (also called Spirit or Mind). The human journey and the journey of the Absolute are reciprocal if not identical, for the evolution of the world Mind is carried through the evolution of human consciousness.

Emergent consciousness is a process of developmental experiences both personal and historical. Hegel's phenomenology, then, is the record of man's ontogenetic development in the light of his phylogenetic development. We observe how man, both personally and historically, moves from the most instinctual sensory awareness (found in infancy and early man), through stages involving increasing perception and the growth of understanding, to a stage of self-conscious reason; until, finally, Mind or Spirit becomes fully conscious of itself, through the human self becoming entirely conscious. In this manner the psyche grows God, so to speak.

Hegel consistently links the epistemological process of self-consciousness with the historical progress of mankind from bondage to freedom evidenced in emerging social institutions. It is the rapid shifting back and forth between the individual's ontogenetic growth of consciousness and the political and cultural phylogenetic growth of humanity that makes this work so brilliantly insightful and evocative. Every mode of consciousness that emerges in the progress of the individual is also evident in the life of a historical epoch. So the degree of self-consciousness that Antigone possesses is equal to the historical ethos of the ancient ideal commonwealth of Greece. In the *Phenomenology,* and later in *The Philosophy of History,* [4] Hegel describes a tremendous unfolding of psycho-historical events from early ages to his own (the decade following the French Revolution). Each and every historical event is an epiphany, an appearance of the Absolute in specific space-time. It is, at the same time, a transitory event, existentially meaningful to the individual to whom it occurs. Some individuals are highly visible as agents of the Absolute. Hegel referred to these as world-historical individuals, those richly endowed people whose personal interests, sensibilities, and passions correspond to the needs and turnings of the time. Out in front or behind the scenes, they become the impresarios of change, the orchestrators of culture and consciousness. In any case they are part of the diary of Mind in time, in which each event is working out some stage of progression toward greater freedom and knowledge, until it reaches the province of Absolute knowledge, in which Mind knows itself. Herein there occurs the union of all consciousness in the universal Mind.

In this odyssey of the world Mind, the primary growth momentum is provided by dialectic: the process of growth proceeds by opposition and reaction, by acquiring new and contradictory insights, and by assembling these into a richer, more complete understanding of existence. The Mind, both personally and universally, cannot rest in any of the stages through which it travels—not because they are incorrect, but because they are incomplete. In the well-known formula, each stage or *thesis* suggests its *antithesis,* and a higher and more complete form emerges in a *synthesis,* which is itself a new thesis. It is only when the self becomes wholly conscious and unified with Mind itself that the process ends, and the dialectical drama of history is finished.

Karl Marx banished Hegel's Mind and, by standing Hegel on his head, was left with the earthly, visible, material world as the scene of the evolutionary struggle. Instead of dialectical Mind, history became the arena for the progressions of dialectical materialism. Most readers are familiar with the Marxist schema of universal history as an economic struggle between social classes. The history of civilization since classical times is seen as falling into three ages: the feudal age, in which a small elite of aristocrats holds the toiling peasant masses in bondage to the soil; the capitalistic age, in which power shifts to the bourgeoisie, who convert the toiling masses into wage slaves; and the age of communism, when the proletarianized masses overthrow their exploiters and establish a perfect society, ending the exploitation of human beings by human beings and transferring the ownership of all means of production to the workers. All of this is seen as an inevitable unfolding of the dialectic in history, the proletariat achieving something not unlike the final stage of Hegel's fully conscious humanity, as human mind, Nature, and culture are reconciled in a higher unity, which Marx describes in virtually mystical terms. One wonders what Marx would have made of the present collapse of communism in his schema of projecting its inevitable triumph.

With the immense increase in cultural and historical knowledge in the nineteenth and twentieth centuries, there arose many brilliant and ingenious systems of viewing the stages of history, especially as they illumined the phases of great civilizations. These perspectives were my own introduction to the philosophy of history; I cut my intellectual eyeteeth in college on Arnold Toynbee's *A Study of History*. Toynbee, along with Walter Schubart, Oswald Spengler, Nikolai Berdyaev, and Pitirim Sorokin, offered complex extended analyses of the spiraling rhythms, fluctuations, and periodicities in the unfolding of sociocultural process. They arrived at surprisingly similar conclusions about the developmental sequence in time of the civilizations and cultural supersystems, as seen in the following chart.[5]

TEMPORAL SEQUENCE

In the Phases of Civilization	*In Prototypes of Culture*
1. The growth or "spring" or "childhood" phase of Spengler and Toynbee.	1. Sorokin's Ideational, Schubart's Ascetic-Messianic, Berdyaev's Barbaric-Religious prototypes.
2. The maturity or "summer" phase.	2. Sorokin's Idealistic, Schubart's Harmonious, Berdyaev's Medieval-Renaissance types.
3. The phase of decline and disintegration. The "autumn" or "winter" phase. Spengler's civilization phase.	3. Sorokin's Sensate, Schubart's Heroic or Promethean, Berdyaev's Humanistic-Secular.

The similarity continues when these philosophers of history and culture describe what occurs during the stage of what I have called the parenthesis period of human history: the time between the decaying phase of a high culture and the emergence of the spring or childhood of a new high culture. Spengler asserts that a "second religiosity" arises at such a time. Toynbee speaks of a "universal church" or new religion born in this period, which then provides the psychological basis for the childhood of a new civilization. Civilizations exist in a cycle of birth and death, but evolution is carried in the spiral ascent of the higher religions that emerge from the decay of civilization. Sorokin observes that, after the decline of the Sensate supersystem, a new Ideational religious supersystem becomes dominant.

There is apparent agreement on the resurgence of psyche in history at these points. It goes along with a growth and revival of ethical values and behavior, as well as a deepening of psychological and spiritual resources.

Since the turn of the century, a remarkable and brilliant array of depth psychologists and students of development have enormously enriched our understanding of the resonance between history and psyche, by virtue of the light they have cast on the ontogenetic stages of human development. Freud joined his formidable knowledge of the meaning and metaphors of classicism to his even more formidable drive to discover the origins and development of pathology, so revealing an archaeology of the self in which aberrations in human conduct were found to be seeded in primal happenings or coded in the now mythic echoes of earlier eras. Additionally, Freud's close analysis of the phases and crises of human psychosexual development and his psychoanalytic observations of the forces and instinctual drives that beset the emerging ego provided the basis for a far more complex and dimensional understanding of the psycho-historical process.

Freud's student Erik Erikson brings history and psyche even closer together in his theory of epigenetic development. He postulates eight stages of psychosocial development, each of which carries with it characteristic needs, tasks, and vulnerabilities critical to the specific stage of growth of personal identity. Each of these stages has an age-specific crisis, the mastery or failure of which influences the future course of development. As these stages have much in common with the

INTRODUCTION: THE NEW DROMENON

Dromenon journey of psycho-historical recovery, I summarize their chief qualities.

According to Erikson, the first life-stage is infancy; its epigenetic crisis develops around the growth of hope and basic trust. An unsuccessful resolution will result in a mistrust that can seriously impair personality development and even lead to psychosis. The second stage takes place in early childhood. Its epigenetic crisis centers on the child's development of a sense of autonomy and will. Failure here results in lifelong failure of nerve, coupled with chronic doubts and a sense of shame. The third stage, the play-age, develops a sense of initiative and creative exploration. The impeding of this initiative leads to a preoccupation with guilt. The fourth stage, the school age, is concerned with the child's developing a sense of industry and confidence in his or her own abilities. A negative resolution of this challenge results in a sense of inferiority and ineffectiveness. The fifth stage, adolescence, covers the crisis of identity; failure in this stage yields identity confusion. The sixth stage, occurring in young adult life, has as its epigenetic crisis the struggle between intimacy and isolation; its successful resolution leads to the ability to love in a deep and sustaining way. The seventh stage is maturity; its ordeal is the struggle between generativity and stagnation. (By *generativity* Erikson means the responsible guiding of the growth of others and the caring and concern for social organizations and other activities.) In this stage, too, a new surge of productivity and creativity is posited over and against depression and frustration. If the positive values prevail, the mature person can come "to the astonished or exuberant awareness of his identity." The eighth stage, old age, is the arena for a crisis between wise integrity and bitter despair. If integral mastery is gained, then the person is truly in a golden age, one in which all the previous stages are consummated, and one realizes a unity with one's self, environment, and life.

INTRODUCTION: THE NEW DROMENON

When we cast this schema on the historical tableau, we note how richly suggestive are Erikson's theses. He himself observes how the successful or failed resolution of an epigenetic crisis, especially on the part of a world historical individual, can have powerful consequences on the age in which he or she lives. Thus he shows us how Luther's identity crisis in adolescence led to a religious revolution and several centuries of social and political upheaval. He has offered a similar perspective on Mahatma Gandhi and the freeing of India from colonial rule. Granted the psycho-historical lens can distort as often as it can illuminate, but there is no question that it provides a remarkable tool in the quest for meaning in psyche and history.

The twentieth century has seen a number of remarkable applications of developmental theory to the understanding of moral development. In his well-known research, Jean Piaget has shown how children's minds tend to evolve through a series of intellectual stages—from sense bound, to emotional, to more rational and abstract forms of expression—as they progress from early childhood through adolescence. My own caveat about Piaget's work is that it was largely a product of research with Swiss children from middle- or upper-class families. It does not adequately include the study of children from cultures in which greater sensory awareness is needed for survival, as is the case in many indigenous societies. An Eskimo woman once complained to me when she was asked by her Harvard professors to demonstrate for her doctoral dissertation the accuracy of Piaget's developmental sequence as applied to Eskimo children: "But these children have a totally different sequence of development. They have to, in an environment that is all white and can float away at any moment!"

Piaget also perceives these stages as attended by related stages in moral development. As psychologist Lawrence Kohlberg reports, "Piaget is correct in assuming a culturally universal age development of a sense of justice, involving progressive concern for the needs and feelings of others."[6] Kohlberg himself presents three major stages of moral development which have relevance to both individual and historical development: the *premoral* or *preconventional stage,* the *conventional stage,* and the *principaled stage.* Each of these stages themselves contain two substages.

In the first substage of the premoral stage, one tries to get whatever one can for oneself regardless of the results for other people. "Whatever I can get away with is right," is this individual's guiding principle. Kohlberg's second premoral stage is one he calls *naive instrumental hedonism.* Here one's actions still satisfy oneself and, occasionally, others. One looks at this stage for rewards and favors which one will, in return, extend to others. A true social contract does not yet exist.

The second or conventional stage also has two substages. In the first, a tendency towards greater stability and socialization is the rule. One looks for approval and tries to conform to a stereotyped image of being "good." The individual's underlying assumption is that such stereotyped images are both upheld and played out by the majority and therefore enhance one's sociability. The second conventional substage revolves around law and order and the maintenance of rules and authority. One gains one's legitimacy by following outwardly imposed rules, respecting authority, and helping to maintain the social order.

The first substage of Kohlberg's third or post-conventional orientation is that of the social contract. At this level of development, moral judgments are based on group derived, democratically accepted laws, rather than on desire for personal gain or religious moral absolutes. These laws are regarded as social conventions that can be changed or amended at any time by an elected body or through the expertise of a judge who is supposed to be impartial in these matters. At this stage, therefore, a hierarchy of authority and experts still dominates the moral scene. But in the second substage—the final stage in moral development—Kohlberg, not unlike Marx or many mystics, holds that one grows beyond the need for outward authority. Rather, one becomes naturally oriented to principles of conscience that speak for a universal good that both transcends and exceeds the demands of social convention.[7] This last is the stage of the law written on the heart and implies the falling away of a state that regulates moral development. The contract is now no longer social but universal, as one becomes one's own moral authority, linked to others by their mutual incorporation of a social contract governed by inner conscience. Surely this condition corresponds in the psychohistorical arena to the return of the golden age or even what, in later chapters of this book, I call the post-individual stage of the planetary person.

Carl Jung, in his own depth probings of the psyche, saw the grand epochs as traditions that continue to dwell as unconscious, timeless, and creative matrices of the human psyche. The Jungian method evokes these traditions so that they become no longer separate but confluent with each other, rising to consciousness as *mythologems* and symbolic motifs of transformation. Jung is far less stage-bound than either Freud or Erikson in his theories concerning the nature and therapeutic power of the psycho-historical structures of the self. He believes that human beings bring with them at birth the ground plan of both their individual and their collective nature. The great prototypical situations that have remained the same for time out of mind are inherited existents in the unconscious self: birth and death, fathers and mothers, youth and old age. Many of the major structures of psychosocial development are givens in the depths of the human psyche. Only the existential levels of consciousness apparently experience these things for the

INTRODUCTION: THE NEW DROMENON

first time. Jung calls these inherited patterns *archetypes* and notes that, since their existence is coextensive with the human condition, they are charged with a dynamism that is prior to the will or personality of an individual human being. They are ubiquitous in time and space and bear remarkable resemblances wherever you find them:

> Comparative religion and mythology are rich mines of archetypes and so is the psychology of dreams and psychoses. The astonishing parallelism between these images and the ideas they serve to express has frequently given rise to the wildest migration theories, although it would have been far more natural to think of the remarkable similiarity of the human psyche at all times and in all places. Archetypal fantasy—forms—are, in fact, reproduced spontaneously anytime and anywhere, without there being any conceivable trace of direct transmission. The original structure components of the psyche are of no less surprising a uniformity than are those of the visible body. . . .
>
> For, just as the organs of the body are not mere lumps of indifference, passive matter, but are dynamic functional complexes which assert themselves with imperious urgency, so also the archetypes, as organs of the psyche, are dynamic, instinctual complexes which determine psychic life to an extraordinary degree. That is why I call them *dominants* of the unconscious. The layer of the unconscious psyche which is made up of these universal dynamic forms I have termed the collective unconscious. [8]

Jung saw these great transpersonal structures as the sediment deposited by the developing psyche throughout its history, and he felt that they derive their impetus from their grounding in ancestral events. But they tended to emerge only in dreams, in the active imagination, or in other arenas in which the psyche was breached by the demands of neurosis or by the stimulus of creative and imaginative discovery. They attested to the subterranean power and continuing relevance of the histories that continue to operate within. Past eras pass into the timeless matrix of forms, and stages of our own particular lives store their achievements in these source levels. There, together, they coexist, the ontogenetic and phylogenetic strata of ourselves, able to be tapped either singly or together for the channeling and transformation of neurotic energies to creative and evolutionary ends.

> And what the dead have no speech for, when living,
> They can tell you, being dead: the communication
> Of the dead is tongued with fire beyond the language of
> the living.
>
> T.S. Eliot, "Little Gidding"[9]

Recent years have seen the appearance of several remarkable and innovative critical studies of human psychosocial development. Perhaps the most comprehensive is that of the Swiss cultural historian Jean Gebser, who, in his monumental study *The Ever Present Origin,* offers a profound analysis of the phylogenetic development of human consciousness.[10] Influenced by Gebser is the work of the brilliant American philosopher of consciousness Ken Wilber. In *The Atman Project* and *Up From Eden,* Wilber offers an ingenius phenomenology of the spectrum and development of culture and consciousness.[11] As Wilber's work is well-known and his books readily available, I will concentrate on the work of Gebser here, referring to similarities to Wilber's thought in passing.

Jean Gebser's archaeology of consciousness uncovers five major stages of social and individual development. He calls the earliest and least articulated stage the Archaic structure of consciousness. Belonging to our earliest hominid ancestors, such societies and their inhabitants were pre-individual, egoless, and identified or continuous with their environment. Ken Wilber refers to this period as the "archaic-uroboric," the era of dawn man, a pre-personal Eden within which consciousness was not separated from its object. (Uroboros is the snake who circles around to bite its tail, signifying, in Wilber's terms, man's embeddedness in nature at this period.) This era stands as the subconscious ground out of which self-conscious humanity eventually arose.

The next stratum to emerge in Gebser's typology is the Magical, a group- or clan-identified consciousness. Here we find consciousness of the self absorbed in the *participation mystique* but with no clear demarcation between inner and outer realities. Consciousness, therefore, is magical, since there is yet little sense of difference between the orchestration of one's inner space and the performance of activities in the outer world. Gebser believes that societies and individuals of this type were psychically gifted, and their way of dealing with the world radically contradicts contemporary notions of how things work. With the Neanderthals and, perhaps, the early Cro-Magnon people, the Magical consciousness reached its full potential. Wilber names this period "typhonic," which refers to the mythical Greek giant Typhon, child of the Earth Goddess, who was said to be half-human and half-serpent. This is the time of shamanic man, deeply involved with his magical totem animal and not yet entirely separated out of his animal past. Dominated by instinct and the pleasure principle, typhonic man corresponds in part to Freud's primary process of infancy, in which body and object are not yet strongly differentiated. Thus, the consciousness of this period, both in its historical and its individual development, is much given to achieving a magical rapport between persons and the ob-

INTRODUCTION: THE NEW DROMENON

STRUCTURE OF CONSCIOUSNESS	CORRELATED STATE	EMPHASIZED BASIS OF COGNITION	MODE OF REALITY APPREHENSION
Archaic	Deep sleep	None/Latency	Originary
Magical	Sleep	Emotion	Pre-rational, identification
Mythical	Dream	Imagination	Irrational (polar) sensitivity
Mental	Wakefulness	Reflection	Rational (causal) abstraction
[Rational]		[This is merely the deficient form of the mental structure of consciousness]	
Integral	Transparency	Concretion	Arational (acausal) integration

This diagram is based on Gebser's synoptic table at the end of *The Ever-Present Origin*.

ject they wish to control—especially telepathic knowledge of the animals they hunt.

With the advent of the Cro-Magnons and their elaborate stone tool technology, there appeared the symbolic sensibility which Gebser called the Mythical structure of consciousness. The essential characteristic of this stratum is the emergent awareness of soul, which, for Magical man, was still sleeping. With the receding of the glaciers, the warmer climate challenged humanity to respond to recreate and reinvent the world. At this stage, women and men joined in partnership to launch a journey of unparalleled discovery: the development of agriculture; the domestication of animals; the creation of permanent and stable communities, villages, and even cities. Also developed were specialized professions, market trade, laws and their executors, arts, crafts—a hundred thousand things. The imagination was critical to all of this burgeoning creativity and, with it, imaginal thinking that carried Mythical humans into their own inner depths. There they met goddesses, and archetypes, helpers from the deep world, who encouraged their visions and charged their creativity. Stories of these archetypal beings abounded in myth and metaphor. Knowledge of their certain partnership prompted the elaboration of ritual, worship, and ceremony, as well as the development of spiritual practices to attain the inner states through which humans could reach them. Since fertility and creativity were often the most critical issues, a great deal of reverence went to the Great Goddess in her myriad forms. Wilber's theoretical framework concurs with much of this analysis and places mythical thinking within what he calls the "membership" stage. The great mythical dramas and symbolic happenings are seen by Wilber to have been created during the time of cooperation or membership between groups of people for achieving long-range goals. In individual development this stage corresponds to a child between the ages of two and four, when she begins to cooperate with others in order to realize her own needs.

The late Mythical period lasted until about the first millennium B.C., according to Gebser. Then the slow shift began towards the emergence of the Mental structure of consciousness. This is the period in which male dominance over the female becomes a major force, and partnership between men and women begins to fade. Culture at this time moves through the anguish of the heroic period typified in *The Iliad* and the rise of power as an abstraction, a tool of self-assertion. Power is no longer numinous, a felt presence of cocreation between humans and gods, but a construct to be legislated and legalized. The expansion of first the Alexandrian and then the Roman empire required such an abstraction of power in order that a cosmo-*polites* might flourish. But spirit became alienated from body, and nature from person under such rule. Philosophies emerged to offer rational ways of dealing with these splits, but more useful was the rising of the mystery cults and religions of inwardness that sought to cope with the chaos of an uneasy ecumenism through an often ecstatic celebration of hope and salvation. Christianity rose in this atmosphere and provided the ethos in which the Roman empire could control and unify its varied peoples. It was during this period, dubbed by the German philosopher-psychiatrist Karl Jaspers the "axial" age, that the "spiritual foundations of humanity were laid, simultaneously and independently in China, India, Persia, Palestine and Greece. And these are the foundations upon which humanity still subsists today."[12] Wilber would seem to place this era within a transitional period between the membership and the egoic periods of human development.

These foundations were eventually depleted of their spiritual vigor, ending the Mental stage of consciousness. In Europe, with the ensuing collapse of the Roman Empire and the subsequent period of darkness, there was to be no rebirth of consciousness until the Renaissance. Then there followed an interim period, which Gebser terms the "vanishing point" of Mental consciousness. This period beginning in the late fifteenth century and running through the Enlightenment was the time of the Rational consciousness, seen by Gebser as a deficient form of the mental structure (and which Wilber refers to as the beginnings of egoic consciousness). Secular and worldly, Rational consciousness found its most thoroughgoing expression in projecting itself in objectified space. Leonardo da Vinci's monograph on perspective provided the basis for not only a development of perspective in painting, sculpture, and music, but extended as well to a whole constellation of world-changing activities. Telescopes and microscopes gave Rational man access to spatial realities never before known; the discovery of intercontinental space forever changed the face and populations of the world; the proliferation of inventions and machines allowed man to dig into physical and geographical space as well as to bring previously separated spaces of the Earth rapidly together.

Promethean in his control of matter, Rational man lost his psychic identity, especially as his ego moved to the forefront of his consciousness so as to better control and manipulate expanses of newfound space. Dimensions of consciousness were lost by virtue of this narrowing focus on ego, and it was only a matter of time before as Yeats said, "things fall apart; the center cannot hold; Mere anarchy is loosed upon the world." Men became champions of the Rational mentality, while women receded further into the background, treated as chattel. Tenderness was directed to the safely untouchable Virgin Mary. Herstory was lost, and with it, soul. Misogyny found its most horrific outlet in the savaging of the female mind and body during the witch hunts, in the course of which untold numbers of women were brutally persecuted. The multidimensional women's psyche, which retained the psychic content supplanted in most men by ego, was both feared and persecuted. Women's devotion to time and process was also feared by space-happy men.

The pathology of Rational man continued into the so-called Age of Enlightenment, when science became transmuted into scientism and the scientific mind arrogated to itself virtually divine powers, becoming both judge and jury on the weight and worth of the world. The quantified, curious cosmos of technology put the coup de grace on the will to power of the Rational consciousness. The erosion of mind and nature that are the inevitable results of Rational man's mania spelled its depletion and tolled its death knell.

The stage was now set for the coming of the fifth period of human development, the Integral consciousness. In his exposition of this stage Wilber completes his review of past development and looks to the future of consciousness. These last are for him the transpersonal, transrational stages of consciousness, the first higher stage of which he calls the centauric, in which the work of integration is accomplished. Herein, man integrates all the parts and pieces of himself into a mature ego, and then is enabled to discover an even higher level of integration and continuity with the patterns of the universe. Such integration implies the state of numinous and noetic illumination and the meeting with humankind's archetypal and eternal nature. The writings and experiences of the great spiritual adepts which tell of this illumination prefigure what may be the common journey for an evolving humanity.

Gebser sees the Integral era as one in which we are not only radiant but also radically immersed in the world. Technology as such is not abolished but rather called back from its imprisonment in rational consciousness. Writing about this stage of consciousness is Gebser's joy and the subject of his most innovative hypotheses. His work is the story of the coming possible human in the possible world. With far-reaching examples drawn from practically every field of human endeavor, especially music and literature, Gebser demonstrates the eruption of a new order of time into consciousness.

The Integral period is the time of the ever-present origin, the creative space-time of the physicists, the timeless time of the mystics. It makes time more an intensity than a measurement; indeed, it allows for freedom for all time forms. Freedom of time forms necessarily implies freedom for space forms. As time becomes achronic, so space becomes aperspective. In 1964, Bell's Theorem showed that in quantum physics, every bonded particle must have knowledge and relationship with every other particle, thus postulating a universe of colossal busybodyness. Everything is implicated in everything else. In David Bohm's terms, everything is spun out of an implicate order that is resonant in all things, in all consciousness. Perspective becomes in this analogy merely a way of lensing the basic interconnectedness of reality so as to make temporary and temporal—common—sense of it. In practical terms, this new vision is a movement away from the old splits and polarities which so haunted the mind and works of Rational consciousness. Integral thought is by implication arational because of its comprehensiveness, its planetary consciousness, its holistic ways of being. In the words of Paolo Soleri, this growing process of complexification-miniaturization works to bring forth all those forces that "characterize the living and the loving: interdependence, interaction, perception, learning, care, cooperation, altruism, feedback, synergy, compassion, transcendence, beauty, integrity, intensity, passion, trust."[13] Ultimately this Emergent form of consciousness is one in which we return to the garden of the ever-present origin, knowing ourselves as cocreators of world and time, partners of God, artists of spirit.

We come finally to Gerald Heard, who, as I said earlier,

offered a novel thesis to account for these psycho-historical speculations in such a way as to make a creative and therapeutic use of five major stages of man's cultural and personal evolution. These five stages will be seen to be similar in scope and intent to several of the previous typologies discussed, especially that of Jean Gebser.

Over the years I found in my own work continuous echoes of the ideas of Gerald Heard. Then, finally, around 1978, I decided to offer an experimental advanced Dromenon workshop in which I would rethink some of the theses of *The Five Ages of Man* in the light of my own subsequent research and findings. The seminar followed to some extent the outlines of Heard's hypotheses, but the major part evolved from my own formulations both as a student of the philosophy of history and as a research scientist. This book is an outgrowth of these seminars. It is at once a book of experiences and a transhistorical journey through the collective human story and through one's own personal history. It begins, therefore, as a search for the pathways that recover old knowings and lead to new possibilities. It begins as a search for Dromenon.

It is, as we have seen, an old but now, surprisingly, revived chestnut (though still contended, especially by Dr. Stephen J. Gould) that ontogeny recapitulates phylogeny. We know, for example, that, owing to the process by which the fetus in the womb recapitulates in its development the evolutionary sequences from simple organism through fish and reptile up to mammal, it is possible to use the data from embryology to explore the missing gaps in the fossil record. I propose that this may also be true of the cultural evolution of humanity and the evolution of consciousness that precipitates those cultural sequences. Many child psychologists like Stanley Hall and his student Arnold Gesell have suggested that the individual infant, child, and adolescent are recapitulating in their individual growth phases the past epochs of humankind's psychosocial evolution. Taking this thesis further, Gerald Heard suggested that the infant, being in a state of pre-individualized dependency and elaborate symbiosis with its mother, helps us to understand the pre-self-conscious state of primitive man with his symbiotic dependency and absorption into the tribal mind. The next developmental state, that of the child or proto-individual, whose protests are aimed at breaking out of the cloying constraints of the nursery culture, can be seen in the psycho-historical perspective to be recapitulating the Heroic age, whose raging attacks and pillage smashed the mother culture in the desire to find a greater self-determination. In the light of more recent evidence, however, it will be seen that this mother culture did not necessarily remain smashed, but in some cases responded to the early attacks by evolving a complex and sophisticated society of partnership between men and women, as well as a pacific and aesthetic agriculturally-based society. It was only in the second wave of attack, as seen, for example, in the Indo-Aryan invasions, that these more evolved mother cultures succumbed to patriarchal and ''heroic'' mentalities.

Heard went on to propose that the third correlation of man's history is the ascetic era, which corresponds with adolescence as the individual's third stage. Herein the adolescent recapitulates a mid-individualistic era of the growth of human consciousness which then leads to a fourth stage of full individuality, characterized by the current humanic epoch and the personal stage of first maturity. Both the ascetic and the humanic eras are marked by correlative growth in psychological development as well as by increasing self-consciousness and by the intensification of individualism.

A fifth stage is projected—a more realized human era that I have called the era of the planetary or ecological person, which corresponds to the post-individual phase or second maturity and the later years of life. The ecological human I perceive as one who has equal subjectivity and objectivity—a far more realized being who exists in an ecological continuum with the realities of inner and outer worlds, and for whom *individualism* is but the chrysalis leading to the emergence of a self that is continuous and flowing with all manner of realities.

The chart on page 39 based on Gerald Heard indicates something of the developmental schema of this thesis and of the progression in consciousness from one stage and era to another.

Becoming Living History

This book is to be read and experienced as a journey of transformation. The goal is the same as it was in the seminars —the psycho-historical recovery of the self, the joining of the breadth of the human story with the depths of each of our personal stories. We begin by being the stage upon which the drama unfolds—we become living history. We try to experience what may have happened in critical junctures in historical epochs and in the recapitulation of these in the stages of our own life. With special exercises and learning experiences appropriate to both past epoch and life stage, we become therapists of history and of ourselves, healing the traumas of ages past and present as we resolve and heal the crises of our own emergent selves. As a result, what may have been lost of the promise and potential of these historical and personal ages may be found again and used in ways that would not have been possible in previous stages. Thus we attempt to "redeem The time. Redeem The unread vision in the higher dream. . . ."

Hundreds of others have gone before you as co-voyagers in this historical and personal journey. Many have returned profoundly changed, and with the creative freedom and courage to use capacities that they barely knew they had. They

HISTORICAL STAGE	PERSONAL STAGE	CRISIS	PATHOLOGY	THERAPEIA
Post-Individual: planetary, ecological human	Second maturity	Meeting the challenge	Involutional melancholy	The Mystery of the Fields of Life: empowering the other, unconditional love
Individual: humanic, self-sufficient human	First maturity	Dualism and divisiveness, breakdown of meaning	Manic depression	The Mystery of Fire: the integration and deepening of the self
Mid-Individual: ascetic, self-accusing human	Adolescence	Withdrawal and self-mortification	Schizophrenia	The Mystery of Air: correcting the drive to mortification, extending and harmonizing the parts of the self
Proto-Individual: heroic, self-assertive human	Childhood	Separation drive of protest, rage	Paranoia	The Mystery of Water: tempering of egotism, communing with nature
Pre-Individual: co-conscious human	Infancy	Birth trauma, leaving the Tribe	Infantilism	The Mystery of Earth: remedying the trauma of birth, becoming the One and the Many

return no longer tyrannized by long-aborted processes in their human development or haunted by imperfect transitions. All of us suffer from these. When only part of us has transited, then other critical aspects are left behind, and these are the parts that continue to impede us and exert an unconscious tyranny. With the psycho-historical journey, however, it appears that many of these parts are allowed finally to blossom. A fullness of identity is achieved as the five ages come full-term in the present moment of one's life.

In this experience, too, people seem to become forever sensitive to the historical process; and in gaining *response-ability* to this process, they no longer feel impotent in the face of rapid change and the complexities of the present historical situation. As a carrier of history, one recovers both the potency and potentials of history. One becomes aware that historical and personal dimensions are not different realities; rather, they are interwoven dimensions within a reality continuum, and each thus creates the other. In this recreation is established the energy for a new creation. For what had apparently been lost was not the energy itself but our awareness that we had it.

To raise this energy, strong measures are needed; and so, in addition to experiences that teach us to use our latent human potentials, we will draw upon modes of myth and ritual that elevate the learning to a higher potency.

We must start, then, by recalling that in many cultures, ritual and ritual rites of passage are the active doors through which one passes into the larger life. I am speaking, of course, of the optimum and creative use of ritual. Too often cultures allowed it to become a confinement instead of a passageway, dead straws choking off new growth. The word *rite* comes from the same root as *art* and *order*. Like all real art, like the movements of sacred dances, ritual provides organic order, a pattern of dynamic expression through which the energy of an event or series of events can flow in an evolutionary process toward a larger meaning or new stage or level of life. It offers us ways in which our transitions may be illuminated. So often we have the breakthrough, the insight, and the graduation—or knowledge of our movement from one stage to the other. But too often in our modern world, lacking as it is in the dramatic and depth acknowledgment of this kind of movement, the transition is lost and falls from grace into the entropy of accident and chaos.

The mystery and ritual, however, make sense and sensibility out of the unknown realms. They serve to mark the exact steps of passage from one reality to another, between our regular lives and a deeper dimension of meaning that surrounds us and yet is a "mystery" because our eyes are closed to it. *Mystery* comes from the Greek word *musein,* which means "to close the eyes or the mouth." "Mum's the word," so to speak. It is the paradox of the mystery that in the course of its rite of passage, the eyes and the ears are opened, as are all the other senses, both physical and mental. The classical requirements for this passage are rigorous: service, commitment, grace, discipline, availability to be danced by the dance of life— in a word, art. Whatever level of consciousness one enters during the course of the ritual, consciousness remains attentive, ready to glimpse the insights and illuminations along the way and make them its own.

During the course of this journey we will go through five such mysteries, employing both their ancient and their modern counterparts, drawing upon the old and classical knowings as well as the most recent discoveries concerning brain, behavior, and the evocation of human potential.

Notes

1. Jane Harrison, *Ancient Art and Ritual* (New York and London: Home University Library: Williams and Norgate, 1913), p. 29ff.

2. Joseph Campbell, *The Masks of God: Creative Mythology* (New York: Viking, 1968), p. 4.
3. St. Augustine, *The City of God*, XII, 14, 21 (London: Everyman Edition, 1945).
4. In the more empirically rooted *Philosophy of History*, Hegel shows how the Absolute or Mind progresses historically through Oriental, Greek, Roman, and Germanic-Christian phases, these being seen as corresponding to the stages from childhood to old age. In this work, too, Hegel illustrates the progression of freedom and consciousness when he demonstrates how, in the first age, only the ruler is free; in the classical age, only some are free; and in the modern world, "man as man is free." Hegel also connects the developing Spirit to the emergence of the political stage in successive organic phases. See Georg Friedrich Hegel, *The Phenomenology of Mind* trans. by J. B. Baillie (London: Allen and Unwin, 1931) and Georg Friedrich Hegel, *The Philosophy of History* trans. by J. Sibree (New York: Wiley, 1944).
5. This chart is adapted from one found in Sorokin's *Modern Historical and Social Philosophies* (New York: Dover, 1963), p. 295.
6. Lawrence Kohlberg, "Moral Development," in *International Encyclopedia of the Social Sciences*, Vol. 10 (New York: The Free Press and Macmillan Co., 1968), p. 489.
7. Ibid, pp. 483-494. Kohlberg's theses are also well summarized in his essay "Moral Development and Identification," in *Child Development*, Sixty-Second Yearbook of the National Society for the Study of Education ed. by Harold W. Stevenson (Chicago: University of Chicago Press, 1963), pp. 277-332.
8. Carl Jung, "On the Tibetan Book of the Dead," *Collected Works, Vol. XI* (New York: Pantheon Books, 1963), pp. 518-519.
9. T. S. Eliot is the supreme examplar of the use of the poly-historic process in poetry. In *The Waste Land*, for example, he achieves a final concentration of the entire past upon the present, and, throughout his other poetry, he always reminds us that:

> Time present and time past
> Are both perhaps present in time future,
> And time future contained in time past.

10. Jean Gebser, *The Ever-Present Origin* trans. by Noel Barstad with Algis Mickunas (Athens, Ohio: Ohio University Press, 1986). An important study of Gebser's work is found in Georg Feuerstein, *Structures of Consciousness: The Genius of Jean Gebser, An Introduction and Critique* (Lower Lake, CA: Integral Publishing, 1987). The chart of Gebser's schema on page 30 is adapted from Feuerstein's book.

11. Ken Wilber, *The Atman Project: A Transpersonal View of Human Development* (Wheaton, IL: Quest, 1980); Ken Wilber, *Up from Eden: A Transpersonal View of Human Evolution* (Boston: Shambhala Publications, 1986).

12. Karl Jaspers, *Way to Wisdom: An Introduction to Philosophy* (New Haven: Yale University Press, 1966), p. 98.

13. Paolo Soleri, *The Omega Seed: An Eschatological Hypothesis* (Garden City: Anchor Press/Doubleday, 1981), p. 225.

ONE

THE
CRADLE OF
AWAKENING:

The Pre-Individual Society and Infancy

*And the old made explicit, understood
In the completion of its partial ecstasy,
The resolution of its partial horror.*

T. S. Eliot, "Burnt Norton"

Pre-individual societies refer by and large to those formed by peoples of both Paleolithic and Mesolithic and perhaps even certain early Neolithic times. From the primitive food-gathering societies of four hundred thousand years ago to the beginnings of the first agricultural societies of 10,000 B.C., they were cultures seasoned by millennia into rituals that served to assure the continuity of the routine, be it for the fecundity of earth and woman or to evoke hunting magic. They often came to exist in a continuum of co-conscious participation in all of the concerns of the group, in what Levy-Bruhl calls the *participation mystique*.

The mind of the individual and the mind of the tribe were indivisible in this mystique. The tribal group acted together and thought alike, and the communal mind was not questioned by the individual members, who did not in any case distinguish themselves from the group. Instead, each and every one tended to be merged in a collective or corporate personality, and this in turn was part of an impersonal and all-pervading power or spirit.

Consciousness, as we have come to value it, is constricted in such a society, or refused development within the rigid social structures ruled by the clan elders. These strictures or taboos constitute the morality of the group and are especially stringent in regard to issues of death, sexuality, hunting and gathering, and other work. The first signs of self-consciousness, self-assertiveness, and egotism are suppressed. In societies of the pre-individual type the members live as a unit and generally hold all in common. They suffer and rejoice together; their agonies and ecstasies, ritual obedience and ritual transgressions, are taken in common; they come to the same joint decisions and have the same awareness of invisible spirits. Together they eat their totem, which is their substance, their emblem, their god, themselves writ large, and are reinforced and strengthened in this act of collective holy communion.

There is evidence to suggest that the early forms of humankind, in their pre-Neanderthal form, existed as beings continuous with the order of nature, mobile plants in nature's seething matrix. Human awareness had not risen to a consciousness of beings as distinct or discontinuous from the world around them. Consciousness consisted of an inarticulate, inchoate sense of an integral world, in which being was continuous with the tapestry of nature. Within the context of this thesis, myths of Paradise and the Fall are seen as widespread nostalgia for the integral world of the childhood of humankind.

Adam and Eve fall out of the unitary continuous world of the garden into a pluralistic, discontinuous one. Look at the account in Genesis of early man and woman being kicked upward out of the paradise of the integral world and what it means for them—what, in fact, it will mean to be human:

> To the woman he said, ''I will greatly multiply your pain in childbearing; in pain you shall bring forth children, yet your desire shall be for your husband, and he shall rule over you.'' And to Adam he said, ''Because you have listened to the voice of your wife, and have eaten of the tree of which I commanded you, 'You shall not eat of it,' cursed is the ground because of you; in toil you shall eat of it all the days of your life; thorns and thistles it shall bring forth to you; and you shall eat the plants of the field. In the sweat of your face you shall eat bread till you return

to the ground for out of it you were taken; you are dust, and to dust you shall return.''

Genesis 3:16-19

The myth promulgated in Genesis provides the paradigm of early human experience—namely, that work, consciousness of death, and the restriction of sexual activity (that is, the moving from unashamed sexuality to sexuality with shame) comprise the range of activities that distinguish human beings from animals. Thus early peoples feel these three structures as religious, in that they permeate their lives as the background to their very existence. The taboos concerning these structures become the earliest forms of the religious experience. What is a taboo but a kind of prohibition that seems to contain its own transgression? The prohibition is given so that it may be violated under certain conditions.

The organized transgression of the taboo then becomes a sacred transgression and supplies pre-individual societies with an authorized period in which they can unleash suppressed urges and become continuous with the violent order of nature. The sacred then becomes the realm of exuberant and unrestrained nature—nature unsustained by order and labor and limited sexuality. The values of the workaday or profane world are inverted. And so human society early discovers itself to be composed of a profane and a sacred sphere. It is defined by the boundaries that limit it—but also by what lies beyond these boundaries. This may explain why religion is often founded on feelings of terror and awe—a kind of nausea and vertigo that seems to be a part of so much religious experience before it is consummated, before humanity loses its discontinuity and becomes one with the continuum of Being. The modern seeker is, after all, still a transgressor, in that the boundaries of the self are transgressed.

Given the clear boundaries and ritualized safety valves of

these societies, it is not surprising that they were looked back on as a golden age, a reign of peace presided over by an ancestral goddess who gave life and fertility to the people and personified their vitality. Eros and empathy were probably the dominant principles here, and many have suggested that the sensory systems of these people were developed to a degree that would to us seem ecstatic and could probably be described by Freud's term for infant sexuality, "polymorphous perverse." This acute sensuality was essential to survival, for it gave the participants in the tribe the heightened perceptual capacities needed to detect food and danger. At the same time, it provided the physiological basis for a deep psychological symbiosis—the participation mystique—which assured the continuity of these kinds of peoples for nearly half a million years.

As we have seen in our Western tradition, the myth of Adam and Eve in the Garden of Paradise reflects our nostalgia for the time before the fall into rational and discursive consciousness, the time when we were co-conscious with plants and animals and each other and had not yet eaten of the tree of the knowledge of distinctions.

Jean Liedloff, who lived with a remnant of these kinds of people, the Yequana Indians in the Venezuelan jungle, makes a trenchant observation about the magnitude of their survival success, as compared to ours, when she writes:

> For some 2,000,000 years, despite being the same species of animal as ourselves, man was a success. He had evolved from apehood to manhood as a hunter-gatherer with an efficient life-style which had it continued, might have seen him through many a million-year anniversary. As it is, most ecologists agree, his chances of surviving even another century are diminished with each day's activities. But during the brief few thousand years since he strayed

from the way of life to which evolution adapted him, he has not only wreaked havoc upon the natural order of the entire planet, he has also managed to bring into disrepute the highly evolved good sense that guided his behavior throughout all those eons. Much of it has been undermined only recently as the last coverts of our instinctive competence are rooted out and subjected to the uncomprehending gaze of science. Ever more frequently our innate sense of what is best for us is short-circuited by suspicion while the intellect, which has never known much about our real needs, decides what to do. [1]

My own experience of having worked with several of these societies that have, to some extent, managed to survive into modern times supports Liedloff's findings among the Yequana of Venezuela. Further, as indicated earlier, these societies have not been caught in a static form but rather, in some cases, have deepened and grown while maintaining their traditional base, so as to encompass a total worldview in which everything is dynamically part of everything else. I have been stunned by the richness of the cosmology of certain tribes in Mali, a view of the universe and its creation with its own metaphors as sophisticated in its own way as any that I've found in the great universities. I have been taught by Amazon Indians how to understand and serve the complex ecology of life. And, among the Aboriginal peoples of Australia, I have been guided along the pathways and songlines into experiencing multiple realities of both landscape and inscape. Quite frankly, much of what we learn in graduate school is kindergarten compared to the knowings and practices of these very ancient surviving cultures. It is all to the good that many anthropologists in the field have ceased patronizing the societies they are studying and are instead learning their ways and internalizing their teachings. In this way, valuable knowledge and old—but to us very new—ways of being are being harvested and applied to help in the critical task of saving the Earth and its species.

Following the proposed pattern of correlation between the stages of developing culture and those of human growth, we can say that the infant, after birth, may well recapitulate this pre-individual cultural era, in some thirty months equivalent to the four hundred thousand years of the whole stage in human development. As the pre-individual was symbiotically co-conscious with his or her group or tribe, so the infant is symbiotic with its mother. The infant emerges from the most total and complete symbiosis within the womb of the mother to continue this symbiosis in a womb relationship outside the body of the mother. These two phases of symbiosis are divided and interrupted by the cataclysmic event of birth.

Many human development researchers are coming to suspect that much individual growth and upwardly evolutionary behavior may be inhibited by the terrible patterning that begins at birth—that frequently difficult passage which most of us go through. Evidence is accumulating concerning imprints left in our brain, body, and psyche by the experience of traumatic entry into the world. One of the earliest of these discoveries was made in 1937, when Isaac Shour of the University of Illinois College of Dentistry reported the discovery that growth rings in human teeth show the incidence of glandular disturbances and other illnesses. Critical to this discovery was the ring called the neonatal ring, which marks the stress of birth.

Since that time, scientists and other explorers of the mind-body connection have produced an impressive array of research papers, articles, and books analyzing all phases of the birth process, from pre-conception to the first weeks of life and the physical, psychological, and spiritual effects of trauma in each or any of these stages. Similarly, much study has been devoted to the various kinds of trauma that can occur, and many forms of treatment and care have been devised to insure that parents understand the importance of their mutual undertaking in bringing a human being to life in today's world. [2]

For adults who were traumatized during one or more of the stages of the birth process (most of the people alive today), the ability to discern and acknowledge these primal wounds may begin the process of healing them and allow for their release in ways which provide a deepened embrace of the life force.

Psychotherapist William Emerson, for example, has pioneered methods of working with babies and young children who have suffered birth trauma and conducts training for adults to heal their own pain and facilitate such healing for others. He teaches his students to look for precise physical and psychological signals that indicate both the type of trauma and the stage of birth at which it occurred and to instigate conscious experience of the trauma through body positions similar to those the baby held when the original trauma happened. Beyond his meticulous attention to skull and facial structure, to the movement and tracking power of the eyes, the tonicity of muscles, the need for expression of the trauma through voice, art, and play, and the importance of re-patterning, Dr. Emerson emphasizes the power of the empathic heart—a major healing force in his work.

All of this attention finally being paid to the most heroic journey of them all, the journey into flesh and blood, throws a painfully bright spotlight on the truth of our initial experience of life—all too often fearful, frustrating, infuriating, and damaging. [3]

The terror before existence, the basic unspecified hostility to the fact of living that many feel, may well begin in these early moments of life. It permeates our days, casting its long pall before the powers of consciousness, checking our initiative, inhibiting creative response, bringing an atmosphere of fear and withdrawal to all our attempts at growth. "Yes, but" becomes the mantram of our souls. The shudder before existence becomes the eventual shuttering of our senses and of the lenses of our minds.

In our philosophies, this terror gives us the alternatives of the agnostic reflex on the one hand and the painful gnosticisms on the other, with their presentiments of human beings as creatures from an alien realm, flung into this world of flesh and darkness, longing to return home again, be it to the seventh planetary sphere of the ancient Gnostic religions of salvation or to the thousand-year reign of the "master race" of the Third Reich. Many religions are no better, holding out as they do the promise of a golden age beyond death or of Coming Home as a state of polymorphous but bodiless bliss in a nirvana attained through exercises of disassociation. That humankind's highest achievements have been both prompted and flawed by its visceral response of terror and alienation gives us pause.

And so, at the beginning of this journey we will take together, I propose that we begin the process of mending our births and then act to mend as well some of the historic trauma that occurred during the breakdown of certain (but not all) tribal groups. Before we do this, however, we must consider further the subsequent stories of the traumas that afflicted both tribe and infant.

The newborn child, emerging from the prepersonal, unseparated life of the womb, feels, under the stress of the alien situation, two conflicting drives. The first is to stop the separation by elaborating a web of dependency ties and rhythms of bonding with the mother, and so establish an external womb situation. This corresponds to the elaborate and intricate rules and traditions of the insular tribe, which reinforce themselves in seasonal rites and in an all-encompassing series of dicta on every aspect of daily behavior, so that novelty becomes blasphemy and innovation is under the rubric of the taboo.

The second conflict arises from the situation of the child, emerging from infancy, who now experiences bonding with the mother as *bondage* and so begins to defy her with a drive of protest and regards any thwarting of impulses as an outrage. This corresponds in history to the drive of protest of the proto-individual, whose innovations were scorned and whose challenges to the traditional order were regarded as an evil to be silenced.

Adam eats the apple in defiance of the Lord, although Eve puts him up to it and the snake has all the lines. Young heroes defy the rules of the old order. The snaking spiral of burgeoning consciousness provokes them to a yearning for a world beyond the unyielding garden.

And so the proto-individual comes to regard the traditional tribe not as a loving matrix but as a prison to be violated, left, and, perhaps, even destroyed. Hence, as Gerald Heard has noted, at the beginning of our self-consciousness lies the fissure of humanity into conservative-reactionary and rebel-revolutionary.

In its own way, therefore, the baby is recapitulating one of the first crises in human history, wherein the primary group further elaborates the rules, making the social pattern more complex and involuted—the participation mystique with few, if any, solo parts—while all the new individuals-in-the-making instigate heroic revolts, getting lost in the babels of their own victories.

If you were to re-create the history of the psyche at this point, what would you do? I believe that we heal the traumas of history and psyche, of birth and the breakdown of the primal society, through a series of experiences that could best be described as therapeutic mysteries and rituals of reconciliation and new growth. It is important that we not dismiss the power of ritual and mystery as atavisms to be outgrown in favor of more "scientific" methodologies. A strictly scientific therapy is, at its worst, a limited, linear attempt to make piecemeal sense out of a complexity of parts that is greater than logic and defiant of all our rationales. At its best, the therapeutic science becomes an art form grounded not in the method but in the rich humanity of the practitioner. The rituals and mysteries, however, are older than antiquity; they are ingrained in the knowings of the self and the galaxy, and provide for the symbolic codings that unlock our latencies and illuminate our transitions.

The first mystery is of the earth and has as its initiatory power the remedying of the trauma of birth, both historically and personally. Its sociohistorical aspect lies in the fissure that occurred when our prehistoric co-conscious and symbiotic society was broken by the eruption of our proto-conscious heroic revolt. Its personal aspect lies in the bad passage, and even worse arrival, that most of us experienced at birth.

It is the premise of these mysteries that these events must be recalled and experienced again in ways symbolic of, and perhaps even similar to, what probably happened. Once we have relived the trauma, we go through these events again, creatively and in the light of the larger order of knowledge that we now have, and which we can now project backward, in order to mend and recover these wounded dimensions of ourselves. In these experiences each individual is recapitulating human history, social and personal, in a new kind of drama—a kind of meta-play. The trauma of birth recapitulates the prehistorical crisis, and the comforting symbiosis is broken in the interest of a developing social ecology.

THE DROMENON FOR THE PRE-INDIVIDUAL:

The Recovery of the Beginning

The experiences are divided into four stages. The first stage recalls the hypnotic symbiosis and comforting securities of the early social group, with the first painful attempt by some members to break away. In the second, one is wrapped in the arms of another, there to undergo a terrible birth of person and hero.

In the third, the birth is raised to its blessed form, and we relive our own births in a method best known in the work of Frederick Leboyer. Here, the atrocities of delivery are refused, and the baby is welcomed without violence and handled with a tenderness and loving insight that subsequently allow the child to develop into an individual at once both serene and creative. In the course of this tender ritual of welcoming, potentials that may well be inhibited at birth are allowed to flourish again.

Finally, the classical mystery of the earth is enacted, to provide a potent and artful ending to the old order and rebirth to the new, thus concluding our ritual drama of transformation.

STAGE ONE
The Remembrance of the Primal Community

Before beginning, the participants will remove shoes, rings, buckles, glasses, and any other similar objects.

The group should divide into two equal parts. One group will sit in a circle, arms linked, and facing each other. Members of the second group will sit back to back with members of the first group and, reaching behind them, will link arms into those of the back-to-back couples on either side of them, so that the entire group is a woven network corresponding symbolically to the interwovenness on all levels of the early community.

The entire group will now close their eyes and sing together the sound:

ah- ah- ah- ah- ah- ah- ah-

The Guide for the occasion should ask them to keep their consciousness completely within the sound they themselves are making as individuals as well as within the sound of the group until, finally, their consciousness becomes continuous with the sound that is the group, and the group which is the sound.

After ten to fifteen minutes of this, during which many of the participants will have entered into a sense of the participation mystique, the Guide will tell them to continue chanting, but that very shortly some members of the group will be touched on the head. Those touched will be representative of the proto-individuals, who are trying to break away from this close and interwoven society.

Those selected should then struggle to break loose, while the untouched ones—those who remain in the primal community—will try to hold them back and keep them from moving out. Some of those chosen would prefer to remain in the circle, while others, not chosen, would prefer to have been touched for the heroic revolt. This mis-choosing, however, has its own purposes and is part of the process.

The Guide should further tell the participants that once

the break has occurred, they are free to explore options for how they will continue to survive.

The Guide will then move around the circle, touching heads at random, or even alternating by touching first a head on the outside circle and then one on the inside—making sure, however, that she does not touch the two heads of a single pair.

At this point the struggle begins, as the individuals-in-the-making attempt to break their bonds, and the primary group fights to maintain the community. The struggle can take many forms, most of which will emulate many of the possible actions and reactions that may have occurred in the early community.

Many of the members of the remaining circle may try to join together with even greater intensity and devotion. Some members of the "hero" group will be celebrating their revolt on the outer perimeter and may even launch an attack on the inner group, trying to drag its members off. Some may form into wandering bands of marauders, fighting among themselves and attacking other bands. Other may find themselves joining together to create new primary communities just like the old ones that they had left. Many other scenarios are possible and inevitably show themselves. But the Guide should be careful not to tell the participants about these, rather letting them rise spontaneously from the archaic recesses of human behavior.

When the Guide sees that the group has resolved itself into various groupings and actions, she should call out in a loud voice, "Stop! Stay where you are. Tell me what has happened to you and what you are experiencing."

The group will then report on their experiences. Some fairly typical responses have been as follows:

"I was so happy in the primal community I didn't want it ever to end. I was warm and sure and safe. There were no threats. It was what I imagine it was like being in my mother's womb."

"I hated it at first when we were all linked there together

and chanting like zombies. I was actually getting claustrophobia and wondering how I could leave. I even thought of sneaking out early and telling the Guide I had to go to the bathroom. But then about ten minutes—or was it ten hours?—into it, I felt the power of the group move through me like a great wave, and there didn't seem to be any distinctions between me and anybody else anymore. So there was no point in leaving.''

"When my partner began to pull away from me, I was terrified. I didn't want her ever to go and felt such rage that she should be trying to leave and break up my perfect world. Then I joined with other members of the inner circle, and we tried to re-create our community again, but it just wasn't the same.''

"My partner really clung onto me when I tried to get away, and when I finally did, I had such a feeling of triumph and went racing through the room, leaping and doing war dances. I tried to find a few others to join me so that we could attack the original group, but they were too disorganized, and we couldn't get our act together.''

"We tried to create a new community of heroes, and in the last ten minutes of discussion, I think we reinvented the laws of chivalry. They were as narrow and hidebound as the laws of the community.''

"I think I'll go back to the womb.''

"I wish the Guide hadn't selected me to be a hero. I never would have left the original community.''

STAGE TWO
Birth as Trauma

After discussion the participants will immediately go into a reenactment of the usual experience of birth as it was enacted in most hospitals in the Western world up until the 1970s.[4] (Creative alternatives have become more recently available, but I believe the incidence of birth trauma has not diminished significantly for hospital births.)

With their original partner from the primal community, they will find a space on the floor, and, lying on their sides, one will be the parent-womb and curl around the other, who will be the fetus.

The Guide will give the following instructions, allowing for appropriate pauses and intervals for the experience to unfold.

The Guide will say: "Those of you who are playing the fetus, and those who are playing the parent-womb, listen closely to my words and respond accordingly.

"We will now enact our births and what happened imme- diately following our births. You, the fetus, have been floating and growing for a long time in your mother's womb. Now, as you continue to grow larger, the walls begin to squeeze you. You protest by kicking, but then the walls release and you can relax again. Again the walls squeeze you. Again you protest and feel terror, and the contractions relax.

"The contractions continue now, more frequently, more rhythmically. They crush you, assault you, and stifle you. Your world has become a prison gone berserk and is demanding your death. But your prison has become a passageway, too, and the passageway a tunnel. Your mother's heart beats in an ever-ascending crescendo, and your own heartbeat joins hers. And, in a paroxysm of fear, you sink down the hell of this passageway."

At this point the Guide introduces the heartbeat sound with a drum.

"Suddenly your fear turns to anger. Enraged, you hurl yourself against this barrier. You must break free. You are trapped between this monstrous force pushing you out and this blind wall holding you back. You twist down a narrowing passageway, your body turning a half-turn, as you struggle to clear this tight, constricting hell. Your head is assaulted and smashed down between your shoulder blades, down into your chest. You cannot survive. It is the time of death, surely. The monster struggles one more time—and suddenly you are free.

"But how horrible this freedom. There is no support; there is no form; there is nothingness. Then, suddenly, someone seizes you by a foot and suspends you over this nothingness. Your spine and head dangling, twisting, you scream, and the world explodes. The cord that attached you from your middle to your mother, which had provided the nutriments and the oxygen to sustain you, is suddenly severed.

"You are smacked sharply on the back, and your lungs open suddenly to the stinging acids of the air. Blinding lights are shined in your eyes. You clench your eyes closed, but they aro forood opon, and dropo of fiory liquid aro oquoozod in. And then your little back, which had only known warmth and curve and softness, is slapped straight on the chill steel of a scale.

"Once again you are picked up by the feet, dangling in vertigo and terror, swung in the noplace where you have arrived. Then you are wrapped in some cloth and abandoned—crying, outraged, and mortally wounded. This is your birth.

"And this is considered a good birth. No problems, no complications—just good, newfangled, steely efficiency. But what this did to your human initiative and to your relationship to the world is beyond telling."

The Guide allows the participants a few more moments to absorb what has happened. Then she tells the partners to switch roles so that the fetus-infant now becomes the parent-womb, and vice versa. She then proceeds to give the same instructions as before.

At the end of the second "birth" the Guide announces the third stage.

STAGE THREE
The Blessed Birth

"We are about to begin the process of healing our births and engage in a blessed birth following the suggestions given by Frederick Leboyer in *Birth Without Violence.* It may be that the previous experience has stirred up for many among you a sediment of memories and traumas that began with the bad birth. Know—and believe for the period of this exercise that it is so—that by reliving our birth according to the principles we are about to experience, we may be able to mend our trauma and go beyond our fears, entering into a life of greater freedom, integration, and initiative.

"Would everyone now please come together, lying on the floor on your sides, bodies touching or brushing against other bodies, not unlike the situation that birds must find in a nest. Relax now . . . and relax still more . . . relax as deeply as you can.

"Beginning now, you are a fetus, being carried in your mother's womb. It is two months after your conception. You are living in the first half, the golden age of being in the womb. You are tiny, and suspended in the boundless sea that surrounds you. You are able to move, beginning with your trunk, and in time the movement spreads to your extremities. You play, agile and lively as the little fish that you are, supported by the great waters all around you. Such freedom and contentment . . . such boundless limits. . . . Only occasionally do you brush against the boundaries of this golden sea where you exist, for the membrane around you, in this first half of the time spent in your mother's womb, grows faster than you do. You never feel confined.

"Gradually the membrane grows more slowly, while you grow larger; and as you continue to grow, your home remains the same size—the golden age has ended. The limitless ocean is gone; the boundaries of the kingdom impinge upon you on all sides.

"One day your mother takes a walk, and you see the sun as a golden halo—a diffused light. You hear sounds of your mother's feet on the pavement, a car horn, and many other sounds, all filtered through the liquid in which you live. The sound is modulated and transformed. There are car noises. She crunches an apple, and you hear her digestive system working. You hear her joints as she moves and the rhythmic reassuring sound of her beating heart. And you hear your mother's voice, its nuances, its inflections and moods. Her voice will be a memory with you forever. Your mother sends you messages of love.

"You continue to grow larger and larger, and you press the walls on all sides. And now it is so tight, it seems that your mother's womb and the curve of your back are one organism. You struggle, kick, protest; but it grows tighter and tighter. Your spine and head curl together like a bending plant, and your whole body makes itself as small as possible.

"The world has become a prison, which suddenly starts to attack. It begins with several crushing hugs, which then release and go away. Gradually your terror departs as the hugs return, this time as playful sensual embraces. You respond with pleasure, arch your back, and allow the embracing pulsations to quiver throughout your body.

"These embraces continue for a whole month, and you grow to experience them as the normal way of being. . . . Then one day the sensual game turns into an assault, and what had been caresses become contractions—wild, out of control, pushing you downward.

"Your fear turns into rage, but then something stops it—your mother is trying to communicate with you and, in the midst of her own contractions, is sending you messages of communion and loving welcome. Your anger somewhat abated, you find your way out of the narrow passageway, and you are born.

"You emerge into a world of silence and darkness, of profound peace and gentle welcome. You, the holy child, have made your entrance. All sounds are soft ones. Time drifts, a kindly patience pervades. You feel soothed by the silence and darkness. You feel the relaxing acceptance, the loving welcome, the slow pace.

"How different this is from the world of intense movement you just left. In the darkness your mother communes with you: 'Welcome, I love you.'

"As you emerge—first your head, and now your arms— you feel warm, strong fingers slipped under each of your armpits, and you are pulled upward. No one touches your head. You are immediately placed in the hollow of your mother's belly, which receives you like a nest, perfectly formed to your shape and dimensions.

"You rest there, receiving. The warm life of your mother's flesh is continuous with your own, still attached by the umbilical cord, which continues to pulse with life.

"You sense that things are different on the outside, but not too different. You feel the new separation. You feel the stirrings of your own individual life rhythm. As you lie there, feeling the rhythm of your mother's breathing, you experience the flow of blood and oxygen through the umbilicus as you always have. This continues for what seems to be a very long time, although actually it is only four or five minutes of clock time.

"Continuing to get plenty of oxygen from the cord, you begin to feel a change in your chest. The flow of blood is beginning to change direction and move into your lungs. Your lungs fill with blood, and your chest, which up to now had been held in by the pressure of the womb, is suddenly released and begins to expand. A burning breath is taken and expelled sharply. You cry out and stop breathing for a moment. But there is no spanking on the back to get you breathing again in the usual way. Instead you are allowed to try your breathing again at your own pace. Gradually, cautiously, you take another breath, expel it with a little cry, pause, and try again.

"As oxygen continues to come to you through the umbilicus you are able to explore the world of breathing at your own pace. Now, with assurance, you begin to breathe rhythmically, in and out, in and out, in and out. You have awakened in a new world, while the memory of the world you have just left fades gracefully. You are breathing fully now, abundantly, easily. You hardly notice that they have cut the cord, and you are separated from your mother. Curled in the hollow of your mother's belly, you begin to pick up the rhythms of her breathing, and a breathing that is a bonding moves between you. Waves of breathing move throughout your little body, coursing from side to side and from head tip to coccyx.

"This movement sets up a pattern of other movements, a pattern that will never end until the day you die. It begins as you stretch out your right arm, touch your mother's belly, and then draw your hand back. Your other hand follows, meeting no resistance in this vast new world of which you are a part. Dimly, you may remember your time in the early amniotic ocean, so long ago, when you could move in a world so vast. But no . . . it is forgotten. Then you stick out one tentative foot and then the other, in a flutter of little kicks.

"You feel the warmth of your mother's hands on your back, one hand traveling over your back and then another, like the sensual caresses you knew in the womb. This slow rhythm of hands traveling down your body soothes you and reassures you as you explore this new world. What remains of the fear you had known a few minutes before in your passage down the birth canal is massaged away by the tenderness of the loving hands. The hands incite you to pleasure; and, with pleasure now, you stretch yourself more and more into the sensual loving world that has come to welcome you, your little arms and legs moving in all directions, your skin alive with sensation, your muscles ecstatic under the tender movements of the deep massaging waves of hands.

"And now you feel strong hands lifting you up again. One hand is under your buttocks, and the other is high up under your back. As these hands turn you on your side, they communicate another kind of tenderness from the soft hands that continue to massage you. Strong hands pick you up and gently lower you into warm water, water that is just as warm as it was when you were inside your mother. You feel weightless and free, and again the comforting memories of another world come back—and you are surprised by joy. What remains of fear or trauma dissolves in this comforting element you know so well.

"For the first time you open your eyes wide, with a look of infinite receptivity. Everything . . . everything that is out there is ready to be received into the deep and unending wells of your eyes. Your head turns from right to left, receiving the visual homage of this world that loves you. And you put your hand up through the water and caress the open spaces of the world in acknowledgment. Your hand drops back into the water, and you raise your other hand and play with the air about you, before it, too, returns to the water. Then a new discovery: one of your hands reaches up and meets the other hand. They dart and play with each other like a pair of courting butterflies. Sometimes they pause together and wave at each other in mirroring currents of oceanic memory.

"One little foot thrusts out, pushing against the edge of the tub, followed by the other. Your body moves in the tub by its own propulsion. What a wonderful game! This new space has all kinds of possibilities—free movement, water, self-propulsion, the space above the water, your own moving hands, your own moving body—and, always, the loving hands.

"Your little hands begin to explore your face, slide over

your nose and mouth, play with your lips. The tongue darts out; your mouth opens; your thumb goes in. Blissful, relaxed, you continue to reach out and explore this world, coming home again to the mouth, where you find such happiness. Thumb in mouth, you make a complete unity, the world out there in union with the world in here.

"Now you are lifted slowly from the water by the strong hands. You feel the gravity of your body weight, cry out, and are allowed to gently sink back into the element in which you feel so secure. Again, and still again, you are lifted up out of the water and returned to it, until gradually you come to feel comfortable with your own gravity and the world outside of the water. You are laid on a warm diaper and wrapped in cotton and wool. Only your head and hands are uncovered, so that they can continue to reach out and play.

"Warm and comfortable now, you are placed on your side. You easily move your head and hands and legs. You feel your abdomen expanding and contracting as you breathe deeply and freely. Suddenly you know that something is wrong. The shifting, moving world has stopped. Why has the world stopped? It has always been in motion, both inside your mother's body and without. You howl in protest. Strong hands again pick you up and rock you, and the fear goes away, as you are again in reassuring motion. You are put down—and again, the fear, the panic. But, still again, you are picked up and cradled and rocked, until at last you no longer find the lack of motion frightening. You lie quietly, open your eyes, and enjoy the stillness. You begin to feel the inner workings of your own body as motion, and outside all is stillness. This is the beginning of the waking and appreciation of your inner life. Moving and awake within, you become fascinated by the stillness without, and lie there considering it.

"You are becoming equal to any of the challenges that

will come your way. You are balanced now, serene, and carried forward in the joy of discovery. Your arms and legs continue to stretch and play in a dance of exploration that need never end. The kingdom of heaven is within. The kingdom of heaven is without. You are the child king or queen in this heaven, the holy infant who now takes up residence in this realm of freedom and all possibilities.

"Your birth has been mended. You are restored to your original potential. Our odyssey has ended."

The Guide might wish to play some gentle music and bring out bowls of simple foods for the roomful of newborns to feed each other.

The Guide announces a half-hour break and gives each participant a handful of clay. During the break the participants are to knead the clay, so that it will be soft and pliable enough for the masks they will make in the final phase of the exercise. After a half-hour the participants come back, and the Guide announces the fourth stage.

STAGE FOUR
The Mystery of the Earth

The Guide asks the participants to stand and chant together a traditional invocation, to prepare themselves to return to the elements of clay and earth. The invocation is chanted in ancient Greek.

Ma ga, ma ga, bo-an pho-be- ron ap- po - tre- pe. (Repeat)
Mother Earth, Mother Earth, turn around our fears.

LIFE FORCE

This invocation is recorded in Aeschylus' *The Suppliants* and is thought to have been part of an initiatory chant for one of the mysteries.

After several minutes of this, the Guide advises the participants to either close their eyes, if they wish, or keep them open just enough to see where they are going, and to move around the room, as in a journey of passage inward, through the labyrinthine tunnels that will take them deeper and deeper under the earth. As they do this, they continue to knead the clay, feeling at the same time that they are kneading their lives and making them more supple and receptive to the coming of new forms.

While they do this, the Guide and an accompanying musician may chant softly in a minor key, or they may wish to chant the traditional hymn that the priests and Initiates chanted during the great Eleusinian mysteries. From what we can recover from Christian commentaries, we know that the initiate underwent some physical and symbolic descent into the underworld, there to die to his or her old self and be reborn into a new self and a higher meaning.

Oide men bio teleutan oiden de di - os-do ton archan.

(This version, given by Pindar, translates: "Happy is he who, having beheld these things, descends beneath the earth: he knows the end of life and he knows the Zeus-given beginning.")

The Guide continues this chant for the next five minutes or so, as the participants continue to move around the room, seeking the passageways to the underworld. (It is best that the room be darkened at this point.)

After this interval the Guide will address the participants as follows, either speaking or singing the words in a minor key:

"Move downward, move inward, return to the earth, 0 initiates. Move downward, move inward, 0 initiates, and prepare to receive the ancient mystery of earth rebirth. Move downward, move inward, until you find that place where it is fitting that you be given back to Mother Earth, restored to your fetal state in her fruitful womb, there to die and be relieved of the old husks of ego and the miscarried life . . . there to be freed of mistaken identity . . . there to redeem the time when the One broke from the Many, and the Many shattered the One . . . there to mend the tapestries of time and history. . . .

"Lying down now, spread on your face the clay that you hold in your hands, and form a mask there. This is to be your earth mask, the earth form under which you are buried . . . and under which you are free and safe to die. Let your body become very still now. Let your mind be stiller yet. Let silence prevail, and soon you will die. Soon you will release and let go the callused husks of the little local self, letting them return to the earth elements, where they need to go in order to be reformed. Dissolve now. Let go. Let yourself die. I will not speak to you for several minutes."

After about three minutes or so the Guide says softly:

"Returning now to life . . . returning now, life moving in you again, but life that has been transmuted and refined in the womb of earth . . . feeling the elements of life flowing back into you, warm and vital currents, the earth returning to you a higher clay. You are reborn now, in this ancient mystery of death and of transformation.

"That which is personal in you knows that you are free to participate in the larger life of the Many and the unique life of the One. They are no longer antagonistic, but complementary. That which is historical in you knows the same thing, and what remains of the great revolts of many millennia past, when

LIFE FORCE

you broke from the *participation mystique* is healed. You are free to know the empathy of the group, as well as the particularity of your own destiny and becoming.

"And so arise now, holding the clay mask on your face as the mark of your initiation. Like Persephone in the ancient Eleusinian mystery, ascend out of the earth, cave, womb, tomb, to become in some sense an immortal—one who knows that birth and death are two names for a single process. Arise and ascend now, and—holding your masks to your faces, making sure there are slits for the eyes—journey back and look at the other initiates who are making the same journey, and sing with me if you choose."

The Guide will then sing—but much more joyously and in a celebrational mode—the Eleusinian chant given above, alternating from time to time with the words given in English. If there are bells and flutes and drums and stringed instruments at hand—if there are instruments that could have been played thousands of years ago—all the better. This is to be an ancient celebration and gains much from the use of these forms.

After a while the Guide invites the participants to place their masks one by one in the center of the floor, building a tower of earth masks, of faces of rebirth. When the tower is completed, the group gathers close around it, arms on shoulders, and chants the opening chant of the exercise.

ah-   ah-   ah-   ah-   ah-   ah-   ah-

Everyone is invited to put in their own variations on the chant, until it becomes the sung equivalent of the variations of the Many within the One. And the exercise ends.

The meal that follows should be a simple, ancient one,

with fruits and cheeses and good breads and perhaps a little red wine—only a little, however, if the participants are planning to explore the next stage of the psycho-historical recovery of the self.

Instructions for Going Solo

STAGE ONE: Ideally, if you are going through the process of The Remembrance of the Primal Community by yourself, you should try to get one other person to join you for this part of the journey. Then just follow the instructions as if you were part of the larger group, taking turns in playing the parts of the one who remains in the primal community and the one who struggles to break loose. If that is not possible, then you must first fully familiarize yourself with the instructions. Next imagine yourself as a member of the seamless web of kinship in the primal community while you chant the "ah-ah-ah" for about ten minutes. Then richly imagine both roles and play them out as fully as you can. Finally, write in your journal your reflections and experience of having been both sides of the conflict in the primal community.

STAGES TWO AND THREE: Again, for these stages, it is highly recommended that you have one other person go through these stages with you. If this is not possible, then make a tape of the Guide's instructions, making sure that you allow for sufficient pauses in order to experience each part of the process of Birth as Trauma and the Blessed Birth. Be sure to record some gentle music to accompany the end of this process. Provide yourself with simple food to eat and clay to knead into a mask. It might be well to have one friend whom you can call to announce your successful completion of the birth process.

STAGE FOUR: Again have the chants and the Guide's instructions on tape. Upon finishing The Mystery of the Earth, you may wish to go outside to a natural setting and lie on the earth for a while feeling Her Great Mystery and your connection to Her. Make sure you write in your journal about these experiences.

Notes

1. Jean Liedloff, *The Continuum Concept* (New York: Knopf, 1977), p.21.
2. The interested reader should contact the Pre-and Peri-Natal Association of North America for further information on this subject. This Association is an educational nonprofit organization dedicated to the in-depth exploration of the psychological dimension of human reproduction and pregnancy and the mental and emotional development of the unborn and newborn child. It publishes a journal as well as collecting, publishing, and disseminating information regarding all aspects of Pre-and Peri-natal psychology. The Association's address is PPPANA, 2162 Ingleside Avenue, Macon, GA 31204.
3. Dr. Emerson's earlier work is discussed in his study *Infant and Childbirth Re-facilitation* (Guilford: University of Surrey Press, 1984). A list of Dr. Emerson's more recent publications, tapes, and videos, as well as listings of his training seminars can be obtained by consulting his center at the following address: Human Potential Resources, 4940 Bodega Avenue, Petaluma, CA 94952.
4. This sequence is adapted from Frederick Leboyer, *Birth Without Violence* (New York: Knopf, 1975).

TWO

THE
SHINING
HOUR:

The Proto-Individual
and Childhood

Go, said the bird, for the leaves were full of children,
Hidden excitedly, containing laughter.
Go, go, go, said the bird; human kind
Cannot bear very much reality.

T. S. Eliot, ''Burnt Norton''

Judged by their duration and staying power, the early symbiotic tribal societies were enormously successful. They provided a balanced—even homeostatic—ecology of skill, community, and belief. A complacent subservience to the unchanging order became the psychological stance of the participants in this lethargic mystique. Social actions that were found to have worked thousands of years before were now seen to be given by gods, and so were crystallized into monolithic forms that brooked no challenge. When everything is sacrosanct, any experiment becomes blasphemy, and variety is impossible. The reader, who is used to the veritable smorgasbord of options for social and individual styles offered in the present hodge-podge era, would find it difficult to imagine how stale and stalemated is the order of the sacrosanct.

Consciousness must grow, however, and many were frustrated in the early symbiotic society. There was nothing left for the growing psyche but revolt or death. Questions had to be raised, adventures sought, challenges offered. Gerald Heard writes, "And as the growing seed bursts the pod, so the pioneers broke their way out, and the emptied husk of their society finally collapsed."[1]

However, in the new annals of herstory, that was not the entire story. As I indicated in the preface to this new edition, in many places, highly sophisticated, agrarian-based societies of partnership between men and women as well as partnership with spiritual powers evolved out of earlier primal societies. As the studies of Marija Gimbutas, James Mellaart, and Riane Eisler have shown, a remarkable culture developed in old Europe in the time between the more primal paleolithic and the explicitly heroic cultures of the post-neolithic era—from about 8500 to 3500 B.C. These civilizations, focused on the rites and worship of the Mother Goddess, demonstrate social, political, artistic, and technological achievements of great subtlety and sophistication. Further, as the findings of archaeologists Mellaart in Catal Huyuk in Turkey and Gimbutas in southeastern Europe reveal, these were basically egalitarian male-female societies, non-patriarchal, with descent and inheritance passed through the mother, and with women playing key roles in all aspects of life and work.[2] The art of this period is non-heroic; indeed, there are no signs of heroes, conquests, or captives. That came much later. Instead the art abounds with scenes and symbols from nature, with sun and water, serpents, birds and butterflies, and everywhere, images, figurines, and votive offerings of the Triple Goddess in one or another of her forms as Maiden, Mother, and Crone. All in all, one gains the impression of a gentle, high culture, nurturing, playful, and pacific.[3] This culture was exported to Crete, where it flourished in populous well-organized cities, multi-storied palaces, networks of fine roads, productive farms, an almost modern system of drainage and irrigation works, a rich economy with high living standards, and the lively and joyous artistic style that can only come out of equality between men and women.[4]

The people of these partnership societies reflect one branch of the proto-individual development. They were far too sophisticated, too skilled in technique, too much the builders and orchestrators of the world around them to be part of the seamless web of kinship with clan and nature that belongs to the earlier, pre-individual, primal societies. At the same time, they were not yet, for the most part, individuated, owing to their continuing alliance with the powers of nature, the subsuming of individual egos in the energies of the Goddess, and their access to depth realities and rituals which may preclude definitive egoic development. They have had neither the suffering nor the alienation that seems to attend the growth of the separated consciousness that haunts the full individual.

The other branch of proto-individual development comes from those marauding bands of Indo-Aryan invaders that helped destroy the peaceable cultures of partnership. *The Iliad*, that grand epic of violence, tells us much about the psychic states and sensibilities of these anarchic heroes and invaders. Much in the epic suggests a bewilderment on the part of the heroes as to where their orders and energies are coming from. *The Iliad* can be read as either a gods-determined document or as a superb psychophysical account of emerging powers and new vitalities that the receiver cannot yet accept as his own.

There is a passage in *The Iliad*, for example, when Athena, during a battle, puts a triple portion of *menos*—a kind of vital life force—into the chest of her protégé Diomedes.[5] When the hero feels *menos* in his chest or "thrusting up pungently into his nostrils," he feels new life and energy rising in him: "My feet beneath and hands above feel eager." He then proceeds to perform the most difficult feats with ease. When he receives *menos* in excess, he even occasionally dares to challenge the gods.

Hector is so possessed of an excess of *menos* that he goes berserk—he foams at the mouth, and his eyes glow.[6] Let us dig further here, as something very important is going on at this juncture in the psychology of human history. For this is not simply the possession and trance state of the earlier hypnocracies, but, as I have suggested, the emergence of a new and critical, if unstable, form of consciousness, one that finds its analogue in the burgeoning energies of the child.

I once read a book that startled me with its ingenuity and curious relevance to this hypothesis. I disagreed strongly with most of the book's premises. Indeed, the margins of its pages are filled with my questions, diatribes, and epithets, with long chicken-scratch commentaries crawling down and around the pages, and frequent and fuming inscribings of "NO!!!" For I'd been reading a crazy book—probably wrong and eccentric in its major premises, but so brilliant and cocky in its scholarship, so lucidly passionate in its arguments, that, like a force field, the book charges and illumines every question that it treats. It deals principally with the change of consciousness during heroic ages and is called *The Origin of Consciousness in the Breakdown of the Bicameral Mind*.[7] Its author, Julian Jaynes, with the energy of a true polymath, weaves archaeology, brain research, literature, history, psychopathology, and a spate of other disciplines to attempt to prove his Brobdingnagian thesis—namely, that prior to the first millennium B.C. consciousness as we know it did not exist. Man and society (by which we must assume he particularly means the earlier co-conscious societies) lived under the authority of the bicameral brain, wherein all mandates, orders, volitions, and other aspects of the cultural superego issued from certain areas of the right hemisphere and were then transferred and heard as auditory hallucinations in certain areas of the left hemisphere, telling man what to do.

Naturally, these hallucinations of the chambered brain were received as admonitions of the gods. This made for a very different kind of culture and consciousness, for, according to Jaynes, in the bicameral era "there were no private ambitions, no private grudges, no private frustrations, no private anything, since bicameral man had no internal 'space' in which to be private, and no analog 'I' to be private with. All initiative was in the voices of the gods."

Regardless of the questionable neurological accuracy,

Jaynes' description does fit the prevailing patterns of consciousness of the early symbiotic societies. Where Jaynes begins
to get fixated on his own hypotheses is when he goes so far
as to suggest that, with such a state of prevailing bicameral
daze, we must read *The Iliad* as the tale of "noble automatons
who knew not what they did." Blind Homer, wrathful
Achilles, all muddled along in a fog in which the left brain
knew not what the right brain was doing. By this interpretation, *menos* was really a gift of the right hemisphere to the left,
with Athena set up as the avatar of the right brain.

Jaynes sees the breakdown of the bicameral mind as occasioned by a series of geological catastrophes, beginning with
the volcanic eruption of Thera around 1470 B.C., and leading
to mass migrations and invasions of peoples all around the
eastern Mediterranean. Meandering bands of hero hordes shattered the bicameral mind.

The ensuing social chaos and cultural exchange, the spread
of writing, the rending of authority, and the declining efficacy
of the local gods led to the birth of subjectivity and the reflective consciousness. The growing silence of the brain-godded
voices made for widespread anxiety, as in these painful lines
from the Babylonian *Theodicy*, poignant foreshadowing of the
Hebrew psalms:

> May the gods who have
> thrown me off give help,
> May the goddess who has
> abandoned me show mercy.

Jaynes' neural theology leads him into many whimsies,
such as his suggestion that the story of the Tower of Babel
was the "narration of the garbling of hallucinated voices in
their decline." To help bridge the decline and the garble, man
took to occultism and sought signs and sureties in omens and

oracles, auguries and divinations. Remnants of the old neural order remained, as in the possession states of right-hemisphere-intoxicated priestesses, prophets, and sibyls. Poetry, too, is but the vestige of bicameral inspiration, the Muses having now been swept "even further out into the night of the right hemisphere."

The effect of all this on me was a state of active neurological ambivalence. I discovered that in my right brain I *knew* he was wrong, while in my left I was *convinced* he was right. Both halves finally got together in concluding that the book is both magnificent and a monument to hubris.

For isn't it hubris to build a whole paleontology of consciousness on brain research that is still in its earliest and most speculative stages? And isn't it hubris to assume that the genius of the past and its artifacts were due only to a simplicity of consciousness and not to a complexity far different from our own? One could offer, for instance, many examples to prove that the ancients were conscious masters of consciousness, able to self-orchestrate along the spectrum of awareness to perform many different tasks. Recent cultural anthropology abounds with evidence of "primitive" peoples with minds as contrary and capricious as our own, and nary a shred of bicamerality.

Mr. Jaynes, I fear, falls into the fallacy of simple location and simple dualism—this/that, here/there, inside/outside, right/left. It is probably much more complicated than that. The ecology of things suggests that we are not located just inside our skulls. Rather, we are organism-environments and, as such, symbiotic with a larger order of Nature. That order may include gods *and* brains and Mr. Jaynes.

But for the vitality of the mind, for the yeasting of the soul, and for the marvelous re-asking of the great questions of time, history, and meaning, better this book by far than the cautious quibbles of scholars who spend their days dissecting the brain of a leech. For Jaynes has added both fuel and format to the issues concerning psycho-historical development. True, there is little neurological evidence to suggest that the relationship between the two hemispheres of the brain changed suddenly thirty-five hundred years ago. But that profound changes in consciousness, behavior, and the manner in which large numbers of people reflected upon themselves evidently occurred is given further credence by Jaynes' work.

In the time of the proto-individual, the dazed and dazzled heroes are witnessing the separation in themselves of those elements in personality that had once been subsumed within the empathic communion of the co-conscious society. Now, separated and alien, their consciousness divided, their loyalties uncertain, they wreak havoc upon those very unities that had been the guiding strengths of the primal and transitional matrifocal cultures. They scorn the pervasiveness of their eroticisms. They muscle and armor themselves against the enticements of their sensuality. They fear, dread, and violate the places and persons who bear witness to the ongoing communion between seen and unseen orders. Cassandra is ravaged. The altar of Athena is defiled.

Then, on conquering, the hero is seized with remorse. Overwhelmed and shocked by the excesses of his own assertiveness, he falls into grief, for still he is tied to the common bonding of the symbiotic communion that he has only recently left. He blames the gods for his irrational behavior but strongly suspects that there is something working in him that, although out of bounds, is still his own.

Thus he feels shame and, not knowing what or who is causing his behavior, moves between paranoid rage and a shame that takes full responsibility. With such anarchy without as well as within, he is frequently driven to suicide. He has lost face, that face which once had been the common face, mirroring all others in the co-conscious society, and now is the mask of a hard-won ego. With no tradition to support and sustain this new "face," with no rites to wash away its violations of taboo, there is no recourse but to self-destruct.

Ajax in his cups slaughters a flock of sheep, thinking they are armed warriors. Shamed by the duplicity of his drunken consciousness, he kills himself. The samurai and the Bushido in Japan, late heroic reentries into the field of history, are afflicted with the same penchant for suicide.

To bear the melancholy of divided consciousness, the hero often seeks relief in the transient unity of mind to be found in drugs or intoxicants. After the rage on the field comes the drunkenness of the evening. After the shame-provoked depressions come the depressants of the fields and forests, the plant narcotics that banish sorrow, which is the meaning of the word *nepenthe*, the drug of the Homeric heroes.

There is much evidence to suggest that the proto-individual Aryan invaders of India brought down with them from central Asia about 1500 B.C. the psychedelic plant *soma*. The plant occupied an integral position in the myth and ritual structure of Vedic religion. It was regarded as divinity and was itself ritually consumed to bring the worshiper to a state of divine exhilaration and incarnation. "We have drunk soma and become immortal," hymns the early Vedic author. "We have attained the light, the gods discovered."

I and others have suggested that as the Aryans moved deeper into India, the gods proved more difficult to discover, because the soma plant, like fine wine, would not travel. I would even suspect that the exercises of the hatha yoga school may have been created as an attempt to fill the "somatic" gap and achieve that physiological state of being conducive to states of consciousness similar to those brought on by the ingestion of the sacred plant. [8] Whereas the soma was likely to have been consumed by the Aryan heroes for the purposes of exhilarating and unifying consciousness, the ingesting of the sacred plant and its subsequent replacement with psychophysical exercises was, by the time of the more stable mid-individual culture, the vehicle for the achievement of higher and even mystical states of consciousness.

Anodynes could only go so far, however, and the hero could not just be a lonely adventurer. After a while he could not stand himself, for he could not live without values, standards, patterns of prestige. He had to have some code of honor, some new forms of commonality. In the Sanskrit *Mahabharata* and *Ramayana*, in much of Genesis, in the Book of Judges, Samuel, and 1 Kings, in *The Iliad* and *The Odyssey*, in the Icelandic *Eddas*, and in so many other epics and sagas of the heroic age, we find the same phenomenon: warriors easily shamed and driven to a code of standards. Lists of thou-shalt-nots, tabulations of censures, and the exhortation to noble acts—these are the patterns that form the moral background of epic literature. The summation that Gerald Heard gives to his discussion of this era is rich with illuminating metaphors:

The Heroic Age was a necessary phase in the human development, a development that has gone on as a spiral process, an oscillation between outer knowledge and inner comprehension, since the end of the preindividual, primal culture. But this proto-individualistic culture was explosive. It was driven out from the land-locked harborage of the tribal estuary that had become a sandbar-blocked, stagnant lake with no more access to the outer ocean. These huddled squadrons, lifted by line squalls of protest, found themselves to be startled navigators, borne over the bar and out onto the high seas. There they found no other port in some island of the blest; only the vast waters welcomed them into a new freedom. And for many this was too much. Unable to manage the gale in their canvas and the waves on their thwarts, they foundered in the storm of passion that was let loose and sank into paranoia.

They became incapable of understanding any but their personal demand for expression. But in the main they rode out the storm with the aid of a sea anchor, that long submarine cable and sack that holds in the buckling ship and keeps its prow facing the storm. Such a sea anchor was the modifying morality which, the sagas and epics show us, was being worked out as a means of educating the boastful hero until (when he does not turn into the Ulyssean navigator) he becomes hammered and tempered into the pattern of chivalry, the honorable knight, the guardian of the weak. [9]

As Heard suggests, there is sometimes a being of transitional consciousness who emerges in the literature of the heroic epoch. He is generally seen as traveler or trickster and is always placed in situations in which he must live by his wits and his cunning, and so move beyond the melancholy as well as beyond the prescriptions of his time. Childlike, he wanders through a world of wonders, beset and tormented by the same forces that overwhelmed and divided the consciousness of his brothers. But he seems to be possessed of a still further complication in consciousness, a kind of third or observing consciousness that renders him relatively immune to the dangers and enticements of either the primal or the heroic worlds on which he is frequently shipwrecked.

The best-known of these is, of course, Odysseus; and the tale told in *The Odyssey* (which reflects a later development of consciousness than does *The Iliad*) is of a child-man, a man of many wiles, who manages to elude the morality of his day and wander from adventure to adventure through a fantastically entertaining world. He is nearly done in, as are his fellow heroes, by his encounter with the one-eyed giant Cyclops—a masterful stroke of description of the mind-set of the heroic age—but escapes that next-to-impossible challenge through an act of simple deception and ingenuity. Odysseus, whose name means "trouble," is the very model of man in the heroic age— brilliant and resourceful, but also greedy, arrogant, and piratical. A much-needed humbling and consequent deepening at the hands of the last representatives of the old partnership cultures devoted to the Triple Goddess (in *The Odyssey*, Circe, Calypso, Nausicaa) is required to end his dark age and to create a new possibility for human development. As I wrote in my book *The Hero and the Goddess:*

> In his involvement with these nymphs, Odysseus receives his first initiation: that of honoring and learning from the female powers that had been so abused by . . . the conquering Greeks.
>
> In a sense, Odysseus' journey into Mystery is about the restoration of the unity of the Triple Goddess through the awesome experiences and initiations of Odysseus. *The Odyssey* reweaves what *The Iliad* had torn asunder—the fullness of the Great Goddess in all her qualities and manifestations. These feminine qualities must be recognized and assimilated in order to enjoy a proper dynamic relationship in which male and female energies meet as partners—that is, equal, but not the same, for the polarity must be there for relationship and creativity to advance.
>
> There are other initiations as well. And in all them Odysseus finds himself tested by a reality that is larger and more mysterious than any he has ever known in his life. The wily and cunning hero, unfailing conqueror of the ways of the external world, is conquered and deepened by the great powers of the internal world. Those very powers that are the domain of the Triple Goddess—powers of insight and imagination, of psychological growth and spiritual awakening. [10]

LIFE FORCE

Thus at the hands of the representatives of the old Mother Goddess cultures of partnership, the wanderer-hero initiates, by virtues of his initiations, a dawning of a new kind of consciousness, one that is the best expression of the positive aspects of the creative delight and wonder of childhood as it corresponds to the dying heroic age. Odysseus stands for the mind of many of those representatives of the heroic Indo-Aryan derived cultures who learned from and adopted the ways and skills of the more ancient Goddess cultures. There is no doubt but that they were nurtured, softened, and civilized by the more sophisticated partnership societies which they conquered. In this way, *herstory* provided the charge and the training for the further development of culture and consciousness away from the anarchies of heroes and into the beginnings of a new order of civilization.

In the correspondence of the historical pattern of heroic anarchy to its analogue in human personal development, it is not difficult to see how the hero-child breaks from the symbiosis with and dependence on the mother into a world of independence and initiative. Like the hero, the child generally faces the problems of anarchy, rage, and fear. These are compounded by the child's growing desire to challenge, explore, and create new explanations—to build the world in its own image.

In his 1940 essay on "The Child Archetype" Jung wrote:

Child means something evolving towards independence. This it cannot do without detaching itself from its origins: abandonment is therefore a necessary condition, not just a concomitant symptom. . . . The "child" is all that is abandoned and exposed and at the same time divinely powerful; the insignificant, dubious beginning and the triumphal end. The "eternal child" in man is an indescribable experience, an incongruity, a handicap, and a divine prerogative; an imponderable that determines the ultimate worth or worthlessness of a personality.[11]

The myths and fairy tales of childhood almost always tell of separation and abandonment. These motifs clearly bear the charge of the stress of separation from the nursery culture and the warm symbiosis with the mother. And so the child wanders, lost in the forest, abandoned in the river, and attempts a task far beyond the child's strength. These myths, fairy tales, and rites of childhood initiation show us clearly that, in spite of the misery and dereliction, a heroic new consciousness is emerging, as are prodigious energies and precocious cunning.

The unique patterns of sensory learning and the passionate form-creating striving of almost every child (even with rigid and conformist schooling) resemble the very impetus of evolution itself in its quest for greater complexity of form. In this way childhood is that point of intersection between biology and cosmology. This enormous potency makes us fearful of childhood. We are ambivalent and uneasy, for something in us still knows that evolutionary energy and morphological striving are condensed in the body-mind of the child.

It is out of this fear that we circumscribe, circumcise, inoculate, and baptize children. Perhaps that is also why we commit mayhem on them, inflicting the modern equivalent of the fairy tales of abandonment and incarceration by cutting off their explorations, stoppering their inquiries, and mocking their sensibilities. In the years since the first edition of this book appeared, the treatment of children has become much worse than it was. Horror and violence have moved to center stage, especially among inner-city children. Reports of child abuse are rampant. The continued breakdown of the family has caused many children to become little more than refugees. In America the shift out of prosperity and the collapse of traditional values and social forms has made parenting much more difficult than it once was. With both father and mother, or the single parent working, children with latchkeys go home to hours spent alone in empty apartments and houses. Psychological as well as physical abandonment has grown to desperate proportions. One hears the terror in children's voices as they call in to late-night radio counselors asking how to get away from an abusive parent.

Children of every economic background are exposed to drugs in school. A growing number carry guns and act out the pattern of violence they see on TV and in the world around them. In the rage that children express is the abuse and violation they feel. Being more vulnerable and less shielded than adults, children understand deceit and have a much keener lie detector than their elders. Being closer to nature, they cannot help but be tormented by the destruction of the natural environment. All this feeds their rage and fuels their desperation.

In the last decade or so education has failed on so many fronts that our schoolrooms have become places for the institutionalization of paralysis, where the genius and glory of childhood is systematically removed, and in its place are put the shrunken shibboleths of reigning culture and consciousness. Herein evolution is betrayed and human possibilities immured. In this context the reader might be interested in reflecting upon a negative meditation that the American poet Rhett Kelly and I once wrote that deals with the nature of the catastrophe. I call it "Consider the Stradivarius."

We are given as our birthright a Stradivarius, and we come to play it like a plastic fiddle. Consider the Stradivarius. Consider the child—the star brighter than any star man's mind can create conception of, this Godstuff rendered freely as spillover of an abundance of which we are largely unaware. This nuclear divinity, which radiates an unnameable glory when it comes, is in fact a creation of such inestimable worth that, were a cosmic scales to be employed, the infant child placed on one tray and all the precious jewels on the other, there would be no possibility of outweighing the child.

Talents to last a million years are the mother lode of its molecules. Its body is celled of mysteries that are incomprehensible, yet existent and responsive to all that is, and therefore is the container and active channeler of all that is. There is no need here to speak of Evolution to come. All the future tunings and turnings are already here, latent givens in the once and future child.

Its arms and legs enter into conversation with the bright of mornings. In perfect diaphany it knows the shapes of nature for its own. Sunbeams shaping grasses, trees parting skies, waters rushing over rock, these are the mirrors and progenitors of all its movings, the visible likeness of its earth-partnered life.

Comes then society's teaching time. The child is ushered into the presence of the Guidepost to the relevant life. And this post, assigned the teaching task, begins the process of informing the child of its smallness in relation to the far larger, its ignorance measured against great intelligences, its ineptitudes contrasted to vast skills, its lacks opposed to fullnesses, its basic inconsequentiality within the context of "things that matter."

Knowledge of its own divine origins begins to be quite systematically removed from its consciousness. First, the fullness of nature is removed. The trees are taken out of its arms, the rushing waters out of its blood. Body and brain are hunched; gates are built in its muscles; its brain becomes a fortress against all vastness, guarding against the remembrance of who it is and where it came from. This done, the child is deemed acceptable.

But it is not yet over. The internal world must be put to rout. At one point, a serious point, the child will be taught that what is imagined is unreal, and an arterial siphon will draw from near its heart that much strength of impulse which was necessary to keep up its commitment to the inner realms. What is imagined, what has a reality of ponderables that simply doesn't lend itself to physically calibrated scales, this is said to be not real, and the child is halved, so to speak.

If the heart siphon is not wholly effective, another siphon is put into the veins of the inner elbow and all that society thinks impractical is drawn from the elbow's crook. Put the various other siphons into alcoved places, the armpits, the groin, the bend of the knee, the arched chamber of the eye-socket.

Tell the little child that the world out there is only this, or only that, or perhaps phrase it merely, make less than worthy the notice of it. Only a tree, and all the trees are cut down; merely a small lake, and the deeps have lost their mystery; only this and merely that, and the magnificences of nature are made into shoddy stage sets. The siphon has drawn nerves of vision from under the roofed brain, taken the full life of seeing from the eyes.

Belittle another human being, categorize him with a label having to do with his color, his race, his lack or surfeit of academic training, his societal affiliations, pin him like a butterfly specimen for the child to inspect minus all his full lifeness, his essential human-divineness, his proper dimensionality; and you've siphoned out generative power that reaches deep into the groin that could have meant the reseeding of the world.

The supreme prerogative of childhood is wonder. If by some chance wonder escapes containment, the child-become-the-adult is able to respond with such totality to the incoming flow of information that he or she is able to organize novelty of pattern and form out of this information. Is it any wonder that so many of the great geniuses and innovators are those who have kept their childhood alive in them? Wonder has a buoyant, exhilarating crest-of-the-wave effect. It is at once an expectancy of fulfillment and an anticipation of More to Come.

"A sense of wonder is the mark of the philosopher," Socrates once said. The aim of the cosmic questions asked by both child and philosopher is to enter into that reflexive state of delight and resonance in which one discovers the answer that tells one that the world is oneself writ large. "I become what I behold!" said the child-man Walt Whitman, echoing the experience of all children, as they seek to understand by incarnating the world.

The engaging, growing child is in a state of continuous creation of mutual relations with the environment. I have termed this state *psychoecology*, by which I mean that the child has leaky margins with the world at large. The nervous system of a child flows into and is systemic with the systems of nature, so nature is experienced sensually as self and cosmos, the one continuous with the other. Should much of this nervous system be shut down—as so much of it is in our northern European-derived education and understanding of intelligence, which discriminates against one whole half of the brain, tending to reward only left-hemisphere-dominant students, who respond well to verbal, linear styles of education—then the child becomes crippled in its critical role as a living metaphor for evolutionary striving.

We are as different from each other as snowflakes; and each of us has, especially in childhood, a special penchant for different ways of exploring our world. In order to preserve the genius and developmental potential of childhood, one must quite simply give the universe back to the child, in as rich and dramatic a form as possible.

Multiperceptual learning, we have found, is a key to this gifting. In school curricula and programs we have helped develop, the child is taught to think in images as well as in words, to learn spelling or even arithmetic in rhythmic patterns, to think with the whole body—in short, to learn school subjects, and more, from a much larger spectrum of sensory and cognitive possibilities. So if a child shows inadequacy in one form of learning—say verbal skills—we direct the child to another, in which the systems of the child's being might be more readily engaged. In sensory motor skills, for instance, a nonverbal child may wake up and be restored to wonder, and then, as the very natural consequence, show a greater facility to learn to read and write more quickly and with greater depth and appreciation. For some children, the growing edge of their exploration of the world is best mediated through visual thinking. For others, it is through music or dance or motion. Much in classical education tends to inhibit these and frequently causes nonverbal thinkers to feel inferior and begin a process of abandonment and failure that will last all their lives. All too often, the saving daimon, fairy, or angel, who could help the abandoned child safely complete its journey through the symbolic way stations of the "bad" culture, is rigorously locked out and denigrated in the current order.

In many years of observation I have never met a stupid child, but I have met many self-righteously stupid and debilitating—and, yes, even brain-damaging—systems of education. As we have discovered, a child can learn math as a rhythmic dance and learn it well, the places of rhythm in the brain being adjacent to the places of order. A child can learn almost anything and pass the standard tests—the modern equivalent of the fairy-tale trials—if, as in the fairy tale, the child is dancing, tasting, touching, hearing, seeing, and feeling information. In school as in the myth, children can delight in doing so because they are using much more of their mind-brain-body system than conventional teaching generally permits. So much of the failure in school and home stems directly from boredom, which itself stems directly from the larger failure to stimulate and not repress all those wonder areas in children's brains and souls that could give them so many more ways of responding to their world.

The changing chemistry of childhood gives impetus to the protest and even rage the child feels at the thwartings that are a child's lot. And perhaps the present rage that children feel, a rage born out of a sense of violation and abuse, serves either to alienate them further from a violent and abusive social order or to repress still further their sense of engagement with the world. It is not surprising that the adulthood of the repressed child is itself so privatized and withdrawn. Autism has become an acceptable way of life. And what with virtual reality machines on the near horizon, withdrawing into private, cybertech-produced fantasies may soon become a norm.

In the normal course of development, however, the small child's first reaction to the repression of a roaming mind, body, and spirit is rage; and that rage reaction, so like a hero's pride of protest, can be correlated with the particular secretion, noradrenaline, found in the core of the child's suprarenals. Noradrenaline causes outward-directed rage, as distinguished from adrenaline, which is the glandular secretion that causes inward-directed rage or guilt. Interestingly enough, chemical studies of those who suffer from paranoia, which often involves regression to childish behavior, show that excessive amounts of noradrenaline are being secreted. The Homeric heroes, given to both paranoia and childish behavior, were undoubtedly overdosing on their own noradrenaline charges. Whether mood precipitates hormone change or hormones precipitate mood is presently a chicken or egg kind of question; but the psyche that has become arrested at a childish, heroical level is in a state of psychophysical regression and exhausts itself by its own excesses. There is no question but that the child, like the hero, needs the motivation of the noradrenaline charge in order to be weaned from the nursery and its condition of dependency ties.

In its creative aspects, then, the chemistry of childhood with its questing curiosity drives the organism into evolutionary striving. But, still at the stage of childhood, the individual confronts the questions that the heroic age handled with such ineptitude, questions that have consequently stymied the further development of our notion and practice of freedom: How is independence to develop without lapsing into anarchy? And how is adventuring initiative to grow without foundering in irresponsibility?

Some of the answer certainly lies in giving the child more to do and more to be. Part of the problem with the old hero cultures is that those who lived in them were so limited in the patterns of their lives. Fight or flight, glory or shame, savagery or limiting chivalry—these were the dualisms that constrained the opportunities and determined the limited choices of the proto-individual. The child, however, always has the marvelous saving grace of being a genius at dramatizing speculation. The human child, unlike the dog or cat, acts out things that can be imagined. The dog and cat don't moo or crow or whinny, (although some transitional dogs I know try). The child can and does. Once it acquires mind and imagination, the child's body—highly sensitized by nurture, by touch, and by its still unshuttered doors of perception—lives in a state in which it is continuously bridging the psychological and the physical distance between the self and the universe.

World-building, whether it be art, culture, industry, or communications networks, is the necessary outgrowth of this special sensitivity and playful genius of the child. These extensions become the prostheses of ourselves, the further organization of nature's materials that transforms the meaning of Nature itself. Because of our neoteny, our prolonged childhood, with its extended allowance for the plasticity and playfulness of our perception and thought, we are able to become co-evolutionists and weave new threads into the fabric of reality. Herein we humans are evolution become conscious of itself; and in this conscious striving to join forces with the universe, our passion and our play move us to extend ourselves into novel forms on the grid of space and time.

In these creative experiences of co-evolution, we may sense these novel forms as the unfoldings of some grand design or mighty purposefulness. They are often carried in the surge of an *entelechy*—a kind of structuring dynamic energy rising from a Source that contains all codings. It is the entelechy of an acorn to be an oak. It is the entelechy of a baby to reach maturity and beyond. It is the entelechy of a popcorn kernel to be fully popped. It is the entelechy of you and me to be God only knows what. When experienced, as it frequently is, in religious, mystical, or other peak experiences, it provides a momentum for change and unfolds as a creative, transforming energy which charges one's life with growth and meaning. From years of study and observation of creative and religious type experiences, I have concluded that the process of entelechy is one of the key ways in which evolution enters into and seeds the manifest world with patterns drawn from depth levels of reality.

The child is the entelechy of the adult, and world-making is ultimately a search for higher levels of synthesis of self and world, drawn from the recognition that outer and inner worlds are interdependent aspects of reality rather than independent states. This is in keeping with a good deal of advanced evolutionary theory, which would see our body-minds as energy systems within evolution, the process that links our individuality with all of nature's strivings toward variation and multiplicity of form. Up to now our joining of this process has been haphazard and a matter, for the most part, of chance or a crisis that leads to innovation. In the complexity and chaos of our current world, we can no longer afford to leave our evolutionary sanctions to such randomness. Here the child is "father to the man"; and the genius of childhood's exploration, if sustained and deepened, gives us many of the tools and qualities of mind and body that we will need to join so vast an enterprise. This is why there is so much emphasis today on embracing the inner child. For we are at a stage of self-reflection in which we are able to sustain, recover, and improve upon our childhood genius.

Recalling the world of sensory splendor known by children, Wordsworth wrote in "Intimations of Immortality," in early childhood,

> There was a time when meadow, grove, and
>   stream,
> The earth, and every common sight,
>   To me did seem
>   Apparelled in celestial light,
> The glory and the freshness of a dream.

Then, lamenting the consequent diminution of his senses, he says,

> It is not now as it hath been of yore,—
>   Turn wheresoe'er I may,
>   By night or day,
> The things which I have seen I now can see no
>   more.

Wordsworth is wrong when he cries that "nothing can bring back the hour of splendor in the grass, of glory in the flower." It can come back, but bearing a different splendor, a different glory. The appreciation felt is more poignant, perhaps not unlike what the prodigal son felt when he returned from his voluntary exile and repudiation of his home. Having come back, he was given so much; his father withheld nothing.

And so it is for those of us who, in our maturity, return to the birthright of our senses. It is as it has been stated in the *Upanishads:* "Abundance is scooped from abundance, and yet abundance remains." There is more now than there was then. The brightness is heightened, because now the shadows are seen, as they were not in childhood. Something is missing in childhood that is given to those who make the Journey.

The connections, when remade, are now felt more keenly. The excitement of paradox acts as constant provocation to self-transcendence, as it cannot in childhood. Realities encountered the second time around have dimensions unperceived before. Eros and aesthetic joy, passion and contemplative intelligence, give to maturity its capacities to cocreate worlds that are true, and ever more true, to our inner vision of what a world can be.

How can we redeem the child within and regain "the glory and the freshness," but on the level of mature and deepened sensibilities? Gerald Heard put the question in its negational form when he asked, "If we would permit the enraged child now buried in our repressed subconscious (just above the birth-wounded infant) to release the pent-up energy, what, in modern terms, would be that procedure?"

Heard suggested that the answer is found in metaphors and practices related to the ancient rites of water initiation.

LIFE FORCE

As we have seen in Chapter 1, the first initiation of earth and rebirth teaches the psyche how to be born into distinctiveness from unison into harmony. The second initiation is to teach the psyche "how to correct the excessive reaction, that the race and the individual still make," against the prolonged nurturing period in mother culture or in the nursery. I would add that it also must involve experiences that teach us how to orchestrate our energies in order to enhance our sensibilities, instead of blocking them in what today might be deemed justifiable rage, but which nevertheless leads to a crippling of the emotional life and subsequent withdrawal.

The first experiences in initiation recalled the violent birth that wounded self and society, and then mended this with a peaceable birth and the ancient rite of restoration to and rebirth from the earth. The second initiation is equally ancient and involves some kind of ordeal by water. In traditional cultures the ordeal can be as dramatic as that of the Siberian shamanic rites, in which the child-postulant is taken to a frozen river. Here he or she has to plunge through one hole in the ice and swim under the freezing water, to emerge some distance away through another hole in the ice. The child might be required to do this nine times, and drowning is always a real possibility. If the postulant succeeds, it is assumed that he or she has been reborn out of the icy womb into a new control of forces within and without.

The discipline and coordination demanded in this ordeal by water requires a tempering of willful egotism, which would only result in excessive struggle and drowning. There must be a transmuting and extension of personality, so that it can join forces with the element in which it is immersed. And in this skillful interplay with water, the initiate not only survives but becomes consciously aware of the self as continuous with nature and with the process and the Pattern That Connects. In this way ego is grounded in essence, and the child gains communion with a larger ecology that is both conscious and chosen. It is a step beyond the unchosen and unconscious ecstasy of that symbiosis the infant experiences.

Baptism, of course, is another form of this. A modern fundamentalist, for whom baptism is a powerful, soul-charging, noradrenaline-raising event, would perhaps protest Heard's easy dismissal of it when he says that "as we now preserve it in a traditional, atrophied form, consisting of the sprinkling of a few drops or at most a quick dip, it is naturally difficult to recognize why such a gently dampening procedure should have been considered adequate to quench the flame of anger or to smooth the contortions of rage."[12] However, Heard's indictment probably stems from the fact that baptism, a practice that is found in many cultures and religions, was often a life-threatening exercise. People could be held under for several minutes until they nearly drowned. Needless to say, when finally they came up, choking and sputtering, they often had a whole new perspective on life. For the ancients believed that to have real change, you have to build real charge. The body had to be pushed to a fairly extreme place to release its habit patterns and to generate the kind of energy from which a major change or rebirth into new life could arise.

James Hillman provides an excellent balance to Heard's dismissal in his review of the enormous concern expressed by the early Church fathers over the critical and transmutational quality of infant baptism:

> When one looks at the early controversies over infant baptism one wonders just what psychological content was so exercising these excellent Patristic minds. Their energy spent on the child is comparable to that of ours spent on childhood in modern psychology. At first, though, they [Tertullian and Cyprian] did not urge early baptism, and Gregory of Nazianzua preferred some degree of mind,

about the age of three, before baptism. But Augustine was adamant. Because man was born in original sin he brought it with him into the world, as Augustine himself had done from his pagan past. Only baptism could wash this from the child. Augustine was sharp about the child's need of salvation, writing: "Those who plead for the mimesis of children ought not love their ignorance, but their innocence!" (Enar. in Ps. XLIV, I.) And what is innocent? "It is the weakness of the faculties of the child that is innocent, not the soul." (Conf., 1, 7, 11). How Freudian: The child cannot perform with its still-too-young faculties, those latent perversities that are in the soul. The soul carried not mere general sin, but the specific sin of pre-Christian, un-Christian impulses of polytheistic paganism which Freud was later to discover and baptise, "polymorphous perverse," and which Jung was later more comprehensively to describe as the archetypes. Baptism could redeem the soul from childhood, from that imaginal world of a multitude of archetypal forms, Gods and Goddesses, their cults and the un-Christian practices they substantiated. [13]

Hillman is rightly drawing attention to the terror of ancients and moderns alike before the power of the fantasy life of the child—of the development of the child's imagery and imaginal mind, which allows the world of wonders within to have equal status with the wonder-filled world without. Freud, like Augustine, clearly regarded this as regressive ("primary process thinking"), while Jung welcomed these visions as a vehicle within which the adult captures something of his childhood fluidity of soul in order to seek a more comprehensive individuation.

THE DROMENON FOR
THE PROTO-INDIVIDUAL:

I Become What I Behold

We will now engage in the experiences and initiation relevant to both the personal and historical stages of this development. Beginning with heroics and an enactment of noradrenaline-charging protest, we will then move into an ordeal by water and follow this by an ancient and powerful *zikkr* of communion.

Finally, we will conclude with an experience that clarifies the knowledge of how we and the processes of nature are the mirror images of each other and how, once we know this, wonder is restored. "I become what I behold," and the child-adult partners nature in a resonance that causes new forms to bloom.

STAGE ONE
The Protest

The following exercise should be performed in a room large enough for all the participants to be able to move freely and swing their arms without hitting each other. The Guide will ask the participants: "What were you able to sense, see, or do in childhood that you are not able to sense, see, or do now?"

The participants will respond, probably referring to the extended sensory capacities that they had as children and no longer have now, as well as to the courage, imagination, and adventurousness of their childhood selves. The Guide will allow about ten minutes for the discussion and for comparisons to be made.

The Guide will then ask the participants to stand up and close their eyes. She then will speak to them, saying:

"We have been crippled and thwarted in our capacities to experience both inner and outer worlds. We are unable, most of us, to see, touch, taste, smell, and hear as well as we once could. Stale habits of perception and the thick, darkened glass of concepts have gotten in the way of our percepts. Similarly, we have been cut off from our freedom to be what we really are by the idols we have made of our habits, by society's expectations for us, by social and professional demands that we shape up to their designs. Francis Bacon once referred to these as 'the idols of the tribe and of the marketplace,' and they continue to cripple us in varying degrees and in various ways.

"Now I am going to give you five minutes of clock time, and during that time many of these idols will rise up before you. These will be symbols of forces that inhibit you, limit your freedom to wonder, to play, to act. In all sorts of ways, since they began in childhood, they have worked to prevent you from becoming what you have the capacity to be, and from engaging in the creative exploration and building of the world that is your natural right.

"As these images rise, you will physically pick up an imaginary but very powerful long-handled sledgehammer or mace. Swinging this instrument, you will rage and protest and smash the idols to smithereens. Make the swinging very powerful, and let your anger and the vigor of your act be proportionate to your need to smash these idols that still haunt you. It is helpful to punctuate each swing with a warrior sound of Yaaaa! Yaaaa!! Try not to hit your neighbors, although in the heat and fury of battle they may remind you of the idols.

"As the idols rise up, and as you strike and smash them, know that at the same time you may be destroying much of their power to affect you any longer. And now begin."

STAGE TWO
The Initiation by Water

For this stage of the exercise, you will need to use a large swimming pool and have standing ready several excellent swimmers, who can pull people out should they get exhausted. (If a swimming pool is not readily available, the exercise can be partially simulated by filling a number of large tubs or receptacles with water. The participants then divide into partners, and one partner holds the other's face under water until the immersed partner indicates the need to come up for air. As soon as he or she has taken a breath of air, the partner allows his or her face to be held under water again. The whole procedure is repeated nine times, whereupon the partners exchange roles.)

The participants will gather in bathing suits around the pool. As this is an ancient and powerful rite of initiation, there is to be no talking or commentary on what is happening. The note of solemnity that marks the observation of the process helps the initiates in the water to continue with the ordeal. The Guide divides the group into subgroups of three to five people. Only one subgroup is in the pool at any given time; the other groups observe. The groups are then told: "You are about to partake of the ancient rite of catharsis and initiation through water. This will be a very arduous process. It is to be done with great concentration and seriousness; draw upon as much skill and strength as you can manage. There is to be no showing off or display of prowess, for to do so would be dangerous.

"Upon my calling you forward, each group will dive into the water and swim underneath for as long as you can without choking before coming up and catching your breath. Thereupon you will dive again and, swimming under the water, repeat the same procedure. This you will do nine times, taking care to stay alert to the process and being aware of the count.

"Each dive will be symbolic of a plunge into your own deeps, there to exhaust, and so release like bubbles, the habits and limitations that confine you. If you tire, come over to the side of the pool and rest until you are able to resume the ritual. As you swim under water, be aware of your personality joining the common element and of your will being put entirely to the disciplines of this difficult and ancient task.

"Let the repressions of your childhood dissolve in the expression of power and movement. If you find yourself anticipating the next breath, concentrate instead on the movement of your right hand or your left foot. This will both focus and distend consciousness and bring you into a fuller relationship to the sacredness of the means instead of to the consummation of the ends of the process.

"If you need help, do not become so prideful and heroic that you cannot ask for it. Someone will jump in and come to your aid. If there are others who can't swim, or who fear water, or who for some other reason do not want to undergo so vigorous a mystery, they will be permitted to perform a modified version of this with a large container of water—following, however, the same psychological principles that have just been described—immersing their heads nine times in the container of water.

"As the members of each group finish in the water, I will ask them to come out and sit or stand quietly by the side, encouraging the others with their silent and solemn attention. No new group will begin until all members of the previous group are out of the pool.

"And now let us begin the ancient mystery of water, and in so doing, allow ourselves to go beyond ego and become one with essence."

After the last subgroup has completed the process, the Guide will invite all the participants to enter the water together and float on their backs. During this time they are to feel themselves becoming continuous with and supported by those very waters to which they had just been given over for extension and release.

STAGE THREE
Zikkr *of Communion*

The Guide will ask the participants to gather around her at the pool and will explain the nature of a *zikkr*. *Zikkr* (pronounced *zicker*) is an Arabic word meaning a kind of exercise or prayer or even discipline that engages consciousness at its very root. The *zikkr* can be negative, and many of us have had long periods of our lives in which the negative *zikkr* went on and on, droning through our days, taking up an enormous part of our awareness and our energies.

Examples of the negative *zikkr* would be a continuous repetition of any one of the following:

I wish I were dead, I wish I were dead,
I wish I were dead . . .

I wish Willy were here, I wish Willy were here,
I wish Willy were here . . .

I wish Willy weren't here, I wish Willy weren't here,
I wish Willy weren't here . . .

I can't, I can't, I can't . . .

I'm inadequate, I'm inadequate, I'm inadequate . . .

I'm not worth it, I'm not worth it, I'm not worth it . . .

I need, I need, I need . . .

The negative *zikkr* becomes so entrenched that it stupifies the brain, poisons the soul, and enters amoebalike, as a huge advancing cancer, to sap our energies and thwart our finest impulses. Much of the collapse and derailment of person and culture is probably due to this repetitive and automatic poison. People call it by many other names, try to uproot and abreact it, curse or cajole it out of existence, but still it hangs in there, a testimony to the powers of entropy. For it has lived in one for too long, been reinforced many times daily, and taken up residence in virtually every nerve and sinew of one's being.

Sometimes the *zikkr* just dies of old age or perishes in the face of some vital crisis or challenge. Mostly, however, it just remains. If we could find a way to teach people to end the negative *zikkr* in their lives, then I suspect the planet Earth would see such an evolution of culture and consciousness as has never been seen before, for upwards of 75 percent of wasted human energy would be available for use and transformation.

There is only one thing I know that can successfully remove or greatly diminish the negative *zikkr*. It is the positive *zikkr*. Traditionally, this has taken the form of prayers or mantrams that become so constant and deep a part of the practitioner's consciousness that the negative *zikkr* is gradually replaced and even destroyed. Best-known are the Sanskrit sound *Om,* or the mantram *Om Mani Padme Hum;* the continuous repetition of the Arabic name for God, *Allah;* the Eastern Orthodox prayer of the heart, *Lord Jesus Christ, have mercy on me;* the Greek Orthodox *Kyrie eleison;* and the jubilant *Alleluia!* The saying of the rosary provides a kind of positive *zikkr,* as do the chants of many Eastern religious groups. All these, however, are predicated upon a specific form of religious belief and worship and would generally not be suitable to one not committed to the understanding and practice of the larger dimensions of this belief, although Westerners have quite successfully been utilizing certain Sanskrit chants with great effect as meditational aids. There is a *zikkr,* a very ancient one, that comes down to us today through the Sufi tradition, and provides a practice that does not demand specific religious belief but nonetheless engages by its power and beauty the heart, soul, body, and mind of the practitioner. The *zikkr* is neither a word nor a concept. It is a universal sound made deep in the throat—a hum of communion: *hmmm hmmm hmmm.* The sound is made three times on each breath and bears with it a great psychophysical power. For it is the sound similar to the one made by babies suckling, to sounds of appreciation, of communication, of pleasure of all kinds—gustatory, aesthetic, sexual, mystical. It is the ultimate approbation, and before its power and beauty, the negative *zikkr* has little if any place to be.

After explaining these things to the group, the Guide will say: "We will engage now in the formal practice of this *zikkr,* although it can be done without this formality in other situations—while driving, while speaking to another person, while engaged in any and all of life's activities. Care should be taken, however, to practice it formally from time to time, to ground it in its sacred and archetypal form.

"To begin, sit on the ground in any position that will keep the spine straight. Close your eyes and breathe very deeply, following your breath all the way in and all the way out. As you do this, allow yourself to be filled with peace and light in the inhalation, and in the exhalation, to send this peace and light out into the world" (two to five minutes).

"Before beginning, we will practice the *zikkr* by inhaling fully and, on the exhalation, making the *hmmm hmmm hmmm* sound deep in the throat. As you make this sound, feel it as a communion with God or Being, whatever your beliefs are, and let the sweetness and beauty of this communion continue throughout the *zikkr*. The sound is to be thought of as the resonance and loving communion between yourself and God or the Essence of Reality. Practice now with me the *zikkr*.

"We will now begin a cycle of thirty-three breaths (ninety-nine *hmmm's*). Do not try to keep the count; I will do it for you. Follow, if you can, my breathing pattern, so that we can all be in harmony together in our *zikkr* of communion. At the end of the thirty-three cycles, I will rap once on the floor and ask you all to inhale and hold your breath, during which time allow the sweetness of the communion to move through your entire being. When again I sound the rap, we will exhale, inhale again, and together do ten sets of the *zikkr*, whereupon I will sound the rap again. Again we will hold our breaths and let the sweetness of the communion prevail. Now let us begin the first cycle of the thirty-three *zikkrs* of communion."

At the end of the cycles of thirty-three and ten, the guide will finish the *zikkr* by saying: "In the tradition it is appropriate to acknowledge and give reverence. If you wish, then, you will bow low, your head approaching the floor, to the God in others. Return. You will bow a second time to the God in yourself. Return. You will bow a third time to the God That Is. Return. And now sit quietly for a while, and meditate in the communion of your experience."

STAGE FOUR
I Become What I Behold

Allow at least a half-hour to pass before beginning the next stage of the exercise, since participants will need time to integrate and reflect upon their experiences.

Shakespeare provided the key to this exercise in the immortal words of *As You Like It:*

And this our life, exempt from public haunt,
Finds tongues in trees, books in the running brooks,
Sermons in stones and good in every thing.

While still in a state of nature and wonder, while still serving as interface between biology and cosmology, the child discovers and exhilarates in the greatest and most hopeful of mysteries: that the patterns in nature provide the lines and whorls, the buddings, blooms, and dyings that reflect and quicken in us a recognition of the similar patterns in our own lives.

In the world of *Unus Mundus* we are, after all—we rocks and winds and waterfalls, we Johns and Janes and Will Shakespeares—analogues of each other, patterned in a field of resonance where everything and everyone is implicated in everything and everyone else. So truth comes in all guises, and everything is right at hand to lead you home. Here is proof, in an exercise of childhood wonder and adventure recast for the adult mind.

Gather all participants around an absolutely splendid log, a regular "Ancient of Days," the kind that has been winded, watered, and weathered to contain all possible patterns fore and aft. Have the members of the group call out spontaneously what they see in the log—eyes, owls, faces, fish.

LIFE FORCE

After a while, ask them to look with a deeper level of themselves and try to perceive mythic and symbolic patterns in the log. Many will see myths unfolding: Buddha meditating, Christ on the cross, heroic battles, meetings of the gods, mandalas, death and resurrection, the story of evolution, partings, passages, and the like. Turn the log around or upside down, and see if this evokes more or different perceptions.

Finally, have the participants look at the log for the patterns and possibilities of their own lives. They may either speak their perceptions or keep them silent, as they choose. Some may see their own life stories. Most will observe the twistings and turnings, the false starts and cul-de-sacs of their personal histories. And for some, the log will reveal mythic dimensions to their lives, metaphors that move them from the personal-particular to the personal-universal.

Divide the group into partners. Each pair now goes outside and finds a similarly potent object of nature. They sit in front of it, reflecting on it, as they breathe deeply. They continue to do this for at least ten minutes (the Guide may sound a gong to indicate the passage of time), allowing their margins to become leaky, so that they feel a flow-through and deep continuity with the natural object. Gradually they allow themselves to become what they behold.

Both partners will now speak for several minutes *as* the object, with the wisdom and knowing of the object, using the pronoun *I* to designate the rock or flower or stream that they now are. At the end of about ten minutes of this (again indicated by the gong sounded by the Guide), they will talk about some particular problem, question, exploration, or concern in their human lives (it need not be the same concern), but only in terms of the patterns they see in the natural object they have just become. At this point they do not look at each other but only at the object of nature, speaking back and forth, careful not to lead each other on or get into a "helpful" discussion, but letting their consciousness maintain continuity with the object, so that meanings can be disclosed and patterns for living revealed.

As an example, let us say that one of the partners (Person A) is concerned with how to develop a writing project, while the other (Person B) is trying to understand a recent death in her family. They are looking at a maple tree in autumn.

> Person A: I see my central theme in the trunk. But out of this grows many branches or sub-themes, which themselves produce still smaller branches. My problem as I see it is that I have given too much attention to a particular branch. If I return to the trunk or the main theme, I will have a stronger novel and a more organic plot.
>
> Person B: Right now the leaves are falling and will soon be earth again. But like the fallen leaves, my Dad has had a full life, has lived through all the seasons, and leaves us now in the full gold and red of his many accomplishments. Perhaps, with a new springtime, he will return in some way. . . .

The Guide will allow thirty minutes to an hour for this, then call the participants back by sounding the gong three times.

When everybody comes back, discuss the experience, especially as it relates to how childhood views of reality can be incorporated with deeper and more mature levels of experience. At the end of the discussion, the Guide will advise the participants that they have completed the therapeutic mystery of childhood and should continue to utilize as many of their insights and experiences as they can in everyday life, so as to move beyond the heroics or withdrawal and into empowerment and communion.

Instructions for Going Solo

STAGE ONE: This stage of protest is readily done alone as you follow the Guide's instructions in the text and rage and smash your own particular "idols." Do not let up in the venting of your fury because no one else is there to participate with you.

STAGE TWO: For this initiation by water you **must have someone else assist you** to be sure you are safe. If this is not possible, then please forego the lake or swimming pool and be content with sticking your head in a tub of water nine times.

STAGE THREE: The *Zikkr* of Communion can be done well by oneself.

STAGE FOUR: This stage of discovering sermons in stones can easily be done alone. Speak to an invisible partner as you perceive the answers to your personal issue in the pattern of the natural object. And, of course, when you complete each stage, write your reflections in your journal.

Notes

1. Heard, p. 26. Heard reminds us, however, of the slow and diffident manner in which this seemingly cataclysmic process occurred and the proto-individual emerged and broke the old co-conscious social order. Remnants of the old order repeatedly rose up to dominate again the cultural mindscape in which they had held so long a sway.
2. Marija Gimbutas, *The Early Civilization of Europe* (Monograph for Indo-European Studies 131, University of California at Los Angeles, 1980, chap. 2, 33-34).
3. An intense but considered description of this culture and its subsequent destruction is given in the remarkable study of Riane Eisler, *The Chalice and The Blade* (New York: Harper and Row, 1987).

THE SHINING HOUR

4. For a critical discussion of archaeological findings and speculations which corroborate this view of ancient Cretan civilization, see the work of Nicolas Platon, *Crete* (Geneva: Nagel Publishers, 1966).
5. *Iliad*, V, 125-136.
6. *Iliad*, XV, 605ff. One of the finest discussions I know of these psychological states as they relate to heroic cultures is found in E. R. Dodd's brilliant work, *The Greeks and The Irrational* (Berkeley and Los Angeles: University of California Press, 1963); see particularly pp. 1-63 *passim*.
7. Julian Jaynes, *The Origin of Consciousness in the Breakdown of the Bicameral Mind* (Boston: Houghton Mifflin, 1967, 1990).
8. Robert Masters and I discuss this at length in *The Varieties of Psychedelic Experience* (New York: Delta, 1967), pp. 247-252.
9. Heard, pp. 39-40.
10. Jean Houston, *The Hero and the Goddess: The Odyssey as Mystery and Initiation* (New York: Ballantine Books, 1992), p. 54.

The underlying continuity of the old matrilinear cultures is found throughout *The Odyssey*. For as Kenneth Atchity and E. J. W. Barber point out, close study of the Homeric epics reveals many traces of an Indo-European "overlay" on the preexisting matrilineal cultures of the Mediterranean and Aegean areas. The most balanced and harmonious "partnership" of the two cultures is revealed in the extraordinary portrait in *The Odyssey* of life among the highly complex and civilized Phaeacians where women play a major role. Apart from the Goddesses and nymphs, the considerable power of the human women of *The Odyssey*—Helen, Penelope, and by rumor, Clytemnestra—points to a pattern in southern Greece and Crete of the time of "influential daughters, daughters who inherit thrones, and sons who go away or are barely mentioned: in short, it seems uxorilocal matriliny." As the authors further indicate, "Aegean princesses were not about to see themselves so easily disenfranchised, as is obvious from the resulting history of marital, political, and theological spats which comprise so much of our corpus of Greek mythology and which dominate the consciousness of Homeric poems." Kenneth Atchity and E. J. W. Barber, "Greek Princes and Aegean Princesses: The Role of Women in the Homeric Poems," in *Critical Essays on Homer* (Boston: G. K. Hall & Co., 1987), pp. 17, 19.
11. C.G. Jung, *Collected Works*, trans. R.F.C. Hull, Bollingen Series XX (New York: Pantheon Books, 1969), IX, 1, pp. 168, 179.
12. Heard, p. 200.
13. James Hillman, *Loose Ends* (Zurich: Spring Publications, 1975), p. 16.

THREE

THE
SEARCH FOR
THE GRAIL:

The Mid-Individual and Adolescence

But all the way, in a dark wood, in a bramble,
On the edge of a grimpen, where there is no secure foothold,
And menaced by monsters, fancy lights,
Risking enchantment.

T. S. Eliot, ''East Coker''

The heroes finally settled down and joined forces with the old agrarian culture, married their father sky-gods to the resident mother goddesses, borrowed hugely from these more sophisticated cultures, and elevated their chief to the role of sacred king and designate of the gods. Slowly, a new order of civilization grew. In cultures developing along great rivers, especially in Egypt and Sumer and old China, the city-state became gradually a kingdom, which became an empire, which became the model of the world.

The priest-king was seen as the loving father, the good shepherd (note the shepherd's crook held by Pharaoh), the protector of all, and the personification of the people as a whole. He must be righteous without faltering or else the people would suffer. We see reflections of this demand in the Greek classical myth in which Oedipus the King has unknowingly committed incest (Is this the unconscious abuse of the Mother Goddess?) and the people of Thebes are struck by the plague. It does not end until Oedipus has discovered his own guilt, put out his eyes, and exiled himself.

In the mythos of the Sumerian and Babylonian peoples in the Tigris-Euphrates valley there are many stories of the humiliation of the Mother Goddess, especially in the tale of the systematic stripping of the goddess Inanna. It begins with the descent of Inanna to earth. In order to assure the continuing fertility of the land, she agrees to marry the shepherd Dumuzi, likely a representative of the invading patriarchal society. She had originally wanted to marry a farmer, that is, a member of the agrarian-based partnership culture. After a passionate and joyous honeymoon during which this Queen of Heaven and of Earth gives her consort royal powers of strength and leadership, as well as the promise of good harvests and continued lovemaking, Dumuzi suddenly reverts to type. He wants the full role of father and king as it is practiced by his nomadic relatives, including little or no partnership with Inanna. This, of course, is the mythic telling of the historical events which replaced partnership societies with patriarchal ones. Needless to say, the marriage soon sours.

Seeking wisdom about these and other matters, Inanna descends through the various levels of the Underworld. At each station of descent, she is stripped of her clothes, crown, and jewels, representing her accomplishments, capacities, cities, temples, and even her very identity, until naked and utterly humiliated, she is killed in the Underworld. As Elinore Gadon tells us in *The Once and Future Goddess*, ''Inanna's descent is a shamanic journey, a venturing into the void, the unknown, into the dark womb of the inner Earth for the wisdom it holds. In this symbolic death, she hangs on a peg, a rotting corpse, but gains essential insight and experience into the full cycle of existence.''[1] Eventually Inanna is resurrected, but she must find someone to take her place in the Underworld. Her husband, Dumuzi, busy with the duties and privileges of kingship, had not even noticed her absence. Furious, Inanna decides that he would make an excellent replacement, and so, like Inanna, Dumuzi is systematically divested of all the accoutrements of his royal power and vitality. But Dumuzi manages to escape the Underworld, and, fleeing from the demons who have pursued him, he returns to the place from which he had begun his adventures, the steppes of northern Sumer.

There he calls on the familiar natural forces—plants and animals— to comfort him. He calls on his mother and sister; he has lost his strength and vitality and can no longer provide for them. Alone without power, comfort or direction, he turns inward and dreams.[2]

Dumuzi's dreams promise only a regression to a primordial state, and only the offer of his sister Geshtinanna to take his place in the Underworld for six months of every year saves him from death. After the harvest, Dumuzi gives up his royal powers and descends into the Underworld, there to enter a period of inward contemplation, meditation, and quiet. This mirrors the new society's reframing of the ancient ritual scenario in which the king, the mortal consort of the Goddess, must die yearly so that a new crop may be sown under the earth. The Goddess sows the seed that is her husband into the womb of earth. There he deepens in his meditations and becomes fruitful in spirit as well as in body and mind. Thus the dreams of Dumuzi are shown to be true, for he must return to the primordial state underneath the ground in order that the crops emerge from the earth. But now, having the knowledge of death, he is able to partner his Goddess wife, who has learned through her own descent the powers and mysteries of life, death, and rebirth. Through her passion play of descent from heaven to earth, and from earth to the land of death, Inanna has truly become the Goddess of the three realities: Heaven, Earth, and the Underworld. The ambivalence inherent in the story reflects the differences and contention between the matrilineal and patriarchal cultures. As Elinore Gadon explains,

Inanna's story confronts us with the great divide between Goddess and patriarchal consciousness. We straddle both worldviews as she travels down to the underworld to experience the mysteries of death. From the vantage of the Goddess the underground is a primal womb, the matrix of all being, but to patriarchy the underworld is an alien place of horror and dread. . . . To the "matriarchal consciousness" of Goddess culture, death is part of the "continuum in which different states are simply experienced as transformations of energy." The Goddess willingly takes part in this process over which she rules. . . .

Inanna, Queen of Heaven and Earth, retained many of the powers of the Great Goddess, but the extent of her domain is ambiguous, and the field is crowded with contenders. The new social meaning of the second marriage ritual is a clue to the way in which the Goddess's powers were co-opted by the patriarchy. Although the union of male and female principles always had been part of the iconography of the Goddess, this relationship was not viewed in Neolithic times as the surrender of power but rather as a catalyst that activated new life within the earth.

In the later Sumerian sacred marriage rite, on the other hand, Inanna transfers her powers to Dumuzi who rules in her place. . . .[3]

The myth of Inanna and her shepherd consort Dumuzi is reflected in many of the myths and ritual structures of the ancient Near East. There the sacred king was seen as assuming the powers of the Goddess as the chief representative and personification of the life of the social organism. It was he who enacted for the people the great cosmic dramas, such as that of the storm god Marduk killing Tiamat, the great mother dragon, seen in the emerging patriarchy as the principle of chaos. Out of the severed parts of this dragon from the sea— the realm of the depths and of primordial creation—Marduk recreates the world. Such ritual dramas confirmed the triumph of history over herstory and the keeping of the feminine depths at bay. An uneasy alliance with the Goddess, in the form of sacred marriage with the priestess who represented the Goddess, was celebrated yearly by these priest-kings. It was hoped that this ritual would assure the renewal of the land and the fecundity of both the people and the vegetation. In such ceremonies, the priest-king becomes the eternally returning Dumuzi and, with the help of the Goddess and the powers she grants him, is empowered to evoke sacred time and space. The site of these mysteries, the temple, is made at once the sacred place—the passageway between humans and gods—and the place where the powers of the great events of creation happen again as if for the first time, in the seasonal return of the eternal cosmic drama.

Through these acts of ritual repetition of the great myths of creation, the world was felt to enter into the eternal present of sacred space and time. In the psychological and religious life of the ancient Near East, ritual repetitions were thought to be essential to maintaining the world. It was held as a matter of faith that the substance of nature would run out if the primary archetypal order was not tapped, so renewing the order of local space and time.

The stability of the empires assured the continuity, for a while, of an interim consciousness rooted in the social microcosm and in the sacred kingship. In some sense the old mother cultures had gained their revenge over the heroic cultures, in the more complex and detailed symbiosis of the great city-states and empires. The burgeoning childlike consciousness of the earlier heroic ages was caught and restrained in the web of these vast interwoven social structures. For the next stage in self-awareness to occur, a different kind of challenge and crisis was needed; and beginning in the eighth century B.C., such a challenge appeared, provoked by the double-edged sword of vast climatic changes and the breakdown of empires East and West.

What resulted ultimately was the democratization of the psyche, the internalizing of forms that had belonged to the sacred kingship or the excluding and exclusive priesthood. As we will see, it was during this period that the Mystery religions began to develop. These were based on the more ancient forms of worship of the Goddess, in which devotees joined her in her descent to the Underworld, there to partake of new wisdom and the promise of immortality. Thus the ongoing influence of *herstory* nurtured the growth of spiritual practices and understandings, which, in turn, furthered the growth of culture and consciousness. Under the impetus of such spiritual charge, men and women began to assume responsibility for their own spiritual governance. The inner life of mind and spirit began to be cultivated apart from the social festivals of catharsis and renewal. Value came to be tied up with personal virtue and integrity. The esteemed ones were no longer the kings but the sages and the enlightened ones. Pythagoras, Buddha, Lao-Tse, Zoroaster, Confucius, and Christ replaced Pharaoh and his tribe. And so the chief figure in the new myth and ritual form became the saving and redeeming divine man with whom one identifies. The long arm of the Goddess is seen in these redemptive figures, for they reflect her mysteries and passion, her dyings and risings, her access to depth worlds, and to dreams, visions, and inward states.

At this juncture humanity began to orient itself no longer by the model and myths of Nature but by the analogue of a transcendent reality that is also to be found within. Powers and principalities were now demoted, especially in the Judeo-Christian tradition. The center of human experience moved from the outside to the inside. In this demythologizing of all and everything, Nature itself was desacralized, as well as desocialized. The gods left their haunts in meadow, brook, and tree. Great Pan was dead. The Holy Temple became a house like any other and carried no sacrality nor cosmogonic power in itself, except as it was accorded by humankind.

Let us look now at some of the ways in which East and West dealt with this rapid precipitation of inward consciousness and self-awareness. In India the Vedic Aryan world-affirming celebration of the forces and principles of Nature has turned by the eighth century B.C. into a suspiciousness about the external world and a preoccupation with inward states. In the extreme climatic changes that occur around this time, the world out there is no longer to be trusted. The monsoons have become more fierce. The desert has encroached upon and ravaged the green world. The climate is enervating. The world has now become *maya*, a mirage of illusions which tempt only to disappoint. Philosophical speculation becomes intense, as we see in the development of the *Upanishads* (700 – 300 B.C.), a fascinating melange of the old sacrificial and prayer formulas of the Brahmin rites and the new speculative consciousness. The principal questions of Upanishadic concern are: What is reality? Of what is the universe an expression? Is it real in itself? Or is it merely an appearance, even an illusion?

In India, too, the law of karma—the principle that all of one's thoughts, words, and deeds have a consequence in fixing one's lot in future existences—took a deep toll. Many students of the social and religious history of India have thought that this sense of inexorable causal nexus served only to reinforce the caste system, with its spiritual sliding scale. The evident lack of interest in social justice and human welfare is also seen as a product of karmic psychology, in that under its laws there is little left to allure one to the venture of making oneself at home in the world.

From this perspective, consider the despair that comes

from viewing one's past and future as an externally revolving wheel of rebirths—a thousand million rebirths conditioned by one's every action. So you're good in this life—you might slip up in the next, and in the third find yourself a swamp rat who would be fortunate to make it back up to an untouchable or a leper.

This led to what Radhikrishna, a former vice chancellor of India, referred to as the continent of Circe—a continent of disease, poverty, and fatalism, with little social change or social conscience, at least as Westerners have understood these terms. Thus, the great and terrible cry: "Oh, would that I could be delivered from the power of my karma over me. Would that I could find my way into a state of being where misery would be at an end and only joy remain."

To be sure, Western critics have painted the law of karma in the bleakest terms, and many Hindu and Buddhist apologists have provided a needed corrective and deeper understanding of the consequences of karma. They show how karma not only gives feedback for mistakes but offers opportunities for growth. They note, for example, the psychological freedom that comes from knowing that one can have control over what one does, and that what one does counts supremely in the nature of things. They note, too, how the enormous sophistication in the understanding of inward states and in the psychology of personal growth and transformation—an evolutionary spiritual psychology for which the West has no comparable development—is the natural consequence of an attentiveness to one's psychospiritual states that comes with karmic concerns. Still, one cannot avoid the fact that for many, the law of karma was trasmuted into a world-evading fatalism from which a way of release was clearly needed. The way out in the East proved to be through the rise of asceticism and devotional philosophies. The coming of the Buddha and the rise of the Buddhist philosophy of mindfulness, nonattachment, and compassionate existence provided one such form, as did the late Hindu yogas, which incorporated Buddhist perspectives and took over the doctrine of the moral desirability of quenching desire, thus preparing for final entrance into Nirvana. Four ways of release from the cumulative karma of existence, four yogas of salvation, were developed, each of which offered practices and philosophies that engaged and deepened the spiritual path and potential of the seeker. What began, in part, as ways of achieving release from suffering, developed into ways of being that explored and enhanced the human potential to an extraordinary degree.

The first of these was known as *karma yoga*—the yoga of works. In its lesser form, it was the plodder's way to salvation, a methodical but cheery way of carrying out rites, ceremonials, and duties that added to one's merit and favorable karma. It became, however, extremely legalistic and, especially with the advent of the code of Manu, prescribed an all-encompassing series of rites and behaviors for every single episode in one's life.

In its more sophisticated form, the yoga of work provided a sensibility in which active people chose to perform their tasks in the spirit of egoless renunciation of the rewards and fruits of their work. This asceticism of renunciation rids a person of the false view that there is a particular ego in whose interests work needs to be done. The results of one's labor must be devoted to the ultimate reality. The life of Gandhi would be an example of the fullest implications of a life lived according to the precepts of karma yoga. This yoga of work and compassionate action is often the path of the social artist.

The second path, the *jnana yoga* or way of knowledge, was developed for the person whose interests were predominantly intellectual and contemplative. It sees ignorance (*avidya*) as the great hindrance to enlightenment (*moksha*). The unseeing and unawakened state is the root of most human misery and evil.

127

There are many notions in Hinduism as to what constitutes this ignorance. The main one is found in the *Upanishads*; the view that our problem lies in thinking ourselves separate and distinct and forgetting that in reality we are Brahma-Atman—as individuals, we are a particular and transient focalization of being, and nothing else.

Countless analogies are offered in this yoga of the relationship between the part and the whole: waves rising from and sinking into the sea, a drop of brine flying across the surface of the ocean for a few moments before it joins the totality of which it is a part. Human freedom comes only with the right understanding of this; and when this understanding happens, the knot of the heart loosens, doubt dissolves, and karma ceases. But the faith in union must become the deep and absolute *knowledge* of union, and this often comes in an ecstatic flash of certainty in the midst of deep meditation. Jnana yoga offers its practitioners an exacting program of intellectual and spiritual development, to prepare the human instrument to be a receptive vehicle for its return to unity.

(Equally exacting is the yoga of knowledge and education offered in the Greek world by Plato, especially in the *Republic*, wherein a most developed and systematic pattern of education turns the mind from a cave-world of darkest ignorance to a light world of absolute knowledge.)

The third path is *bhakti yoga*, the yoga of love and devotion. This is the way appropriate for those whose feelings and emotions are uppermost in their personalities. It assumes the form of warm, loving, and often passionate devotion to a personal god or goddess, or even to a guru, as the way of release. If the aspirant surrenders completely to the divine one, then, it is thought, selfish desire and egoism will be overcome; from the devotion of all to the god comes union with god, until all egoism is removed. The personal god becomes the stream or the river that leads one to Brahma and a unity with all being.

The first literary recognition of bhakti yoga was made in the *Bhagavad Gita* or "Song of the Blessed Lord." It is one of the great classics not only of religious literature but of the history of the development of consciousness. The hero-soldier Arjuna takes no pride in the pattern of prestige and is sick at heart at the thought of the carnage he must shortly inflict in battle. His charioteer, who is actually the great god Krishna, teaches him the yoga of love as well as of duty and gives him access to the ascetic modes of meditation and psychophysical training, in order that he may perceive the larger patterns behind the meaning of existence. (The yoga of love again finds its correlation in the Greek world in Plato. In the *Symposium*, lover and beloved evoke in each other a development that leads to both a knowing and a cocreation of the good and the beautiful.)

The fourth way, *hatha yoga*, prepares the body to be a refined vehicle for the mind. Herein the Sanskrit psychophysical philosophers developed enormously sophisticated systems of physical and psychological techniques to allow for the acquiring of states of consciousness that would orchestrate the body and focus the mind in ways that would cause the adept to transcend local conditions and attain enlightenment in the oneness of Brahma.

Whereas many in the Eastern world tended to take the inward path of intense ascetic disciplines, in the West the precipitation of self-awareness began by taking a more overt and public form. In Greece it began in the remarkable interaction that occurred between the Apollonian way of order and the Dionysian festivals of ecstasy. Order and ecstasy blended to create one of the greatest triumphs of the human spirit—the ancient Greek tragedy.

These were no mere theatrical spectacles. They were virtually religious festivals, in which all the citizenry participated, in which meanings that eluded one in daily life were found and the hidden order of things was understood. Herein the marriage of order and ecstasy spawned philosophy and the dialectical questions that were to change the nature of the Western mind for the next twenty-five hundred years.

Using the myths and symbols of the old hero culture as well as the older Goddess cultures, the tragedies permitted people to think obliquely about their own problems and not repress the growing questions asked by the transitional inward-turning psyche. In ways very different from the quietistic meditations of Eastern man, the more muscular psyche of the Hellenic Greek engaged in a kind of public psychodrama, asking questions of power and fear: "Is the universe alien from me? What are the limits of human power? Is it possible, if not to be happy, at least to be unafraid?" The agon of the drama projected the agony of the soul, the terrible woundings of the great tragic heroes reflecting the breaching of the comfortable old order of psyche and society and the birth pangs of the emerging psyche of the mid-individual.

All of the great tragic dramas dealt with the myths and characters of the past heroic age, but they took these rather unconscious rowdies and bullies and filled them with soul. Even clumsy, cloddish Ajax, the archetypal jock, becomes, in the crucible of the tragic drama, a deeply introspective soul, reflecting on the nature of his own misery. Clytemnestra, who had been in the old myths a force of evil and chaos, becomes in the drama the representative of the rich subtlety and deviousness of which the soul is capable. In these ways the robustness of the old heroes becomes a psychic agility, the growing complexity of the self reflecting the change in Western personality, the agon of the drama and of the soul charging the old myths with the transformative power of pathos.

The Sophoclean treatment of the myth of Oedipus illuminates the stages of the transition from proto- to mid-individual. When we first meet Oedipus, he is grounded in the ruthless realities of the old heroic era and has yielded to the tremendous primary sin of his own heroic nature. Told in a prophecy that he would kill his father and marry his mother, he sought to avoid such a fate by not returning to his adoptive parents. The inevitable happened nonetheless. Oedipus met a man at three crossroads, knocked him down, and killed him, not knowing that the man was his real father. Here we see the excesses of the old heroic order and of childhood—the too-muchness of noradrenaline rage and overreaction in the face of conflict. Shortly thereafter Oedipus fulfilled his tragic destiny by marrying a lovely older woman, neither of them knowing that they were mother and son—the ultimate shame and result of unthinking mindless heroism. In the course of the Sophoclean drama, the hero becomes the most intellectual of tragic avatars, pursuing with consummate legal logic the secret of his own identity.

One sees in the course of the play the development of those deductive logics and investigative probings that became the hallmark of Greek logos and philosophy. Oedipus moves from the implacable confidence that is the last statement of heroic success through inward and outward questings, deepening reflectiveness, and involutional turnings, to discover himself —and, by extension, the heroic way of being—guilty and finished. Not a god but Oedipus himself then bears the moral responsibility and initiative to punish himself.

With the philosopher-dramatist Sophocles, human response and responsibility became both more inward and more uniquely individual, apart from the laws of nature or the mandates of the social order. And so, in a profound symbolic act, Oedipus puts out his eyes, so that he can now live in the inward world. For many years he wanders blind through Greece, accompanied by his young daughter Antigone, until he comes to the grove at Colonus, where he is welcomed by Theseus, the young King of Athens. Theseus reverently acknowledges

Oedipus for who he was and what in his wanderings he has now become. Theseus, the step beyond Odysseus (wily and cunning like Odysseus, he knew how to follow Ariadne's thread through the Labyrinth and kill the Minotaur of the old order), acknowledges the hard-won wisdoms and psychic depths of Oedipus.

Blind in the labyrinth of the byways of Greece, Oedipus has found the highways of his own soul and gives to the prepared and willing psyche of Theseus—and to Athens—the knowledge and wisdom of these inward journeys. In this gifting, Athens becomes symbolic of the *Unus Mundus*, the place in the Western world where outward events are grounded in the deeps of inward ones. In this mythologem Sophocles gives us, with extraordinary power and insight, an understanding of how self and society can be transmuted to create the groundwork for a flowering of culture and consciousness such as the world has rarely known.

But this Golden Age of Greece did not last and, as it died, psyche was plunged even more deeply into itself. The outward forms that necessitated the inward journey were desperate and chaotic. Euripides, writing in that time of plague, war, and breakdown, tells it best:

> So I have a secret hope . . .
> of someone, a God, who is wise and plans,
> but my hopes grow dim when I see
> the deeds of men and their destinies.
> For fortune is ever veering,
> and the currents of life are shifting,
> shifting, wandering forever.[4]

This is the wandering psyche that no longer knows its home, the rising of the inward depths that are no longer grounded in social forms. The choral lament of Euripides tells the tale of an age. Its brief lines are a microcosm of the social and spiritual chaos of the late fifth century B.C. Poet and polis alike are united in the death of confidence in the old order.

The Periclean promise of the Golden Age, the Sophoclean *telos* or sense of purpose, the citizen's vision of a world understood by human intelligence and controlled by divine purposiveness—all have collapsed in the horrors of the internecine Peloponnesian War, in the corruption, in the multiplication of intrigue, and in the grim misery of a plague, unexpected and inexplicable, that killed more than half the population of Athens. Anarchy is deified. The gods themselves are abandoned as inadequate. The universe ceases to be felt as a cosmos, an order, governed by either deities or discoverable natural laws, but stands revealed as a desperate chaos, shifting, shifting, wandering forever, governed only by the terrors of blind chance and an emerging psyche that does not know its form.[5]

The form was soon to be sought in developments that laid the basis for the Western mind. After listening to the dialectical reflections of Socrates, the young playwright Plato burned his plays and sought the explication of meaning in life in a more inward drama of the soul and mind. His pupil Aristotle did likewise, but brought back the Ionian philosophy of Nature into these inward inquires, so linking physics and metaphysics. The spirit of tragedy and the breakdown of culture created the psychic environment in which philosophy became a necessity. Philosophical speculation, however, was generally suited to people with special social and educational advantages. The parallel drama and exploration of the masses was equally radical and profound and, more than philosophy, created the dominant forms of mid-individual consciousness.

We must remember what happened in the Western world following the conquests of Alexander the Great, the spread of the Diadochian Empire, and the expansion of the Roman

Empire. The collapse of the ancient empires of the Middle East, the loss of independence for Israel, the Hellenic and Syrian city-states, the population shifts, the deportations, enslavements, and repression of the local culture and religions, all reduced men and women to a sense of powerlessness over the proceedings of their lives, and to an extreme state of forlornness in the subsequent world turmoil of intellectual, cultural, and spiritual disorientation.

The loss of meaning that resulted from the breakdown of institutions, civilizations, and ethnic cohesion made it necessary for many to attempt a regaining and understanding of the meaning of human existence in inner terms. Additionally, the political uprooting and the policy of colonization under Alexander led to a cosmopolitan consciousness and even to unconsciousness.

The gradual collapse of political boundaries within the Roman Empire gave rise to a relative freedom of movement. Egyptians could take up residence in Greece, Syrians in Rome; inhabitants of Asia Minor could settle in Gaul, and Africans moved to Spain. One was no longer a member of a local city or state (a *polis*); one was no longer a *polites* or citizen, but now had become *cosmo-polites*, free to pursue the spiritual and psychological realities of other cultures.

No longer tied to state or regional cults, general principles of religion acquired a life of their own and unfolded their deeper implications. Archetypes and universally resonant symbologies could develop. Thus religions that had grown out of the old civil state religions now became, in the cosmopolitan reality, infinitely more interesting, varied, and psychologically evocative than they had been in their provincial forms.

The state Babylonian religion, for example, after being hellenized and liberated, became an extraordinarily complex religion of archetypal symbols and astrological science. In other developments the myths and images of Oriental thought were married to Greek conceptual thinking, resulting in the curious philosophical arcana of the Gnostic religions. Within gnosticism, too, the realms of Oriental magic were translated in the language of stoic cosmology, and Iranian dualism was dressed in the themes of Platonic thought. As the sensuous imagery and symbologies of Oriental thought were put into the crucible of Greek rational consciousness, a new form of metaphysics and archetypal psychology emerged, one in which the realms of inwardness came to have as much ontological status as did the external world.

Perhaps the deepest and most satisfying aspect of this syncretic and cosmopolitan public pursuit of private salvation was in the spread of Near Eastern mystery cults throughout the Hellenic and Roman world. These were ecstatic forms of piety that borrowed much from the earlier Goddess religions, but now were transfigured by the Hellenic-Roman spirit into dramatic inward journeys of anguish, grief, loss, redemption, joy, and ecstasy. Within these dramas the feminine story and ethos continued to develop, but now could be presented as ways of taking vast numbers of people down into the womb of regenesis. What had gone underground during these dark days of *herstory* remained so, but there in the mystery religions, which often were celebrated in caves or in labyrinths beneath the ground, those who sought meaning and a new consciousness met and were remade. Mystery religions provided the alienated individual lost in the nameless masses of the Roman Empire with an intimate environment and community of the saved. There a man or woman counted as a real person and found a deeper identity. Identifying with the God-Man or God-Woman of the mystery cult, one died to one's old self and was resurrected to eternal life and personal transfiguration.

Still, for many, a darker sensibility of their place in the world pervaded their self-concept. Again we remember that the majority of the inhabitants of the Hellenistic Roman Empire had no opportunity of participating in the government of the state or exercising any influence on it, as had been possible in the Greek Attic democracy or the Roman Republic.

In the large cities and towns of the entire Mediterranean area, the individual was submerged in the great collective—lost, a nameless nothing in the standardized mass. Throughout the Gnostic and ascetic liturgies are exclamations like "I am flung, thrown, hurled into this morass." The primary experience of the world of the Gnostic mid-individual was of an alien place into which one had strayed, a prison from which one wanted to escape. Thus the constant entreaty of the period: "I am an alien in this world, and this world to me. Who has conveyed me into the evil darkness. . . . Deliver us from the darkness into which we are flung."

The mid-individual of this drama of alienation is filled with self-blame and wracked with desire for salvation. Knowing that one's body and psychology belongs to the order of the world, the one hope is to escape this fallen situation and this alien vehicle. One is impelled to seek deliverance because spirit is immortal. The labor of salvation, then, entails a rigorous discipline of mind and body and, at the same time, the gathering and freeing of the powers of the spirit, as a way of going beyond the old world into the new.

With the rise and spread of the Christian religion of transcendence, which both grew out of and incorporated many of these movements of the Hellenic-Roman world, the ascetic demand grew stronger and more organized. Rigorously disciplined monastic communities were created to contain and support the salvational yearnings of mid-individual men and women. Large numbers were drawn into monasticism, many of whom did not belong there. And this led inevitably to relaxed orders and the discrediting of the ascetic pattern of prestige.

The state, however, learned from these orders, utilizing in its armies those energies generated by repression, those propagandas, drills, trainings, and uniforms, to control and coerce a self-consciousness that could be made efficiently loyal by exploiting its sense of guilt. In this way some of the excesses of modern military statecraft grew out of the pathos and pathology of the world-denouncing form of the mid-individual.

How do we in adolescence recapitulate this stage of the mid-individual? Adolescent inwardness is prompted by growing changes in body size and chemistry. The complexity of physiological transformation that occurs in adolescence is certainly as dramatic and complex as what happens in growth during the first three years of life. With these vast changes and with the emerging sexual feelings, the adolescent awareness turns in on itself and begins to break the spontaneous world-self continuum of the child. Whereas the child becomes what he or she beholds, the adolescent stands apart. The bonds with nature have been broken, as the bonds with nature were broken by the rise of the historical dramas, religions, and philosophies of inwardness and transcendence during the corresponding historical era.

The play of the child, with its form-creating striving, becomes in adolescence games and athletics, which provide a more savage and ascetical control over the burgeoning internal processes. Thus it may not be advisable to have children under ten imitate so closely the games of their adolescent brothers and sisters. A lot of seemingly innocent football and baseball savages the spirit and importance of creative play in childhood. The adolescent needs the order, the logic, even the Logos of these highly structured games, in order to temper and diffuse the rising intensities of eros. In most cultures we do not find complex gaming before puberty. Indeed highly

LIFE FORCE

structured games are often part of the mysteries into which one is initiated shortly after the rites of puberty.

The adolescent often desires to be trained and to submit, to be drilled and uniformed, to be lost in the anonymity of the group. The cult of music and of rock concerts creates a group ecstasy in which they can both express their discontents and absolve their darkness. These desires spring from adolescents' ambiguity about themselves as their increasing self-consciousness turns in on itself—as it also did in the inward-turning cultures. How much of today's consciously grotesque dress and hairstyles among teenagers reflects this ambiguity and search for a unique identity? And then there are the questions of gender and its preferences. The things that were once taken as axiomatic about human life and sex are no longer so. Many of the adolescent pop heroes in the music and entertainment fields are androgynous, and unisex fashions are *de rigeur*. The spread of AIDS has made sex dangerous and has caused adolescents to ask real questions about relationships.

As long as training and drills can be kept as modes of tempering and honing, they can channel the growth and deepen the forms of the emerging individuality of the adolescent. If too coercive and autocratic, however, they lead to a slamming down of the gates in body and mind, and adolescence begins the long process of the repression and stultification of who they really are. But when the self-concern of the adolescent becomes, as it almost always does, self-disappointment, and this becomes obsessional, a failure of nerve and guilt-ridden seeking of suffering for suffering's sake can occur. In watching the latest Olympic games one is tragically reminded of this as one observes teenage performers who are offered almost as temple sacrifices for public consumption. Female gymnasts, for example, are expected to maintain an adolescent's body way past the normal age, and many become both bulemic and anorexic as a result. They are deified for not developing, for becoming a perfectionist toy that performs the gymnastics routine perfectly. How different is this from the requirements of the early Greek Olympics, where one was encouraged to be able to perform a variety of physical skills and sports as well as give a thoughtful speech, dance, sing, and write an ode to the gods. Overdeveloped bodies and massive musculature were considered anathema, the emphasis always being on grace and harmony in physical proportions.

Adolescents become geniuses at putting themselves into situations guaranteed to provoke their own humiliation and suffering. Suffering is almost sought to anesthetize the sense of sin. Perhaps that is why their games are so fierce and often guaranteed to do real physical harm. That is why the seeking out of humiliations is so devious—witness the rise of eating disorders among teenage girls. And, of course, the adolescent often finds an outer authority to legislate this suffering and humiliation, be it the drill sergeant, the coach, the best friend, or the gang. These last two provide plenty of opportunities for humiliation, not only of the body, at whose appetites adolescents feel disgust, but also for the growing intelligence, curiosity, and will, before whose emergence they feel fear. (Sit between 3:30 and 6:00 P.M. at the local hamburger joint near the high school and listen to the teenagers intone their litany of disgust.)

Compare the sensorial delight and generalized eroticism of the child with the muscular violence of the adolescent. Watch how children touch each other in a very generalized and offhand manner, and compare it with the cautious and extremely limited touching that passes between adolescents. A personal sense of guilt is the adolescent's main conviction of sin. This sense of guilt may be nature's corrective to the too-muchness and intense specificity of genitalized sexual feelings.

Nature's way is to have a much larger palette to draw

upon, and adolescents too often become focused on just one or two colors. When one is wreaking havoc upon the body, brain, and nervous system, then perhaps quite rightly one feels guilty. Since this same sense of guilt seems to rise cross-culturally and also in very permissive societies, it well may be nature's way of informing us of the need to restore in adolescence a wider spectrum of mental and physical awareness. The sense of guilt surely has much more complex origins than in social sanctions alone. It may well be the ecology of things trying to right itself.

The aim of life in cultures of the mid-individual is often seen to lie beyond life, where one is no longer plagued by human desire. Be it the Eastern fear of returning to this world via the wheel of karma or the Western horror of enduring an eternity of physical suffering in the world to come, both express the dread felt by adolescent, mid-individual cultures before the ambiguities and torment of life in the body.

Consider the success of simplistic religions and esoteric sects among adolescents. The rise of the Jesus freaks and various forms of ecstatic fundamentalisms—the following of a Reverend Moon or of a young Indian boy as the "perfect master"—these are the pursuits of a simplistic esotericism and a desperate seeking for authority. These, in my observation, frequently lead to emotional highs and a conviction of having attained "the Truth"—but at the cost of new adolescents' ecstatic reacting to the larger field of the world around them as if they had undergone psychological and social lobotomy. We might consider also the quasi-religious ecstatic effects that certain electronic rock groups have upon adolescents, numbing their minds with noise. Having become part of the pan-aesthesia of the electronic, amplified environment, they are no longer either individual or guilty.

What if a church comes along, claiming inevitability, universality, and supremacy over morality? Part of the success of the now defunct communist ideology was its appropriation of these kinds of church mandates without the theological components. Appealing to ascetically fixated people, the communist ideology fulfilled the three requirements of the ascetic type—utter anonymity, the historical inevitability of the process, and the finality of the process and its ultimate resolution in world universality. Here again we see the pressures being attempted in both the religious movements and the former Communist party, which in the great ascetical age produced (1) people who accuse themselves, denounce their own actions, and inform on others, (2) examiners of conscience and spiritual judges, and (3) the one revelation absolute and final.

The form of madness that this takes is not the paranoia of the child and the heroic era but the schizophrenia that haunts the adolescent and ascetic personality, a split of mind and body brought about through the pressures described. The *therapeia* needed would be a more total and humane psychophysical development—not just a strong body but a fluid one, not just a tough mind but a comical and resilient one—that would seek to grow into a state of generalized tenderness and temper the genitalized eroticism.

A sensual ease and tenderness should be encouraged at puberty, in order to avoid the tragic split between mind and body that often occurs at that time. The adolescent should be educated in such a way as to continue extending the sensorium of the child, so that the world of Nature and the world of others can be perceived and appreciated from a larger sensory spectrum. Similarly, the adolescent could be taught to have sensuous bouts with ideas, learning to see conceptual realities in terms of their sensory roots. Above all, the adolescent should be entrusted with real challenges and given real tasks to perform to make a better world. When encouraged to become social artists and give their opening hearts to service and compassionate action, there is almost nothing that these young people cannot do. One thinks of the constant refrain of endless commencement speakers at high school graduations. "You can change the world," they say. As they should. For it is true.

THE DROMENON FOR
THE MID-INDIVIDUAL:

The Castle of Constraints

The earth burial permits the rebirth of the psyche into a cooperative empathic society of the One and the Many. The water catharsis is the means of moving beyond the anger-distended, childish heroic ego into the one who becomes what one beholds. Just so, the therapy of air causes the ascetic and adolescent to correct their drive to mortification and life rejection. In its variations the therapy of air always showed postulants that they were not depraved, that in them dwelt the living breath, but that owing to their new individuation and self-consciousness, they had lost their *inspiration* and were subject to illusions and withdrawals. We will therefore perform an epic of adolescence and the mid-individual that is at once a mystery of air and a way of going beyond the castle of one's own constraints.

All great tales of the mid-individual tell of the Journey of Transformation, in which one quests at world's end for freedom and meaning and finds, for a time, the emblems and metaphors of one's own constraints. The kingdom that keeps the Grail, the path to the pearl of great price, the place of one's heart's desire are hidden in wastelands, guarded by demons, locked in dungeons. In the trials that attend the seeking, one is caught in the bowels of the castle that harbors one's own constraints, there to work through one's inertias and toxicities before being able to proceed to freedom and discovery.

We begin with the call, the lure of becoming. What beckons you forward on the evolutionary journey? In contemporary terms, what is your tropism? Plants are tropistic to sunlight

LIFE FORCE

and turn their fronds and petals toward the fires of heaven. Root systems are tropistic to water. Salmon, near the end of their lives, feel a powerful tropism to swim upriver to spawn in very special waters. Parsifal was tropistic to the Grail, Arthur to the perfect court, Buddha to detachment and compassionate awareness. My father, a comedy writer was tropistic to making people laugh; my dog has an irrepressible tropism to leaping after Frisbees. Margaret Mead had a tropism to new experiences and to making the world work. Day is tropistic to night, and night to day.

Tropism is the natural movement toward entelechy and away from the forces of entropy. Without tropism the planet would be a dead round stone lost in space, while we would not be at all. Tropism primes all becomings and gives us the passion to pursue a larger reality known by the heart, if not yet by the head. Tropism is evolution's gift to emerging humanity.

STAGE ONE
Finding the Tropism

The Guide speaks the following:

"To clear yourself for receiving the call of your tropism, begin by shaking yourself all over for at least five minutes. Let your body pass from gentle shivers to large quakings and back again, breathing in many different patterns. As you continue to shake, let your breathing become rapid, deep, slow, and then rapid again, allowing the body shakings to then begin to pattern the breathing. After a while, if you like, add a vocal component as well.

"Then sit down, letting your arms lift gently like branches,

144

your fingers becoming tendrils seeking the tropism. Ask yourself, 'What is my tropism?' Feel it as a subtle movement in the fingers, a metaphor in moving hands for the transmission of knowings deeper than your intellect and more potent than your dreams. Let the tropism pass from hands to heart and head as feeling tones of meaning.

"As images or thoughts arise, let the tropistic movement of your hands seek the 'rightness' of the image and, like the flower, move away from the shadows of inappropriate goals (if you should be reflecting on these). Be drawn to the sunlight of those ideas that embody the deeper tropism.

"In this way a singular but telling feedback occurs between the knowings of the body and the wisdom of the psyche, and one glimpses both the roots and the heights of one's evolutionary possibilities."

STAGE TWO
The Dungeon of the Castle of Constraints

The Guide continues:
"In the world of the psyche we can telescope time and space and so move quickly to other significant stages of the Journey. After the call, the quest begins and subsequently founders, caught in the tangles and prisons of one's own making. For this stage close your eyes and follow your breathing all the way in and all the way out, while listening closely to my words.

"You will now find yourself locked up in the dungeon of the Castle of Constraints. It is a dark, dank, altogether miserable place—cold, wet walls, fearful stenches, and an atmosphere thick with futility. Terrible as this place is, you also know that it is a prison of your own creation. Each iron bar represents the blocks, the stalemates, and the negative intentions in your life, which keep you from acting with freedom in the world. For the next several minutes reflect on what it is that keeps you in this dungeon. You may even see in each bar some of those images of yourself that incarcerate you" (two minutes).

"There is a legend, which is said to be true, that once in a long while a large and beautiful cake is delivered to the inmate of this cell. If you look around you, you will find that this cake has arrived in your cell. Something tells you that there may be a file inside of the cake. Choose whether you are going to thrust your hand into the cake and retrieve the file to saw your way out. Make your decision in the next few minutes, knowing full well the implications for personal freedom that go with this decision.

"If your decision is to file your way out of this dungeon, start filing through the first bar or stalemate now. Make an actual physical filing movement, working as hard as you can, filing through one bar at a time.

"Working with as much physical intensity as you can summon, breathe deeply, and coordinate your breathing with this physical effort—at the same time calling upon as much mental and emotional passion as you have for getting out of the prison. If anxieties and fears arise, keep pushing, filing, and forcing your way out. You will find that as you saw through the bars, these once intractable fears may be undercut as well."

Here the Guide observes the participants closely and gives them as much time as is needed.

"When you have succeeded in sawing through as many bars as necessary, give a final push, and crawl or walk through the opening you have made.

"Standing up now, know yourself as freer than you were before. In filing through the prison bars, new possibilities have been opened to you and have made you freer and more completely yourself than you were before.

"You are not, however, free enough, for the dungeon leads to a room filled from end to end and from wall to ceiling with an immense spiderweb, which symbolizes further constraints in your life to freedom and becoming."

STAGE THREE
The Spiderweb

Throughout this stage of the experience, the Guide will play a piece of music that suggests struggle within the web and eventual triumph. (An excellent recording to use for this is Michel Jarre's *Oxygene,* Side A, NTI 824746.) The Guide continues:

"There is no way to pass through this room without being caught in the web, and you find that soon you are held in the center of it. There are many lines and threads of great strength that in different ways inhibit you or otherwise control you, and you see that they extend outward from your body. These lines that entrap you and cripple you and impair your freedom in so many ways are all symbolic forms referring back to persons or events from the past that still exert significant influence on you.

"But I want you to know that these forces do not have to control you—that you have the possibility of really being free, and some of the lines of this web really have little strength at all. They were strong once, but now they restrain you only because you are in the habit of being restrained by them and do not really question their power. And as you begin to move around this room on the spiderweb, follow some of the weaker lines to their source in people or events or perhaps even in yourself. Give a little tug, and they will come free. If you meet with much resistance, then stop, breathe deeply, and feel your powers become more integrated as your deep breathing balances and centers you. Then pull on the line again. Continue for a while doing this, pulling out these weaker lines that bind your freedom to be; and as the music plays, if you feel like it, engage in a dance of the Release from the Lesser Lines" (two minutes).

"Continuing to pull out these threads, listen at the same time very carefully to my words. Know that you are free to accept or reject what is about to be said, and that you can incorporate everything acceptable and appropriate to you into your own value system, into your most basic value system on every level of your mind-body.

"And know now that you are essentially free to use your body as an instrument of your own creative will, so long as you use that body in what you know to be an ethical way with mindful regard for other beings. You are free to develop the enormous potentials of your body. You are free to release and nourish its capacities for radiant health and abundant energies. You are free to enhance its senses, its skills, its capacities for healing. You are free to stop regarding it as some poor creaturely clod upon whom you dump the punishments and rejections that you and others project onto it.

"And you are free in your mind. You are free to think whatever thoughts you might want to think, have whatever imaginative or subjective experiences you might want to have. You are free to dream, to envision, and to create with the enormous potentials of your own mind and the inspiration of Mind at Large. You are free to acknowledge and accept your own growing intelligence, and no one has any right to try and diminish your sense of your own mental capacities. No one has any right to exercise any dictatorial controls over what you do with your mind and no right to impose guilt or any other penalties on you for your thoughts. You are bound only by your own ethical responsibilities for your mindful life.

"You are free to recognize and celebrate your own accomplishments. If there is confusion and denial of these accomplishments, then pull out these threads of confusion and denial —knowing, however, that all activities in this universe of ours are confluent and convergent, and everyone's activities and accomplishments are interrelated and are themselves the seeds that inspire others to further accomplishment.

"We are enacting a drama of release from error. We are pulling out those threads, spun out so long ago by ourselves and others, that have led to self-denigration and low self-esteem and have crippled our freedoms.

"And you will understand now the nature of this web in which you have been caught. It is very largely a product of such error and confusion. Being more conscious at this moment of your capacity for freedom, take note now of the stronger lines of bondage still attached to you. And you will follow each one of these powerful lines of crippling influence outward, until you come to the source, the emanating point of the particular line. That source then will be revealed to you—the persons and experiences, whatever happened to create that particular line in the first place. And you will proceed to that source walking or dancing there from the vantage of your present maturity, and with great power and strength you will take hold of that line and pull it out. Use as much mental, emotional, and physical power as necessary to track down and pull away each of these lines.

"In discovering these sources, these source persons and events, you may find that it was your own error that created the crippling line of influence that ever since has linked you to the past. Or you may discover that you were genuinely

wronged by someone, and if so, that it is important and bene-
ficial to express forgiveness now, either to that other person
who wronged you or to your own past self who wronged and
crippled you. By doing this, the past will cease to contain the
resentments and other strong negative feelings that keep you
in bondage.

"You will go to these sources and pull out these lines as
often as need be, trying, if possible, to extricate yourself completely from the web and, in any case, becoming by this symbolic behavior much freer, more completely yourself, more fully
human than you were before. You have about ten minutes of
clock time to complete this dance and drama of freedom. Do
whatever is needed—pull, yank, dance, confront, forgive—until
finally you are free."

STAGE FOUR
The Dark Forest

"You have freed yourself from the room of the web. Now
ascend the stairs and enjoy wandering through the great halls
of the castle for a while" (two minutes).

"Go now into the courtyard, enjoying the feeling and the
knowledge of liberation that now are yours.

"And yet, in this place there is one last barrier to freedom,
symbolic of remaining forces that inhibit you—the Dark Forest
that surrounds the Castle of Constraints. Here dwell the dra-
gons of jealousy puffing their toxic fumes, the fascinating flowers of evil, the mires of erosion, the quicksands of despair.
Demons on the path will await you there, blocking your way
to the forest, mocking your power to love, sapping your will to
continue. But remember—although this is a dangerous journey,

you have just come through two trials in the Castle of Constraints and are now much freer and more resilient, and therefore more creative and imaginative, than you were at the beginning of this adventure.

"Still, you do not want to enter the Dark Forest without special preparation; and all the great stories and sagas of knights-errant and wise women tell us that at the edge of the forest you must pause and perform an internal act of catharsis, a banishing of your own inner forms of self-hate and self-destruction, which will soon be met in demon forms in the realm of the Dark Forest. By first performing these powerful internal banishing procedures, you will be less likely to be overwhelmed by what you meet in the Dark Forest.

"Begin, then, sitting down at the edge of the Dark Forest, your eyes closed, and open your mouth as wide as you can. Then discover that you can open it still wider. Inhale very deeply, breathing down into the pelvic plate. In this inhalation feel yourself scooping up with breath the negations and toxicities that plague you. Upon exhalation, with wide-open mouth and a sound of *ahhh,* bring them up, conscious of their progress every step of the way. Exhale them, mindful of what they are, of what is their feeling tone. Sometimes they will be specific, sometimes not.

"Continue to do this, inhaling deeply and scooping up that within you which you wish to banish. And with wide-open mouth on the *ahhh* exhalation, rid yourself of these inner demons, following their progress of catharsis from the lower trunk up through the rest of the body and out of the mouth" (twenty to fifty times).

[This is a very powerful procedure and may be too strong or inappropriate for some participants. The participants should be told ahead of time about what is to happen at this stage and take responsibility for determining whether they feel able to go through this procedure or not. The strain is not just men-

LIFE FORCE

tal, but physical as well, and the hyperventilation involved would not be recommended for people with various kinds of physical disorders, especially those that relate to heart or lungs, or proneness to seizures.]

"Now close your mouth and breathe normally through the nose, letting your whole being become quiet. Be aware of a new dimension to your freedom, one that has a gallant and even debonair quality and that will now allow you to meet the forces in the Dark Forest with a gracious and even merry spirit. After all, these forces are merely constellations of energy that have gone awry and probably are not very happy with their lot.

"You may find frogs that need to be kissed in order to be turned into princes, creeping horrors that need handfuls of salt thrown on them to dissolve into the earth and reform themselves as higher principles, ghosties and goblins and things that go bump in the night, gorgons and zombies and minotaurs and cyclopes, gollywogs and withle birds, and even a stray swamp gaboon or a tree squeak or two. They are there to be slain or stroked or kissed or salted or acknowledged or even transformed. Some will need combat. Some you will fight; some you may even kill. Most you will outwit, love, transmute. Enter now into the Dark Forest in this manner, meeting the demons on the path."

At this point the Guide will put on a suitable recording for passing through the Dark Forest. The guide should not worry about any lagging of attention; the building cadences within the music will help sustain the adventure (twelve to fifteen minutes). (An excellent cassette recording for this is Vangelis'*Heaven and Hell* RCA 5110, Side A, track 2. The experience of the Dark Forest and of the Kingdom should be structured so as to last as long as this track on the cassette plays—about fifteen minutes. The Guide is free, of course, to select her own music.)

"You are now out of the Dark Forest, and you have entered into the Kingdom, the realm of perfect freedom. To live in the Kingdom is to live in the extended life fields, to play in the fields of the Lord. Look around you at the beauty and abundance and at the wealth of reality at hand. It is the place of love and light, these being the principles that pervade life in the kingdom.

"Love is the core of life in the Kingdom. Light is its messenger. What else, or who else, is there for you to discover for yourself. Go now and explore the Kingdom, and find out what sustains its beauty and meaning. You have several minutes of clock time, equal to as much time as you will need subjectively to explore this realm of light and love."

The Guide now gives the participants five minutes of clock time.

"Go now in this Kingdom to a place where you are aware of a rare attunement to the harmonies of love and light. Sitting there with your eyes closed, enter the silence, breathing deeply. Let the breath carry with it a stilling that permeates all your parts. In the breathing, a deep quiet moves through your body and stills your mind, until mind and breath seem to be one thing. And now your breath becomes filled with light, and as you breathe, you feel your body begin to be filled and enveloped by light. As you do this, feel the deep connection between your outer self and the high being within.

"Focus your attention on the area of your heart, allowing it to become as a radiant sun. Let that sun stream out a light that is love, that is joy, that is the abundance of being, to every organ and artery and cell of your physical being. Let that sun radiate in concert with the rhythms of your body and breath until there is no part of you that is not suffused with light. Tune the light to even greater brilliance, so that it streams clear and triumphant into even those dark mental and emotional crannies that remain. Every cell and system and organ sings with light; every brain wave and blood beat and thought stream is filled with the deep and powerful oneness of this light which is love.

"There is a meditation on light that is appropriate here; repeat it to yourself as you choose. I will give it to you phrase by phrase:

I am a being of Light . . .
I love the Light . . .
I serve the Light . . .
I live in the Light . . .
I am protected, illumined, supplied, sustained
by the Light and I bless and sustain the Light . . .
The Light and I are of the same being."

The Guide may wish to repeat this one or more times. Several minutes should then be allowed for participants to sit in quiet meditation on the Light. After a while the Guide will say:

"You have come a long way today in this journey. You have encountered the symbols of your own constraints and dealt with them as you must. You have worked to heal the guilt, the divisions, and the constraints that afflict the adolescent and the mid-individual. Many of you have experienced the intimations or even the actuality of the expanded nature of freedom. You have known the love and illumination that come of dwelling in the Kingdom beyond the Dark Forest and the Castle of Constraints. But this mythic and classical journey has one last stage, for in the higher order of things, in the rule of love, it is natural and seemly that one return to the dark realms and give to these places and their inhabitants some of the good that one has gained.

"Your return is from a very different order of being than the one you may have had when you left. For know that the Kingdom is now within you—where it was all along, but you have not had the freedom to recognize it. Bringing this Kingdom and its order of loving wisdom to the dark realms, do what you will, act as you must, that you may help seed and transform these realms until they, too, become part of the Kingdom. You may dance this sequence or enact it or sit quietly and perform it within the realm of your active imagination."

The Guide allows as much time as seems necessary for participants to do this. If she chooses, she can play at low volume an appropriate piece of music (five to ten minutes). (Recommended for this stage is Vangelis' *Heaven and Hell* RCA, 5110, Side B, track 5, or Pachelbel's *Canon in D,* Musical Heritage 106Z.)

At the conclusion of this sequence, the Guide welcomes the participants back from the Journey, and if it seems appropriate, they share their experiences.

Instructions for Going Solo

All of the stages of this scenario of the Dromenon for the mid-individual can be done by oneself. You just have to put the Guide's instructions on tape, along with the appropriate accompanying music. Be careful to allow yourself enough time and pauses in order to get the full benefit of the processes. And be sure to chronicle your journey in your journal.

Notes

1. Elinore W. Gadon, *The Once and Future Goddess* (New York: Harper & Row, 1989), p. 130. This work is an excellent source for re-thinking herstory.
2. Diane Wolkstein and Samuel Noah Kramer, *Inanna, Queen of Heaven and Earth: Her Stories and Hymns from Sumer* (New York: Harper & Row, 1983), p. 163.

3. Gadon, pp. 139, 141.
4. Euripides, *Hippolytus*, 1105-1110.
5. In Thucydides the annals of life and war from 431 to 404 B.C. appear as a chronicle of *kinesis*. The historian describes a momentum of constant upheavals unparalleled for the quality and the quantity of the misfortunes it brought upon Hellas:

> Never before had so many cities been taken and laid desolate . . . never was there so much banishing and bloodshedding. Now on the field of battle, now in the strife of action. Old stories of occurences handed down by tradition, but scantily confirmed by experience, suddenly cease to be incredible; there were earthquakes of unparalleled extent and violence; eclipses of the sun occurred with a frequency unrecorded in previous history; there were great droughts in sundry places and consequent famines, and that most calamitous and awfully fatal visitation, the plague. All this came upon them with the late war, which was begun by the Athenians and Peloponnesians by the dissolution of the thirty years' truce made after the conquest of Euboea.

Thucydides, *The Peloponnesian War*, trans. R. Crawley (New York: The Modern Library, 1951), 1.23.

FOUR

THE
FOOTSTEPS
OF MIDAS:

The Individual and First Maturity

Wavering between the profit and the loss
In this brief transit where the dreams cross
The dreamcrossed twilight between birth and dying . . .

T. S. Eliot, ''Ash-Wednesday''

In the West the ascetic ideal lasted on as the pattern of prestige until the early fifteenth century. After the Crusades, the revival of learning, the spread of guilds and industries, and the coming of the Renaissance, a new kind of consciousness was needed to deal with the growing complexity of the outward world. But until this time, the ideal of the individual who is self-sacrificing to save others had become, almost globally, the noblest concept for thoughtful, sensitive, and responsible people.

Consider the remarkable similarity of the two great archetypal images that dominated the mid-individual consciousness. The Eastern archetype sits in an agony of ecstasy under the banyan tree, in self-effacing, salvational *samadhi*. The Western archetype hangs on a tree in an ecstasy of agony, in self-sacrificing, salvational offering. Both direct humanity to a different reality from the one conditioned by the given structures of space and time.

In many parts of Asia, and especially in India, the ideal of the ascetic became widespread. Asia, by and large, did not move into the individualized personality, but remained absorbed in the inner-worldly aspects of the psyche. The tradition of self-assured individualism that asceticism had compelled the hero to abandon always remained a deep undercurrent in Western consciousness, and it was not long before it surfaced again, in a much stronger but more sophisticated form. To the people of India, introduced to the willfulness of the enterprising ego by the purveyors of the British East India Company, this form of individualism seemed to be so preposterously irrational as to be impossible, a figment of maya. Unfortunately, however, maya persisted and grew, weaving its phantasms in the self-aggrandizing colonialism that turned great parts of the world into objects to be exploited and enervated.

In China another variation occurred. Her concern with the Tao and the social cosmos made the independent hyperindividual appear a monster. In addition to the *Tao Te Ching*, the *Analects* of Confucius and the writings of Chuang-Tzu, while technically not ascetic literature, are urbane and witty commentaries on the self-effacing life of right relationship, in which ego as we know it has no place; and person, society, and cosmos flow together in the most intricate and subtle harmonies.

Chinese folk tales make this point further in their characterization of those who overstep these bounds and fall into the ravages of ego as enemies of the Tao, be they feudal chiefs or dragon demons. I even wonder whether the success of Mao Tse-tung over Chiang Kai-shek was due to his equating of the communist collective to the ancient flow of the Tao and then contrasting these to the Western-learned individualism and practices of Chiang Kai-shek and his cohorts.

The birth of the modern consciousness and its unique dilemmas is a fascinating and intricate tale; and as it is the story closest to our own experience, I would like to explore it at greater depth than I have used for the previous stages. Gerald Heard states the themes that haunt the development of humanic self-sufficient man as it is illustrated by the West when he writes:

> The foreconsciousness of Western man was almost completely insulated from his deeper total consciousness, and

this drove him to the search for objectivity. The search for objectivity centered his interest in the outer world and led to his discovery of the scientific technic. This gave him (1) the physical powers that permitted him to threaten all the world and conquer much of it, (2) the economic increases that allowed him to raise his biotic standards, and (3) the physiological information that gave him the ability to get rid of much disease, multiply population, lengthen his life, and increase energy and output. Such apparent victories made it possible for him to believe in progress and an earthly Utopia. Now the West, by its very striving to discover objectivity, has reached psychology and is trying to study the self, which constructs the environment it would modify. While the East, with scientifically armed assault and with scientifically discovered and commended aid, turns to attempt the humanic phase and to abandon asceticism. In studying the West's experience of the humanic phase of extreme individualism we are, then, studying not the private story of aberrant occidental man but the first attempt of mankind to be a complete individual. And this is an inevitable step in the evolution of the human consciousness as it strives toward complete understanding. [1]

The modern consciousness can be seen to have begun with the death of the old story and the attempted emergence of a new. The old story, as the ingenious theologian and speaker for the Earth Thomas Berry has noted, sustained and shaped our emotional attitudes, provided us with life purposes, energized our everyday acts. ''It also consecrated suffering, integrated knowledge, guided education. We could answer the questions of our children. We could identify crime, punish criminals. Everything was taken care of because the story was there. It did not make man good, it did not take away the pains and stupidities of life, or make for unfailing warmth in human associations. It did provide context in which life could function in a meaningful manner.''[2]

Now, the traditional story has become nonfunctional, and it works only in a limited orbit. It is extremely limited both sociopolitically and psychodynamically. We see its dissolution in every phase of our lives, and the quickie replacements of modern programs are tangential, ephemeral, incapable of sustaining the life situations that we need. Clearly we need a new story, a new set of orderings, but that belongs to a later part of our discussion.

Berry has suggested that the old story was functional until the fourteenth century and the coming of the Black Death, which took perhaps two-thirds of the lives of Europe and lasted in some form until its last great rampage in London in 1655. In its early stages it brought about a decline in the whole of Europe and ended the comforting harmonics of the interrelated hierarchies of the medieval world. There were several profound responses to this experience of the plague and the decline of the old story, which shaped the forms of individual men and women and the modern consciousness. These were seen in the reactions within the believing religious community, in the dissolution of the interrelated hierarchies of the old order, and in the rise of a secular scientific community. The responses in these levels of society pushed the psyche of Western humanity into recesses from which it was not to reemerge until very recently.

During the late Middle Ages and early Renaissance the believing community had recourse to Hermetic traditions and to the renewal of esoteric pre-Christian philosophies. These were often very elegant and sophisticated, as in the philosophies that informed the work of Marsilio Ficino, the speculations of the Neoplatonists of the Italian Renaissance, and the scientific speculations of Giordano Bruno and Tommaso Campanella. They could also be as primal as the eruptions of the older religions of the earth, nature, and the great Mother, now recirculated in the widespread resurgence of the craft of wicca. In wicca, the ancient practices of union with spirit and nature found a new continuity and development. Highly experiential and often ecstatic, filled with practices that served to link inner meditations on archetypal principles with the energies and potencies of nature, the craft of wicca was especially appealing to women, who found in it not only the feminine face of God but also a more useful and vital spirituality than was to be had in the Church. But whereas a high-blown esotericism sapped the vitality of the one, the Inquisition, always fearing the eruption of feminine spirituality, took its bloody toll of the other. The believing community found its mainstream in the redemptive mystique, with its strong conviction of the depravity of human nature and a widening gap between the Creator and the creation. The sense of human beings in some kind of partnership with the creative principle, which had been an important tradition in Christianity, was abandoned.

Additionally, the basic pattern of the medieval and Renaissance worldview, so comfortable in its interrelation of cosmological, natural, and political orders, was being destroyed. In the God-ordained hierarchy of medieval theory, everything existed in relationship to everything else, a scheme that was absolute for the entire universe. The social hierarchy thus reflected the psychological hierarchy, the cosmological hierarchy, and the celestial hierarchy.

This reflective attitude was contingent on the workings of allegory. Allegory was a single thread interwoven throughout the vast tapestry that was the medieval universe of the old story. Allegory gave the universe divinity, beauty, and meaning, spinning a pattern whose many figures artfully mirrored the details of each other. The whole, seen in perspective, could be taken as a celebration of order.

Perhaps the finest summation of the importance of order in the medieval and Renaissance tapestry of interrelated hierarchies is to be found in Ulysses' famous speech on order in Shakespeare's *Troilus and Cressida*. To get the full flavor of the mind of the time and the power of its sentiments, the reader perhaps should read the speech aloud, allowing the thundering drama of its cadences to speak through him or her.

> The heavens themselves, the planets, and this centre
> Observe degree, priority, and place,
> Insisture, course, proportion, season, form,
> Office, and custom, in all line of order:
> And therefore is the glorious planet Sol
> In noble eminence enthroned and spher'd
> Amidst the other; whose med'cinable eye
> Corrects the influence of evil planets
> And posts, like the commandment of a king,
> Sans check to good and bad: but when the planets
> In evil mixture to disorder wander,
> What plagues, and what portents, what mutiny,
> What raging of the sea, shaking of earth,
> Commotion in the winds, frights, changes, horrors,
> Divert and crack, render and deracinate
> The unity and married calm of states
> Quite from their fixture! O!, when degree is shaked,
> Which is the ladder of all high designs,
> The enterprise is sick. How could communities,
> Degrees in schools, and brotherhoods in cities,
> Peaceful commerce from dividable shores,
> The primogenity and due of birth,
> Prerogative of age, crowns, sceptres, laurels,

But by degree, stand in authentic place?
Take but degree away, untune that string,
And, hark, what discord follows. Each thing meets
In mere oppugnancy. The bounded waters
Should lift their bosoms higher than the shores,
And make a sop of all this solid globe;
Strength should be lord of imbecility,
And the rude son should strike his father dead;
Force should be right, or rather right and wrong.
Between whose endless jar justice resides,
Should lose their names, and so should justice too;
Then everything include itself in power,
Power into will, will into appetite;
And appetite, a universal wolf,
So doubly seconded with will and power,
Must make perforce a universal prey,
And last eat up himself.[3]

Far from being merely an eloquent testimony to the unity of the interrelated hierarchies, Shakespeare's speech provides an ominous prediction of what would result should a displacement of this unity occur. The downfall of one aspect of the universe would occasion the downfall of all the others. As Richard Hooker said, ''Let any principle thing, as the sun, the moon, any one of the heavens or elements, but once cease or fail, or swerve, and who doth not easily conceive that the sequel thereof would be ruin both to itself and whatever depended on it.''[4]

What were the alien conceptions that shattered the medieval and Renaissance confidence in rational order and cosmic harmony? The Black Death and its attendant horrors, which periodically ravaged Europe for some three hundred years, served as the background from which new conceptions could more easily emerge. Also, the scholastic traditions of the rising universities had sanctioned a process of making rigid distinctions between modes of thought that had once been seen as continuous and coextensive with each other. It was a process that culminated in the work of the nominalists, who declared that there are no universals or abstract entities, that only individuals and separate objects exist in reality.

Herein was laid the dangerous tradition in which integral realities were considered unknowable to critical and analytical intelligence, and the individual was thought incapable of discerning the field of relationship between the self and other beings, except that of concrete physical objects and contacts. Herein, too, was planted the detachment of the full individual whom we are here calling Humanic man from the worlds outside and inside himself, so that he ultimately became a dispassionate and dangerous observer, a manipulator of both these worlds.

But it was an even more complex series of inquiries into the nature of reality that hastened the disintegration of a medieval synthesis and drove Humanic man into a radical self-sufficiency. Along with Theodore Spencer, I share the hypothesis that the major interrelated orders—cosmological, natural, and political—were shaken by the works of, respectively, Copernicus, Montaigne, and Machiavelli.[5] The result was a final coup de grace to the old order, and the establishment of a skepticism and detachment that seeded many of the subsequent concerns of the modern age.

The new cosmology of Copernicus dethroned the earth from its central position in the universe, and the whole harmony of the spheres became discordant. With the razing of the Ptolemaic system, the allegorical coherence of the universe structure and the parallel reflections of the three great orders were demolished. The great chain of being fell apart. The microcosm-macrocosm relationship dissolved, as did its resonance in the human psyche.

We should not, however, overestimate the effects of the Copernican revolution on the general public. Its far-reaching implications were not to be felt until Galileo confirmed its hypotheses by his perfection of the telescope. Indeed, the Galilean discoveries exceeded those of Copernicus in dismembering the medieval superstructure. For it was Galileo who totally rejected teleology as the governing worldview, putting in its place a universe that was no more than a succession of atomic motions in mathematical continuity. With this notion, causality or purpose could only be regarded as inherent in the motions of atoms themselves, and everything that happens, as the effect solely of mathematical changes in these material elements. In his brilliant study *The Metaphysical Foundations of Modern Science*, E. A. Burtt gives a concise summation of Galileo's message to his time:

> Teleology as an ultimate principle of explanation he set aside, depriving of their foundation those convictions about man's determinative relation to nature which rested upon it. The natural world was portrayed as a vast self-contained mathematical machine, consisting of motions of matter in space and time, and man with his purposes, feelings, and secondary qualities was shoved apart as an unimportant spectator and semi-real effect of the great mathematical drama outside. [6]

The disenchanted consciousness was shaped even more profoundly by the moral anarchy suggested in the writings of Montaigne. In his undermining masterpiece "Apology for Raimond Sebond," Montaigne attacked the ramparts of the natural order and tore down the standard of man's superiority in the hierarchy of living creatures. Published in 1569, the "Apology" was a pretended defense of Sebond's *Natural Theology,* a conventional scholastic glorification of man's place in the universe and the uses of reason. Montaigne's essay is a study in irony. Under the mask of apologetics, Montaigne appears to condone the naive and monotonous ideas of Sebond. This he does without obscuring his real purpose—to point out the arrogance and vanity of man—in a method that makes short work of the orthodox clichés contained in the *Natural Theology*.

His mask is quickly abandoned, for early in the "Apology" Montaigne states that his intention in writing the essay is to make people "feel the inanity, the vanity and nothingness, of man; to wrest from their hands the puny weapons of their reason; to make them bow their heads and bite the ground beneath the authority and reverence of divine majesty."[7]

Schooled in the methodology of ancient skepticism, Montaigne was a brilliant and rigorous critic of the Renaissance and scholastic notion of man's central place in the universe:

> Let us consider for the moment man alone, without outside assistance, armed solely with his own weapons, and deprived of divine grace and knowledge, which is his whole honor, his strength, and the foundation of his being. Let us see how much presence he has in this fine array. Let him help me to understand, by the force of his reason, on what foundations he has built these great advantages that he thinks he has over other creatures. Who has persuaded him that that admirable motion of the celestial vault, the eternal light of those torches rolling so proudly above his head, the fearful movements of that infinite sea, were established and have lasted so many centuries for his convenience and his service? Is it possible to imagine anything so ridiculous as that this miserable and puny creature, who is not even master of himself, exposed to the attacks of all things, should call himself master and

emperor of the universe, the least part of which it is not in his power to know, much less to command?[8]

Presumption, according to Montaigne, is man's worst failing. "The most vulnerable and frail of all creatures is man," he wrote, "and at the same time the most arrogant. He feels and sees himself lodged here, amid the mire and dung of the world, nailed and riveted to the worst, the deadest, and the most stagnant part of the universe, on the lowest story of the house and the farthest from the vault of heaven, with the animals of the worst condition of the three; and in his imagination he goes planting himself above the circle of the moon, and bringing the sky down beneath his feet."[9]

Armed with the same presumption, man declares himself equal to God, allotting to himself the earmarks of divinity. At the same time he consigns to animals a portion of stupidity and lowliness, taking no heed of their possible "secret internal strivings." Montaigne sees his task as one of turning the tables on this unwarranted allotment, for "When I play with my cat, who knows if I am not a pastime to her more than she is to me?"[10] Man is in fact little more, and perhaps even a little less, than animal. "He is subjected to the same obligations as the other creatures of his class, and in a very ordinary condition, without any real or essential prerogative or preeminence."[11]

Montaigne asks if it is not better "to remain in suspense than to entangle yourself in the many errors that human fancy has produced?"[12] He answers his own question by presenting an ironic survey of some of the more outlandish notions man has created to serve in his apotheosis. Chief among these is man's idea of God. Montaigne ridicules the idea that God in any way resembles man and that man and his petty affairs are central to God's concern. He need only amplify Xenophanes' remarks about animals creating their gods in their image and likeness to find the most damning conceit:

> For why shall a gosling not say thus: "All the parts of the universe have me in view: the earth serves for me to walk on, the sun to give me life, the stars to breathe their influences into me; I gain this advantage from the winds, that from the waters; there is nothing that the heavenly vault regards so favorably as me; I am the darling of nature. Is it not man that treats me, houses me, serves me? It is for me that he sows and grinds. If he eats me, so indeed does he eat his fellow man, and so do I eat the worms that kill and eat him. [13]

In a similar vein Montaigne demolishes the arguments about man's supposed knowledge of nature, reason, and the soul. It is rank presumption on man's part to see his own clumsy machinery as providing the model for the architectonics of the heavens and then to ascribe to himself all kinds of fanciful paradigmatic and microcosmic functions.

As for reason, it is the source of much of the pathos inherent in the human condition. It smothers instinct, sophisticates the appetites, undermines custom, and, all in all, puts man at a great disadvantage in relation to animals. Further, because of its imperfect character, reason is more often than not an instrument of self-delusion rather than truth. The only true and useful knowledge that can be had must be sought for in the ultimate realities that lie beyond human comprehension.

Montaigne concludes his skeptical tirade with the admonition that man can only rise from his nothingness by renouncing his so-called powers and abandoning himself to the mercy of divine grace. A metamorphosis is occasioned only by such miraculous and celestial activity.

By stressing the absurdity of the natural order when left to its own devices, Montaigne rendered all the other orders absurd. How could a society, much less a universe, be comprehended by the miserable and lowly creature that Montaigne demonstrates to be man? The earlier Renaissance had compared man to the angels and thus assured him of his place in and knowledge of the natural and celestial hierarchies. With Montaigne and the writers who followed in his wake, man's only analogue was bestial and the hierarchies became foolishness. The result, at the beginning of the seventeenth century, was the same as that which Robert Frost has described as indicative of the crises of our own day:

As long on earth
As our comparisons were stoutly upward
With god and angels, we were men at least,
But little lower than the gods and angels.
But once comparisons were yielded downward,
Once we began to see our images
Reflected in the mud and even dust,
'Twas disillusion upon disillusion.
We were lost piecemeal to the animals,
Like people thrown out to delay the wolves. [14]

The most flamboyant subversion of the hierarchical order was prompted by the political writings of Niccolo Machiavelli. Writing at a time when Italy was divided and ravaged by faction, the helpless prey of foreign mercenaries, Machiavelli was led to formulate what was to become a basic political postulate of sixteenth-century Europe: the necessity for a strong, centralized, national authority embodied in an absolute prince. Machiavelli, the supreme realist, acknowledged the despotic ideal and saw the salvation of Italy as dependent upon the coming of a ruthless, ambitious, and powerful Prince, one who would have to seize and maintain power through his own strength and cunning.

The tenor of Machiavellian realism was such as to further the growing rift between politics and metaphysics. The body politic was brutally dismembered from the hierarchical system, and any remaining theocratic principle was vitiated in the wake of the harsh realities of Machiavelli's political experience.

It was Machiavelli's contention that political power was entirely removed from any divine ordinances, and rather than deal with visionary models of republics and principalities, one need only go to the "nature of things" to destroy the feudal hierarchies and theocratic systems. [15] With Machiavelli, the state is a completely autonomous, morally isolated thing, severed not only from the spheres of metaphysics and religion but from all other forms of ethical and cultural life as well. [16] It stands alone in empty space, marking its lonely vigil by a constant negation.

As one critic has put it, Machiavelli's interpretation of the state is of necessity based upon "the assumption of weakness, ingratitude, and ill will as essential elements of human character and society, upon the acceptance of religion only as the means of making a people docile to their governors, upon the open admission of cruelty, parsimony and betrayal of faith as necessary (if regrettable) instruments." [17]

Machiavelli based his rule of conduct on a firm conviction as to the basic depravity of man: "Men do not go in the direction of God unless they are forced to it by necessity." [18] The much-sanctified *ought* becomes the target of Machiavelli's ridicule:

> But my intention being to write something of use to those who understand, it appears to me more proper to go to the real truth of the matter than to its imagination . . . for how we live is so far removed from how we ought to live,

that he who abandons what is done for what ought to be done, will rather learn to bring about his own ruin than his preservation. A man who wishes to make a profession of goodness in everything must necessarily come to grief among so many who are not good. [19]

He concludes that it is "necessary for a prince, who wishes to maintain himself, to learn how not to be good, and to use this knowledge and not to use it, according to the necessity of the case." [20] For Machiavelli, the acceptance of the belief in the deep moral perversion of man is the beginning of political wisdom. The illusion of man's original goodness is but a romantic absurdity. "Whoever desires to found a state and give it laws," he cautions in *The Discourses*, "must start with assuming that all men are bad and ever ready to display their vicious nature, whenever they may find occasion for it." [21]

This being so, the Prince can rise to greatness only by being a more astute and cunning practitioner of the vices of his subjects. He must rule by dissembling. He must master the arts of craft and treachery. He must learn to play both the fox and the lion. In the notorious eighteenth chapter of *The Prince* he writes as follows:

You must know, then, that there are two methods of fighting, the one by law, the other by force; the first method is that of men, the second of beasts; but as the first method is often insufficient, one must have recourse to the second. It is therefore necessary for a prince to know well how to use both the beast and the man . . . the one without the other is not durable. . . . A prince, being thus obliged to know well how to act as a beast, must imitate the fox and the lion, for the lion cannot protect himself from traps, and the fox cannot defend himself from wolves. One must therefore be a fox to recognize traps, and a lion to frighten wolves . . . therefore a prudent ruler ought not to keep faith when by doing so would be against his interest. . . . If men were all good, this precept would not be a good one, but as they are bad, and would not observe their faith with you, so you are not bound to keep faith with them. [22]

The standards Machiavelli accords to his picture of a vigorous society are "low but solid." Its symbol is the Beast Man as opposed to the God Man. It understands man in the light of the subhuman rather than that of the superman. It takes its bearings from necessity, and necessity soon reveals the discrepancy between how people live and how they ought to live. Necessity has little patience with imagined republics and imagined principalities.

The *realpolitik* of Machiavelli gained its power and justification by attacking the old story, the ontological system of the age—in this case the elaborate structure of the interrelated hierarchies. The teachings of Machiavelli banished all inherited doctrines grown from the soil of the medieval ontology and shattered the mirror of reflection through which human beings in society found their relevance to the order of the cosmos.

Abandoning the conventional belief in the law of Nature and denying the providential government of the world, Machiavelli recognized only the claims of practical necessity and, in so doing, rent the ontological fabric of the medieval world. Again, the destruction of one hierarchy implied the destruction of the others as well.

These three new theories, then, finally shattered the foundations of the old order; but their full impact can be understood only from centuries of historical retrospect. Only through that long-range perspective do we come to see that as a legacy of these three theories ambiguity became the way of life. Indeed, the theories can be seen as a kind of prototype of the chronic questioning that has haunted the modern age in the Western world.

Much in the modern consciousness may have grown out of the crises and events that occurred following the collapse of the mighty scaffolding of the old order. One effect of this crumbling of the traditional worldview was the religious situation. The tendency to see human beings as unworthy creatures divorced from the orders of heaven and earth added fire to the religious revolutions of the sixteenth and seventeenth centuries, especially to the growth of the Puritan movement in Protestantism and to the Jansenist movement of the Counter-Reformation in Catholicism. The disassociation with the Church of Rome in the early sixteenth century also called into question all of those ideas sanctioned by the Church, which had by now become an intricate, if not an indivisible, part of the culture as well. To doubt these precepts was not merely to doubt the ecclesiastical system, but to provide some of the momentum behind a full-scale attack upon the very foundations of Western civilization and consciousness.

The coming of Protestantism forced many to bear a psychological and ethical burden that would have been unthinkable under the medieval Church of Rome. Medieval Catholicism placed the brunt of ethical discipline upon the institution of the Church, which interpreted God's law, authorized its observance, and punished its transgressors through its juridical authorities. Additionally, the sacraments of the Church gave to practicing believers a means by which they were assured a continuity of grace and a way of reconciliation with all of the orders of reality. The Reformation shifted the burden of moral discipline to the individual conscience, a shift that some have felt put more responsibility on human nature than it could stand at the time. The manifestations of dualism and paradox, the confounding of knowledge with knowledge, the growth of individualism, were in some sense prompted by the new psychological burden that Protestantism demanded.

As Max Weber has shown in his critical study *The Protestant Ethic and the Rise of Capitalism,* the burden of psychological disenfranchisement led the new Protestants to curious ways of coping with their condition, ways that created the basis for the rapid spread of capitalism, industrialism, and technology. Born guilty and daring not to explore their inner depths lest they discover themselves as denizens of Hell, with little assurance of an ultimate place in the scheme of salvation, they made themselves the focus of tremendous if neurotic energies with which they sought to prove themselves by laboring in the vineyard of the world, there to justify their existence through objective works. Wealth and the accumulation of material goods became the partial proof of their redemption. A rigorous and even isolating self-sufficiency became the mark of their identity. Consciousness became synonymous with objects, and as consciousness became objectified, even more energy was directed onto the outer environment.

The enormously influential *Wealth of Nations* by Adam Smith reinforced these attitudes, saying that the self-evident policy for humankind is that reason should always be followed, and enthusiasm and the emotional life dismissed. Herein, the critical analytic method grew to become the chief means whereby human beings could understand and conquer their objective and objectifying universe. The obsession with the rule of reason during the Enlightenment was but the natural outgrowth of the dissociation from the complex spiritual and psychological involvement with the world of the interrelated hierarchies.

It is significant to note, for example, that while Protestant northern Germany became industrial, Catholic southern Germany remained agricultural, a telling commentary on the outward manifestation of psychological change. We must recall as well that America in these early days was largely settled by those Protestant sects who believed themselves to constitute a redemptive community—the band of the (possibly) saved. This sectarianism functioned well for institutional efficiency and even for moral efficacy, a state of affairs that dominated the American mind-set until fairly recently.

Meanwhile, the rising standards of living, the spreading distribution of the benefits of large-scale production, and the exploitation of non-European areas and peoples—together with humanitarianism at home—made the idea of progress a distraction from the growing malaise and un-nurturement of the psyche. Economics and rationalism dominated the Western mind-set from the end of the Napoleonic wars until very recently. But some of the effects of the celebration of reason since the eighteenth century have had devastating effects on both psyche and civilization.

When reason gains too great a rule, then dreams and prophecies, psychological insights and unconscious forces, go underground and fester. Rationalism's success in cutting off access to our deep psychic and spiritual dimensions suppressed half our lives. And suppression proverbially acts like the unrelieved pressure cooker. Sooner or later it blows up. It may well be that the holocausts of the twentieth century—the irrational rages of persons and nations, the closed and malevolent political systems, the "authorized" killing of millions—are partly the direct result of the rationalizing zeitgeist that relegated one-half of human nature to the subconscious stockpile, where it spawned hothouse chimeras, before reemerging through the back door onto the playing field of history, seeding the world with chaos and the demonic.

It may even be, as George Steiner has suggested, that the devastations of World Wars I and II, and most particularly the destruction of the Jews, were the natural outcome of rational-ism's rule over the nineteenth-century consciousness, which then generated a restlessness and an itch for chaos. "The col-lapse of revolutionary hopes after 1815, the brutal decelera-tion of time and radical expectation, left a reservoir of unused, turbulent energies." This, together with the immense growth of cities and the monetary-industrial complex, effected the alienation of self-sufficient consciousness on the part of nineteenth- and twentieth-century individuals, creating the necessary conditions for the coming debacle: "Outwardly bril-liant and serene, 'la belle epoque' was menacingly over-ripe."[23]

Another response to the breakdown of the old story led eventually to the scientific, secular community, which sought a remedy to the disaster through the understanding and con-trol of the forces of nature. Western culture's philosophy of power over nature began quite early. At a time when Western Europe was a small primitive outpost of the great centers of civilization, Western peasants and artisans were technologically precocious. By the year 1000 A.D. they were applying water power to industrial processes other than the milling of grain; and shortly thereafter, with inventions such as the stirrup and the horse plow, they were gaining a sense of manipulative power over nature virtually unique in the history of human cultures. "By mid-thirteenth century a considerable group of active minds, stimulated not only by the technological suc-cesses of recent generations but also led on by the will-o'-the-wisp of perpetual motion, were beginning to generalize the concept of mechanical power. They were coming to think of the cosmos as a vast reservoir of energies to be tapped and used according to human intentions. They were power con-scious to the point of fantasy."[24]

By the middle of the fourteenth century these fantasies prompted the invention of all kinds of mechanical contraptions and laid the groundwork for the galaxy of technological effects that followed in the wake of Gutenberg. The pace accelerated so that in the year 1444, a visitor from another culture (one could almost say another planet)—a highly cultured Greek ecclesiastic, Bessarion—visited Italy and suffered from an early version of future shock. He encountered a vast display of ingenious mechanical devices, witnessed the superiority of Italian ships, arms, textiles, and glass, and was astonished by the vision of waterwheels sawing timbers and pumping the bellows of blast furnaces.

Succeeding centuries saw a steady acceleration of the extension of "the empire of man over things." The genius of Bacon, Galileo, Newton, Descartes, served to deepen the estrangement of humanity and nature; a nature now seen as a measurable, mechanistic function, to be interrogated with power. Perhaps Bacon was the principal architect of this process, for it was he who gave to the Western mind-set the most thorough justification for the principle of domination, affirming that "the command over things natural—over bodies, medicine, mechanical powers, and infinite others of this kind—is the one proper and ultimate end of true natural philosophy."[25] It was Bacon, too, who joined his New Philosophy to technology and mechanical innovation, assuring us that men would go on to create "a line and race of inventions that may in some degree subdue and overcome the necessities and miseries of humanity."

The ecological critique was announced by the poet John Donne, a contemporary of Bacon, who sounded an alarm that was to become prophetic for the events of the twentieth century:

And new Philosophy calls all in doubt,
The Element of fire is quite put out;
The Sun is lost, and th'earth, and no mans wit

Can well direct him where to looke for it.
And freely men confesse that this world's spent . . .
'Tis all in peeces, all cohaerence gone;
All just supply, and all Relation. . . .[26]

Despite the warning, the spending of the world's substance and the loss of supply and relation were not perceived
by the technological heirs of Francis Bacon. They insisted on
maintaining Bacon's illusion of unlimited power and unlimited
progress, which in turn led to illusions that prolonged the
dualistic agony of a humanity separate from nature. If power
is achieved, the dictum went, then one can continue to master
the world outside—and if unlimited power was achieved, then
unlimited mastery. As Thomas Berry tells us:

Scientific inquiry became the controlling human preoccupation, pushed by obscure forces in the unconscious
depths of western man. The telescope and microscope
were invented. New forms of mathematical expression
were created. A scientific priesthood came to govern the
thought life of our society. Men looked at the earth in its
physical reality and projected new theories of how it functioned. The celestial bodies were scrutinized more intently,
the phenomenon of light was examined, new ways of
understanding energy evolved. New sciences emerged:
The Novum Organum of Francis Bacon appeared in 1620,
the *Principia* of Isaac Newton in 1687, the *Nuova Scienza*
of Giambattista Vico in 1725.[27]

Prometheus, so the legend goes, had a brother, Epimetheus—a fey, benighted fellow whose name means "afterthought." Zeus, furious over Prometheus' giving of fire—and
thus some measure of control over the powers of nature—to
humankind, sent Pandora to be Epimetheus' bride, complete

with a dowry of the famous box. It is interesting to note that late Renaissance thinkers identified strongly with the figure of Prometheus, but only insofar as he was the agent of new knowledge and new power, not as being ultimately responsible for the bride of Afterthought and the unleashing of an unimagined series of woes.

The Pandora's box of a "scientific" control of Nature was given in the seventeenth century, but it was not really fully opened until the nineteenth century, with its radical acceleration and extension of industrial and technological changes in all avenues of life. The Industrial Revolution compelled a destruction and transformation of all the traditional ways of being, knowing, having, living. It was perhaps the most intense assault the world has ever seen on the traditional image of humanity and the notion of what it means to be human. Cumulatively, the number of changes resulting from the growth of population, the expansion of industrialization, the birth of many new sciences and modes of investigation, and the revolution in social, familial, and value structure, constituted a quantum jump in the whole fabric of human existence, as well as in the psychodynamics of human experience.

It was especially in the arena of economic change that the most drastic effects on human self-understanding occurred:

The social effects of the Industrial Revolution markedly transformed the lives and actions of individuals in Europe, especially by the mid-nineteenth century. For example, the emergence of the concept of "factors of production" (land, labor, and capital) had revolutionary implications for the Western image of humankind. Humans (the labor component) were no longer a part of the organic whole of society; rather, the person, the laborer, became an objectified and standardized component of the production process. The tendency to see people as mere units in the production process, bought in an impersonal market place and forced to submit to the dictates of the factory in order to survive, was reinforced by the post-mercantilist socio-economic ideology of laissez-faire, which discouraged government intervention in economic activities. The image inherent in this setting could reasonably be described as "economic man": rationalistic (able to calculate what was in his own self-interest), mechanistic (a factor of production), individualistic (with great responsibility to take care of himself), and materialistic (with economic forces acting as primary if not exclusive reward and control mechanisms). [28]

Such an objectification of human personality and needs in terms of factors of production served to discourage the search for a subtler and more organic guiding process for the industrial era. Again, it was the larger sensibility of the poet and novelist who detected the greater ills to come. Here, for example, is a passage from The Duke's Children, in which novelist Anthony Trollope describes a group of aristocratic fox hunters discussing the perils of hunting "in these modern days." The passage was written in 1880:

. . . not the perils of broken necks and crushed ribs . . . but the perils from outsiders, the perils from new-fangled prejudices, the perils from more modern sports, the perils from over-cultivation, the perils from extended population, the perils from increasing railroads, the perils from indifferent magnates . . . and that peril of perils, the peril of decrease of funds and increase in expenditures! [29]

This late-Victorian scenario proved predictive of the kinds of problems that were soon to plague the twentieth century. On page 183 we find a table of selected successes and asso-

THE FOOTSTEPS OF MIDAS

S.R.I. Table of Selected Successes and Associated Problems of the Technological/Industrial Era[30]

"Successes"	*Problems Resulting from Being "Too Successful"*
Reducing infant and adult mortality rates	Regional overpopulation; problems of the aged
Highly developed science and technology	Hazard of mass destruction through nuclear and biological weapons; vulnerability of specialization; threats to privacy and freedoms (e.g., surveillance technology, bioengineering)
Machine replacement of manual and routine labor	Exacerbated unemployment
Advances in communications and transportation	Increasing air, noise, and land pollution; "information overload"; vulnerability of a complex society to breakdown; disruption of human biological rhythms
Efficient production systems	Dehumanization of ordinary work
Affluence, material growth	Increased per capita consumption of energy and goods, leading to pollution and depletion of the earth's resources
Satisfaction of basic needs	Worldwide revolutions of "rising expectations"; rebellion against non-meaningful work
Expanded power of human choice	Unanticipated consequences of technological applications; management breakdown as regards control of these
Expanded wealth of developed nations; pockets of affluence	Increasing gap between "have" and "have-not" nations; frustration of the revolutions of rising expectations; exploitation; pockets of poverty

ciated problems of the present technological era prepared by the Stanford Research Institute's Center for the Study of Social Policy. The table is contained in the center's brilliant study *Changing Images of Man,* a telling realization and compounding of the fears of the nineteenth-century social critics.

With the implications of this table, we come to full term in the ancient but constant state of objectifying and dominating Nature. Reinforced by medieval fantasies of power, given philosophical and mechanical force by the Promethean individuals of the late Renaissance and early modern period, proliferating everywhere in the last century, it is now, finally, laden with the near-apocalyptic results of excessive success. It is an enactment on the field of history of the story of the sorcerer's apprentice. The apprentice, understanding almost nothing of the subtle dynamics of the powers he is dealing with—and of himself in relation to these powers—is overwhelmed by his evocation of the automated brooms. He is nearly done in by the sheer excess of his success.

What was lacking in the apprentice, and in the history of Western technological success, was a sense of the vital ecology that links inner and outer worlds. The dominant social paradigm of reality perceived largely in economic and technological terms is deficient, in that it is bound only by the objective, "outer" dimension of things, and thus contains no internal limiting factor. But the outer environment is itself strictly limited in its resources, and so each solution yields ten new problems.

Lacking the full complement of Nature in all its parts, technology and its stepchild, materialism, are frankly *unworldly.* One could almost say that they are not only unworldly, but are in fact *unworlding.* The singular present drama of ecological, social, political, and psychological breakdown, much of which owes to the doings of the technological apprentice, is as powerful a drama of the unworlding of a world as one could ever see. These are the footsteps of Midas, the heritage of a world that turns metallic and dead at our touch.

Why have we turned into Midas? Why are we unworlding ourselves at such a catastrophic rate? Why are our successes such failures? A great deal of blame lies with our psychological inadequacy and abuse of success. As has been seen, the natural continuum of humanity and Nature, as well as the richness of human psychological and spiritual process, was ignored and derided during the recent reign of quantity. The premises of technology proved inhibitory and hurtful of human personality, based as they were on nineteenth-century attitudes and principles that were psychologically naive, linear, insular, and exploitative. As E. F. Schumacher has noted, "The economics of giantism and automation is a leftover of nineteenth-century conditions and nineteenth-century thinking, and it is totally incapable of solving any of the real problems of today."[31]

Then, too, we have the fact that the glorification of *demonstrable proof* led to the structuring of the more humanistic disciplines such as psychology and social science in terms of the operational mechanisms of nineteenth-century science. Ironically, however, the intensification of this method drove individualized men and women to studies that lay closer and closer to themselves and their own unconscious. Still more ironically, when Freud, the rediscoverer of this hidden continent of the psyche, deals with it, he sees it as the permanent antagonist to reason and good sense. Freud in many ways was holding on to the ideal of the critical analytical intellect of the individualistic person.

In physics, the great science of mechanistic attachment was transformed from 1895 on by field concepts. With the concept of quanta came the understanding that is leading to the disappearance of what had been the goal of thought since the rise of Ionian science twenty-four hundred years ago—the goal of absolute objectivity. Finally, the coup de grace was delivered with the Heisenberg principle of indeterminacy and Einstein's principle of relativity.

Discovery of the developing sequences of life was brought to its first full expression by Darwin in his *Origin of Species* in 1859. After Darwin, the new physicists, in their study of light and radiation, came almost simultaneously to an understanding of the infra-atomic world and the entire galactic system. In biology the new science of ecology and its systemic understanding of the exchange of energy systems marks, along with the new physics, the end of analysis as being the exclusive method of understanding the nature of life.

Presently we are living at a time of extraordinary insight into both the microphase and macrophase of the phenomenal world. With the concomitant expansion of our ways of knowing, a new story is finally beginning to become available in its basic outline. As Berry has written:

> The scientist-priest-prophet-mystic suddenly became aware that the opaqueness of matter had dissolved. His science was ultimately not the objective grasping of some reality extrinsic to himself; it was rather a moment of subjective communion in which man saw himself less an isolated, olympian, knowing principle than a being in whom the universe in its evolutionary dimension became conscious of itself. . . . The final stage has been to see that man himself is not a detached observer of this development but that he is integral to the entire process. Indeed man may now be defined as the latest expression of the cosmic-earth process, as that being in whom the cosmic-earth-human process becomes conscious of itself. [32]

THE FOOTSTEPS OF MIDAS

The sheer intensity of present reality has caused us to turn a corner. We are living, I suspect, in a time when the convergence of complexity with crisis is creating a *tertium quid*, a whole new mind-set on how we know and deal with our reality. Times in which the dominant paradigm or way of understanding reality shifts or undergoes substantial change have been called times of "transvaluation of values" (Nietzsche), "hierarchical re-structuring" (Platt), "conceptual metamorphoses" (Thompson), "cultural mutations" (Bois and White), and "new-system functions" (Korzybski). My own term for what is now happening on a global scale is "whole system transition." The study of paradigm shift and the growing interest in its phenomenology owes much to Thomas Kuhn's ground-breaking study of such shifts in science. His book, *The Structure of Scientific Revolutions* has become a kind of bible (which he neither sought nor intended) for understanding changing paradigms in many fields. [33] An historian of science, Kuhn offers many examples to demonstrate how the scientist's methodology is strongly influenced by the prevailing paradigm about how the world works. The scientist's point of view then, is likened to a pair of glasses which give a particular lensing to whatever the scientist is exploring. However, whenever a paradigm shift occurs, the glasses get broken, and the scientist is forced to look at the world differently.

We may now be in the early stages of a qualitative and quantitative departure from the dominant technological paradigms. There are signs that we are finally moving out of the objectifying, manipulating philosophy of power that reigned for too long. The ecological crisis alone is doing what no other crisis in history has ever done—challenging us to a realization of a new humanity and a new way of dealing and working with our world. The rise of women to full partnership with men in the whole domain of human affairs, after more than a millennia of subjugation, is providing a whole new chapter in *herstory*. In fact, the rise of women may be the most important thing to have happened in the last three thousand years, and will have the most extraordinary effects on changing human consciousness and the ways in which we do things. This is explored in the next chapter.

An holistic perspective and understanding is emerging—an ecological ethic, along with a new partnership between men and women, in which the human acts in concert and in partnership with Nature to bring about more symbiotic ecological relationships. The ecological ethic and the emerging equality between the sexes also aids in achieving a necessary synergy between individual and organizational microdecisions, providing a healthier basis for the macrodecision to emerge. It provides, too, an organic basis for interdisciplinary and intercultural coordination.

These are some of the stresses and challenges that confront our time of first maturity. Developmentally it is a time when one is often torn with conflict between the relief of independence and the distress of isolation. Responsible, compelled to make choices, mature men and women cannot seek the ultimate authority to give them their orders, as could the adolescent. Out of the plurality of choices offered by the culture, individuals must decide for themselves which are the best ones. They are faced with choosing between all the various "isms" and "ologies," between all the varieties of closed minds.

Even without certainty, Individual man has been able to produce powerful, predictable, and profitable results in the outer world. But the isolationism of his mind, its truncation from its deep psychic roots as well as from the feminine side of himself, causes him to jettison every belief and practice that cannot with immediacy be shown to be experimentally accurate. Shaped and manipulated by the technological environment, modified and treated by education, social plans, and therapies still based for the most part on obsolete mechanistic models, many people in first maturity have come to think of themselves as prosthetic extensions of the technological process, instead of seeing technology as a prosthesis of the human process.

It is therefore enormously significant that the current crisis in consciousness among Individual man—the loss of a sense of reality felt by so many, the rising tides of alienation—occurs concomitantly with the ecological destruction of the planet by technological means and with the repression of the psyche by an inadequate vision of human possibilities. The long repression of women during the era of Individual man has intensified the pathology as well as the stresses on both person and environment. Without women's ways of knowing, the world has fast become an ecological disaster, and the genocides of people, species, and nations have grown to epic proportions. These kinds of stresses prepare the ground for the emergence of the manic-depressive personality. As Ruth Benedict has indicated in *Patterns of Culture*,[34] our society is predominantly manic-depressive in outlook and so often welcomes the manic-depressive individual. The overly energetic, manic young person is always courted in the job market and even in the public forum. Witness, for example, the candidates in recent presidential elections. Indeed, they can successfully project their conflicts onto others in that confusion of misunderstandings and thinly disguised ill will called *politics*.

A new kind of holistic outlook is necessary, to help Individual man recover the parts of self and society that he has abandoned and then integrate these into his independent knowing and reason. Mature men and women need programs of reeducation in the extended use of body and mind, to make themselves less vulnerable and more prepared to receive, contain, and deal with the overloads of our technological era.

As I have tried to show throughout this book, the greater

use we make of our physical and mental capacities, the more we will manifest a tendency to growth and a rich unfolding of the self. With regard to the latter, it is especially important for Individual man to experience those levels of the psyche where the images are archetypal, mythological, and possibly transpersonal. To know these aspects of ourselves is to restore the ecological balance of inner and outer worlds that individuals so desperately need. It is to gain a wider use of the self and a larger measure of self-knowing. It is to move beyond the conditionings and the cul-de-sacs and the diminishments that our technological environment and our culture-bound dread of the deeps has imposed on us. It is to extend the frontier of inner space, which, unlike outer space, has inexhaustible resources.

THE DROMENON FOR THE INDIVIDUAL:

Mea Machina, Mea Mandala

The Dromenon for the individual will be one that joins the conditioned and mechanistic aspects of men and women to the unconditioned deeps of which they are a part. It is an experience that joins together the power of the two realms with the mystery and *therapeia* of fire. The emanations of the fires of the sun or the ignited fires of the earth are evoked in order to burn away the obstructions that keep the self in a state of chronic divisiveness. In the illumination that follows, at the point beyond the burning, a new form is discovered to contain the mystery of one's deepened maturity.

It is curious and revealing that Individual man has shown such a tendency to glorify robots. For over a hundred years humanic Western culture has been preoccupied with a morbid fascination with androids, cyborgs, and buzzing, whirring mechanical monsters in whom sentiment still flows and love can bloom. The mechanical man is the child prodigy of technology; movies, novels, and toys testify to the special and mythic place he holds in our hearts.

The pause that we feel before the specter of preprogrammed, steel-girt obedience is tempered and romanticized by a creature with the psychic qualities of a very brilliant and loving dog. Pinocchio longs to change his wooden body for that of a real boy. The Tin Man in *The Wizard of Oz* yearns for a beating heart. The robot heroes of *Star Wars* are in manner and morals far more humane than their human masters and are almost mystic in their quest for each other. Data, the android officer on *Star Trek: The Next Generation* practices laughing in front of a mirror in a touching attempt to cultivate a human sense of humor. The spaceship computer ''HAL'' of *2001* falls into a tragic bout with paranoid schizophrenia before he is ''lobotomized'' by the human engineers. When the TV robot drones ''It does not compute'' to the sillies for whom he is responsible, he does so out of a deeper caring than theirs and a larger perception of the nature of reality.

Strong, resourceful, inventive, fairly obedient, and capable of freedom—these are the images of mechanical man that are currently so prevalent in the cultural mindscape. What had begun in the last century as a literary and metaphorical attempt to enshrine conditioned behavior and to imprison a Caliban in an iron suit, what was meant to be the ultimate prosthesis of the machine age—the mechanized version of our very selves—has now become in the current cultural myth its exact opposite: angels with spare parts, steel-and-silicon seraphim, objects ablaze with psyche. And now with high-powered computers in the hands of many and virtual reality machines just around the corner, we are entering into the most intimate symbiosis with the cyborg reality.

To me, the promise this holds is extraordinary. Ethologists and behaviorists beware, for what had been vaunted as the allegory of our own conditioned and automatic behavior has now—as all good allegories will—stopped dead in its aluminum tracks, spun round, and with great dignity declared its own freedom. In its current telling, the myth of the robot is revealing of the changing reality of our attitudes toward ourselves.

I am robot, true. A great deal of my behavior in my body and brain responds with a Pavlovian regularity that would delight the inmates of any Skinner box. Yet if I did not have a good many of these automatic behavior loops, I would not be able to dress, drive, or feed the dog while discoursing on metaphysics, do all the right things when my husband gets stung by a bee and passes out, attend to a thousand tasks. I am robot. The synaptical circuits of my brain and body are as automatic as any servomechanism. But, like the robots of the contemporary myth, I know that I am possessed of a mindfulness that can direct my automata and put their ancient and immense powers to work for me.

All this I am proud to call *Mea Machina*—the knowings of the old brain; the survival skills of lizards and lemurs remain with me still. *Mea Machina* is the conduit of the crafty instincts of the early mammal that I was and the tree-topping monkey that I became. Millions of years of successful codings are available for selection by that part of me which is biocomputer. Ingenious and genial, *Mea Machina* provides me—when I grant it a modicum of awareness—the worthy and brilliant crew that gives me the motive power of centuries and a prodigious array of options and opportunities. *Mea Machina*, if reconceived, is a key to higher freedom and to an awareness of the Pattern That Connects. If divorced from mind, however, and left to its own devices, it binds us in a lethargy of sameness and unfreedom. Our splendor is imprisoned by inevitable behavior. Our progress is programmed into self-fulfilling prophecies and musty cul-de-sacs.

In order that this not happen, it is necessary to employ procedures from time to time that will allow for the greening of the *machina* and its grounding in the roots of freedom. Which brings us to the subject of the *mandala*. And what is a mandala? Well, the earth is a mandala, as is your eye, as is your galaxy, as is a flower, as is a spider's web, as is a snow crystal, as is the cross section of a tree, the pattern of Stonehenge, the Aztec calendar, the Dromenon on the floor of Chartres cathedral.

When we consider the nature and practice of the mandala, we discover that it "consists of a series of concentric forms, suggestive of a passage between different dimensions. In its essence, it pertains not only to the earth but to the macrocosm and microcosm, the largest structural processes as well as the smallest. It is the gatepost between the two. . . . Through the concept and structure of the Mandala, man may be projected into the universe and the universe into man." [35]

Almost every culture has its artistic and religious representations of the mandala. One sees them in Persian carpets and in Nordic runes, in Celtic frets and in the stone chiselings of Australian aborigines. With their basic properties of a center, symbolic of the eternal potential, the matrix of forms, and some kind of bilateral or dynamic symmetry, and the establishment of points of reference—either cardinal in number or infinite, as in a circle—these renderings are so universal that one suspects that the mandala is more than a statement of relationships between dimensions of reality. It contains the geometry of meaning and serves as a call to awakening and a coding for continuing evolution.

In Eastern cultures and especially in Tibet, the mandala has long been used as a ritual process of meditation, leading one into ever-deepening reflections on the nature of reality, until finally the square—symbolic of earth and human-made life—is traversed, the innering circles of initiation into higher phases of psychological and spiritual growth are absorbed, and one enters the Center, the abode of the One, the place of mystic integration with cosmic reality. In the course of this mandala journey, there occurs the healing and the wholing of body and mind, as it does also in the Navaho sand painting.

Here, the mandala serves as a method in which the powers of Creation and the Beginning of Things can be constructed and evoked in the vicinity of those needing help and healing. The person to be healed sits in the Center place, while the shaman-painter works the colored sands around him or her into a mandala recalling the cosmogonic event. As this is being done, the long chant that tells of this mighty event is sung, and the friends and relatives sing their belief in what is taking place. The one to be healed becomes reoriented in reality, receiving a cosmic consecration from heaven and earth, the cardinal directions, the moment of Creation, time past and time future, eternal now. Centered in the mandala, the one to be healed is rewoven back into the fabric of Being, the faulty parts healed, as they join a tapestry of larger connections. Even harsh polarities are reconciled, and there occurs a union of those very opposites that may have caused the mental or physical distress. [36]

In our own time the mandala has again come into its own, chiefly through the explorations of C. G. Jung, who saw in it a therapeutic device with the most far-reaching implications for structural integration and transformation of the mature human personality. [37] In all traditions, however, the mandala serves as a passageway for energy that unifies and heals and gives us back our citizenship in a universe larger than our aspirations and richer than our dreams. It reminds us, as Dane Rudhyar has suggested, that each organism is a focalization of the entire universe at one given space-time interval, and likewise, each space-time interval is such a focalization. Thus, as I am robot, I am also Mandala. I am Mandala, and that means that through deep centering, I can reach that place in myself where universals become consonant with daily existence.

I offer you, therefore, an exercise that joins together the power of two realms with the therapy of fire. It brings the ancient strength of timeworn habits to the even more ancient freedoms and illuminations of the form of wholeness that resides within but extends and informs all without. In this procedure, which I have called Mea Machina, Mea Mandala, that which is strong and static and that which is fluid and dynamic are bridged and integrated. Finally, at the conclusion of the exercise, one sits before the fires of heaven, or of earth, allow-

Mandala of Samvara

People with Long Hair

ing the vestiges of the divided self to be symbolically burned away and the new form of one's deepened maturity to be fired and made firm.

We begin with *Mea Machina*.

STAGE ONE
Mea Machina

On a good-sized piece of paper draw a large box, to which are attached arms and legs. At the top of the box draw a stylized version of your own head. Label this drawing *Mea Machina*.

As if you were drawing the inner workings of a robot, draw inside the box some of the habituations and conditioned behavior patterns that cause you to spend a good part of your life on automatic. Be aware of the mechanism as a whole, drawing in those habits and behavioral patterns that you like and those that you dislike. Try also to do this in such a way that you portray the linkings and circuitry that caused one part of your habituated behavior to influence another part. In this way you become aware of many of the automatic patterns of connection that govern your life. You might indicate, for example, with appropriate circles, grooves, and gears, how being disacknowledged by someone spins you into an automatic depression, which then causes you to disacknowledge someone else, which then spirals you down into a compression chamber of regret and self-hatred, which then causes you to be vulnerable to colds, headaches, and stomach cramps.

The pattern could also be positive—one that starts with acknowledgment and leads you into acknowledging others, which brings you into a state of receptivity to new ideas, which leads you into a state of health and vitality, which causes you to take a creative risk or to start or finish some piece of work.

LIFE FORCE

Leave room inside the structures you have drawn to describe the habit patterns in your own words. You could also write them at the side of the big box, with an arrow indicating the part of the drawing to which they belong. Do not in any way feel bound by these instructions—you may prefer to make a more symbolic drawing showing the nature and connectedness of your patterns of automatic behavior.

Take at least thirty minutes to do this exercise, and if you finish before then, review your *machina* to see if you haven't omitted other critical patterns. (I have included in these pages two examples of *Mea Machina* and *Mea Mandala* drawn by seminar participants, to indicate some of the varieties possible in this exercise.)

Now ask yourself these questions:

What have you learned about yourself by objectifying your *machina* in this drawing? What connections have you noted between behavioral patterns that you hadn't observed before? What do you remark about the many levels of habituation and their interconnectedness? We often are aware of only our most obvious automations and remain obtuse to the more subtle ones, which may be even more deeply ingrained and have wider consequences.

How can you, by maintaining conscious awareness of these patterns, begin to control and orchestrate them, instead of letting them rule over you? It is useful to do this exercise about once a month, to keep abreast of your habituated behavior. Many of my students have found that by objectifying this behavior in a drawing, they can consciously choose the connections they wish to further, as well as direct the power and energy of their own *machina* toward gainful purposes and growthful ends.

Allow yourself a short break and then begin the next part of the experience, *Mea Mandala*.

STAGE TWO
Mea Mandala

The preparation for discovering the mandala within yourself is to be done very slowly and as a meditation. Have ready in front of you a large piece of drawing paper and your art materials. Use whatever drawing materials or instruments you like—paints, watercolors, crayons, colored pencils, felt-tip pens, rulers, compasses. It is often useful to have plates of several sizes available should you want to house your mandala in an exact circle. The Guide now says:

"Sit in a comfortable position, preferably on the floor and with good balance with respect to gravity. Close your eyes, and slowly follow your breath all the way in and all the way out. As you continue to breathe in this manner, be aware of the space that surrounds you—front, behind; left, right; above and below. Try to feel these spatial coordinates within a radius of four feet from your body. Experience if you can the place in your body where these coordinates touch and meet. Relate these coordinates to the cardinal directions.

"Continue to breathe slowly and deeply. Let the rhythm of your deep breathing remind you that you are part of the cosmic process. Your breathing links you to all the forms and forces that sustain the universe—expansion and contraction, the taking in and the giving out, advance and withdrawal, the filling and the voiding, birth and death" (two minutes). "As you continue to breathe so, know yourself as one with this universal life, living and dying with each cycle of breath so that soon you can ask yourself, 'Am I the breather or am I the breathed? Or does it make any difference?'

"Continue to breathe in continuity with the cosmos; but when you come now to the end of an exhalation, remain without breath for a few moments, entering that spaceless, timeless place where consciousness is without an object and where there is nothing but pure awareness" (one minute).

"Continuing to breathe slowly and deeply, let a circle arise in your mind. Allow the circle to expand and contract with the rhythm of your breathing. As you reflect on this circle in your mind's eye, allow yourself to meditate on the ancient saying: 'God is a perfect sphere whose circumference is nowhere and whose center is everywhere. . . . God is a perfect sphere whose circumference is nowhere and whose center is everywhere. . . . God is a perfect sphere whose circumference is nowhere and whose center is everywhere. . . .'

"Let this thought subside, but know that one center of the perfect sphere will arise in you. . . . Allow your own circle to expand further, becoming a luminous sphere containing your head, your throat, and the area of your heart. If extraneous thoughts occur, gently release them on the exhaling breath and know yourself more deeply as a unique sphere that is itself a center for the perfect sphere.

"Gradually, effortlessly now, the sphere grows, encompassing the rest of the body, until your entire physical being is contained within it. The expansion continues, the sphere now surrounding your coordinates in space four feet away in every direction.

"Let your consciousness be without an object. Let your mind rest in pure awareness at home in the core of all Being centered in the Source itself. At this timeless moment, in this spaceless space, you are Mandala—the beginning and origin of all form, the seed of all potential, the matrix of all mattering, the soul of all spirit. You are Mandala. You are the lens through which is focused the energy of creation. If waves of energy or surges of light and color come into your awareness, then sense these as primal currents that stream from the source levels bringing life to all being.

"You are Mandala. You are the bridge between being and becoming, between the external now and the flowing of time, between essence and existence. You are Mandala, the place of perfect wholeness, the resolution of all polarities. You are Mandala, the source of healing, of growth and transformation.

You are Mandala." (Allow two to five minutes for this meditation.)

"When you are ready, open your eyes and gradually come to relate to this world while maintaining awareness of the world of mandala, so that it becomes natural to be in the two realms at the same time.

"Staying in this experience, let the mandala flow through your hand, heart, and mind by making a simple drawing of a mandala which represents something of what you now know and feel about your place in the cosmic order. Remember, the making of the mandala is both a discipline and a sacred act that links you to a larger reality. This act therefore demands a thoughtful concentration as well as a willingness to channel the wholeness that is there within. Do not worry whether or not your artistic skills are able to translate adequately the fullness of this vision. What is important is to make something that reminds you of the dimensions of your experience. Should you become distracted, simply allow yourself to recall and become present again in the reality of the luminous sphere and the world of mandala, then resume your drawing. Allow yourself as much time as you need for this execution. In seminar situations most participants tend to take about an hour, although if your drawing is very elaborate you may need much more time."

When you have finished, discuss or reflect upon what you have done. If members of a group have done this exercise together, they may wish to share and discuss their drawings. In any case, some consideration should be given to a comparison of the messages given in the *machina* and the mandala.

STAGE THREE
Blending Machina and Mandala

This portion of the exercise will need a Guide and a drum, although technically it is possible to put the instructions as well as the drumming on a tape recording.

The Guide now tells the participants:

"Sitting on the floor; place the drawings of your *machina* and your mandala side by side in front of you.

"Look at the drawing of the *machina* while breathing deeply. As you look and breathe, become aware of the automatic patterns and mechanisms of habituation that compose your *machina*. Do not judge these; simply allow yourself in the breathing to become attuned to them.

"Now do the same with the drawing of the mandala. Breathe deeply and attune yourself to it.

"By my drumbeat I will signal the switch from breathing and taking in one drawing to breathing and taking in the other. I sound the drum now—look again at the *machina* and breathe deeply with it" (twenty seconds).

"Now I sound the drum and you look at the mandala, breathing slowly and deeply, taking its essence into yourself" (twenty seconds).

"As the drumbeat quickens, continue to move from mandala to *machina,* allowing your breathing to remain deep, but becoming more rapid in rhythm with the drum."

The Guide now shortens the time between drumbeats, and the breathing and looking from one drawing to another gradually becomes faster and faster. The Guide should take from three to five minutes to accelerate the process to the point where the drumbeat is continuous and without pause, so that the participants are moving their heads from side to side with great rapidity as well as breathing very quickly. At this point the Guide gives one final loud beat of the drum and says:

"Lie down and close your eyes. Let mandala and *machina* flow and blend into each other. Let mandala give its powerful creative energies to *machina* and let *machina* give its everyday liveliness and patterns of ordinary existence to mandala. Let the mingling of *machina* and mandala create in you the Form of the possible human. Become aware of this inner form as that which contains and shapes your deepened and integrated nature" (two to five minutes).

The Guide now directs the participants outside if it is sunny and warm and there is a pleasant place where they can sit and view the sun. If this is not possible, then the Guide should have a fire prepared outdoors or indoors, and tell the participants to sit in front of it. The Guide should arrange for the participants to get to the sun or the fire as quickly and as quietly as possible, reminding them to keep their awareness on their new inner form. Drums, bells, and other musical instruments can be provided to be used if desired later in this exercise. When the participants are all sitting under the sun or in front of the fire, the Guide instructs them:

"Breathing deeply, take the sun (fire) into yourself, letting it pervade every part of your being, burning away the obstructions and separations and divisions until you feel yourself at one with all of your parts" (one minute).

"Passive and receptive now, let the sun (fire) be within you and around you, firing your new and higher form to strength and beauty like a vase in a kiln. Let the integrated form of the *machina*-mandala be brought to completion within you in the kiln of the therapeutic fire. As you feel this happen, feel free to sing or speak aloud or even dance or play your awareness of the transforming fire. When it seems appropriate, let it become a celebration of transformation. Greet and celebrate the new form in others as you greet and celebrate it in yourself" (ten to twenty minutes).

When the time seems right, the Guide should gather the participants and ask them to discuss and reflect on what has happened.

Instructions for Going Solo

If you are doing the Dromenon for the individual alone then you should tape record the Guide's instructions and follow the inductions and processes carefully. Make sure that you have appropriate drawing materials at hand. As there are a number of long meditation instructions, please be careful to give yourself enough time to experience these. Also, try and regulate the drumbeat in the section on blending the *machina* with the mandala so as to get the full benefit of the accelerating rhythm of the drumming. After you have experienced this process several times, you will find it easy to direct your own meditation without the need of a Guide or a tape recording, adding whatever suggestions will serve to deepen or improve your own experience of evoking the mandala.

Notes

1. Heard, p. 58.
2. Thomas Berry, "The New Story," Teilhard Studies, No. 1 (Winter, 1978).
3. *Troilus and Cressida*, 1, iii, 85-124.
4. Richard Hooker, *Laws of Ecclesiastical Polity*, 1, ix (London: Everyman's Library, 1907).
5. Theodore Spencer's version of this thesis is found in his book *Shakespeare and the Nature of Man* (New York: Macmillan, 1951), pp. 1-50 *passim*.

6. E. A. Burtt, *The Metaphysical Foundations of Modern Science* (New York: Anchor Books, 1954), p. 104.
7. Michel de Montaigne, *The Complete Essays of Montaigne*, Vol. II, trans. Donald M. Frame (New York: St. Martin's Press, 1960), p. 125.
8. Montaigne, p. 137.
9. Montaigne, p. 130.
10. Montaigne, p. 130.
11. Montaigne, p. 13.
12. Montaigne, p. 189.
13. Montaigne, p. 223.
14. Robert Frost, "The White-tailed Hornet," *Robert Frost's Poems* (New York: Pocketbooks, 1971).
15. Niccolo Machiavelli, *The Prince*, trans. L. Ricci (New York: Modern Library, 1940).
16. J. W. Allen, *History of Political Thought in the Sixteenth Century* (New York: Barnes & Noble, 1960), p. 477.
17. Una Ellis-Fermor, *The Jacobean Drama* (New York: Vintage Books, 1964), p. 12.
18. Machiavelli, *Discourses*, Bk. I, ch. XI.
19. Machiavelli, *The Prince*, p. 56.
20. Machiavelli, p. 56.
21. *The Discourses*, Bk. I, ch. 3.
22. Machiavelli, *The Prince*, p. 64.
23. George Steiner, *In Bluebeard's Castle* (New Haven: Yale University Press, 1971).
24. Lynn White, Jr., *Medieval Technology and Social Change* (London: Oxford University Press, 1967), pp. 133-134.
25. Francis Bacon, "Sphinx or Science," in *The Works of Francis Bacon*, Vol. VI (London: Longmans, 1870), p. 40.
26. John Donne, "An Anatomie of the World: The First Anniversary," in *The Complete Poetry and Selected Prose of John Donne*, ed. Charles M. Coffin (New York: Modern Library, 1952), p. 191.
27. Thomas Berry, p. 11.
28. *Changing Images of Man*, a report of the Center for the Study of Social Policy, O. W. Markley, Project Director (Menlo Park: Stanford Research Institute, 1973), p. 54.
29. Quoted in J. B. Schneewind, "Looking Backward: Technology, Ways of Living and Values in Nineteenth Century England" in *Values and the Future*, ed. Kurt Baier and Nicholas Rescher (New York: The Free Press, 1971), p. 110.
30. Reprinted from *Changing Images of Man*, p. 7.
31. E. F. Schumacher, *Small is Beautiful: Economics As If People Mattered* (New York: Harper and Row, 1975), p. 70.

32. Berry, p. 11.
33. Thomas Kuhn, *The Structure of Scientific Revolutions* (Chicago: The University of Chicago Press, 1968).
34. Ruth Benedict, *Patterns of Culture* (Boston: Houghton Mifflin, 1961).
35. Jose and Miriam Arguelles, *Mandala* (Boulder: Shambhala, 1972), p. 12.
36. Studies concerning the American Indian sand painting of the Southwest include David Villasenor, *Tapestries in Sand: The Spirit of Indian Sand Painting* (Heldsberg: Naturegraph Press, 1966); Mary C. Wheelwright, *Beautyway: A Navaho Ceremonial* (New York: Pantheon Books, 1957); and Gladys A. Reichard, *Navaho Religion, A Study in Symbolism* (New York: Bollingen, 1963).
37. The most informative and important of Dr. Jung's procedures and commentaries as well as reflections on the therapeutic use of the mandala are found in *The Collected Works of C. G. Jung* (New York: Pantheon Books, 1959), especially *The Archetypes and the Collective Unconscious* (Vol. IX, part 1) and *Psychology and Alchemy* (Vol. XIII), and in the commentaries he provided for Richard Wilhelm's *Secret of the Golden Flower* (New York: Harcourt Brace, 1931).

FIVE

THE
LARGER
SPIRAL:

The Post-Individual
and Second Maturity

Old men ought to be explorers
Here and there does not matter
We must be still and still moving
Into another intensity
For a further union, a deeper communion . . .

T. S. Eliot, ''East Coker''

With the breadth of life behind one, the depths are now at hand. The post-individual of our second maturity is the inheritor of this breadth and the bearer of these depths. For many of us, our years are being extended as our options and opportunities are being increased. We now have the time to become who we are; no longer men and women working a few short years in search of subsistence, we now are gaining a life span that allows us to become sages, richly actualized human beings able to transcend the particularities of our local selves, able to deal wisely and creatively with the enormous personal and planetary complexities of our time.

Let us briefly recapitulate the stages of our journey to this point, in order to better understand the place where we now have arrived. Four distinctive epochs of the history of humankind have been presented as a possible typology upon which to project and understand four successive stages of humanity's psychosocial development. The spiraling evolution of consciousness implicit in these developing epochs has involved a series of profound changes in which humankind uses and reflects upon its humanness.

In re-visioning these four stages as a spiral of evolutionary development, we sought the beginnings in a primary culture in which the members were co-conscious and pre-individualistic. A few of these intensely symbiotic societies still exist in fragmentary form in several parts of the world. More sophisticated partnership societies also evolved during the neolithic period, often matrilineal in focus, with worship centered on the Goddess. Such cultures tended to be proto-individualistic in their human development. The complex culture of ancient Crete was given as an example of this. Both of these cultures may have been followed by brief episodes of heroic ages. Boastful, wrathful, and shameful, as well as childishly ignorant of their own weaknesses and faults, these heroic proto-individuals spent their fury upon the old primal culture as well as upon the partnership societies and helped to end the Eden of pre-individualistic man.

The third age involved a desire for self-improvement, a penchant for rigorous self-discipline—an inward-turning that questioned the nature of the self. A passion for transcendence marked the philosophies, psychology, and religions that developed out of the needs of this era. The feminine infrastructure still influenced these cultures and found a spiritual outlet in the developing mystery tradition, wherein one enacted the passion play of the god or goddess and found through them a larger reality and a deeper life. The story of the descent of Inanna provided the template for such spiritual journeys. The Eleusinian Mysteries celebrating the dramatic agon of Demeter and Persephone are another example of this archetype as are the sacred mysteries surrounding the cult of Isis and Osiris.

This ascetic, mid-individual condition then passed into the fourth stage, in which individualism attained its majority and the humanic phase of human development was launched. During this period *herstory* was often repressed, or went unseen, or was safely channeled through the worship of Mary—preserved in stone in all of those medieval cathedrals named "Notre Dame."

At this point, the spiraling of development, which appears to move from a form of consciousness with little self-reflectiveness to a stage of awareness in which self-consciousness is intense, seems to have come to its natural completion. I believe that this completion signals the beginning of a new spiral in the development of consciousness and culture, one that incorporates in its first turning the previous four stages but also adds the full component of the feminine.

The completion of one spiral and the beginning of a new one may have grown inevitably out of the inquiries into the nature of reality on the part of the individualized men and women of the late Renaissance and early modern period. Ironically, their Promethean ambitions to conquer nature and steal fire from heaven and earth led them eventually to inquire into the realms of time, history, and inner and outer space, where even more potent fires dwelled. In looking backward, they discovered their animal origins and kinship with all of life, so confirming the metaphoric truth their ancestors had known when they gave their gods beaks and claws and lion faces. In aiming their lenses at stars and molecules, they found that they were not at the center of it all but were, rather, co-extensive with all of the wheelings of the universal dance.

Through this knowledge, the individualized men and women that we had become experienced a failure of nerve and feelings of loss—until an exhilaration set in, and we began to realize that a cosmic democracy is implicit in all our parts. The old Hermetic traditions told us, "As above, so below." The secret teachings of mystery schools of millennia past, which gave us the symbolic keys to know of the sacred conjunctions and identity between microcosms and macrocosms, have now become explicit and knowable by both reason and imagination. Our brains are star gates, our bodies celled of mysteries, which when unraveled, give us citizenship in a universe richer than our aspirations and more intriguing than all our dreams. Our psyches have dimensions as large as these and are able to sustain a flowering of life and consciousness far greater than any we presently know.

Since much in these inner dimensions transcends self-

LIFE FORCE

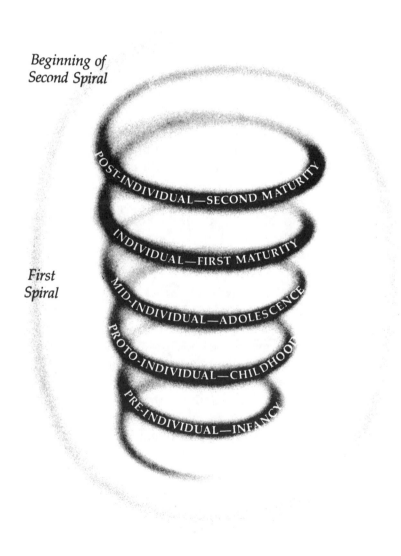

*Beginning of
Second Spiral*

POST-INDIVIDUAL—SECOND MATURITY

INDIVIDUAL—FIRST MATURITY

*First
Spiral*

MID-INDIVIDUAL—ADOLESCENCE

PROTO-INDIVIDUAL—CHILDHOOD

PRE-INDIVIDUAL—INFANCY

consciousness, we are walking the edges of an ambivalence that can either destroy or transform. We are among the first members of self-conscious humanity to become conscious of nonself-consciousness. When these depths arise and are ignorantly accorded the status of archetypal powers, feeding the demonia of a particular nation or ideology's will to power (e.g., Hitler's use of the Germanic myths of blood and power, or the "inevitable" triumph of dialectical materialism as the archetypal agent of communist ideology), then the *beyond within* becomes just another Pandora's box, seeding the world with chaos and the demonic.

But if we begin to join our present perspective to the transformative task of gaining the capacities to live with these depths, then we have entered a new phase in human evolution and a new era of human consciousness, one that could be termed that of the post-individual or the era of ecological humanity.

With the coming of the post-individual, we become symbiotic with the wider ecology of things, linked in the depths to the great integral realities that inform our little local selves and call us at the same time to a remembrance of the universals in which we share. The implications of this are staggering, but in some sense they have always been known. Indeed, they have been predicted in the great mythic tellings of the time after the end of time when Arthur will wake in Avalon, when Quetzalcoatl will return from the West, when the hero and the heroine with a thousand faces will come back from their journeys in the far-flung dimensions of the soul, when all of us sleepers will awaken to who and what we really are. In recent times the vision was stated with great poignancy by Thomas Merton, who said, "My dear brothers, we are already one, but we behave as if we were not. What we have to recover is our original unity. What we have to become is what we already are."

LIFE FORCE

What we already are, if we would but become, are beings who can be both uniquely ourselves and members of a larger community. We are capable of marrying the integral depths of the self, with its rich matrix of forms, to the analytic observations of existential life. When this happens, then creative thinking and imaginative and efficient problem solving become the normal way of life, making the extraordinary the ordinary and natural way of being. Then the cooperative flow between ourselves and others will also become natural, replacing the competition and violence that stand in attendance upon our present limited and limiting selves. The great forms of union, whether religious, sexual, or aesthetic—or the communion that occurs in the genius of friendship—will become for the many the modes of evolutionary transformation.

I do not mean to suggest that all this will ever happen or will be an obvious and easy next stage. As we grow in consciousness, we grow also in freedom to accept, reject, or modify all of our options. We are even free to doom ourselves. Thus this step is much greater than any previous step. In the words of one prescient writer, we are at the turning point of human history.[1] All of the other steps called only for an increase in individual self-consciousness, an intensification of self-awareness. For thousands of years we have been learning to live more powerfully in ourselves, albeit with the loss of sensory acumen and other ways of knowing and being that could prove so valuable to our extended development.

Now the process joins an even greater spiral. The vastness of the human potential, most of which has remained latent, reveals an even greater vastness behind it. Having been crystallized out of this immense ecology, humanity now has the perspective to see it for the first time, and in so doing, to join a larger spiral of it. It is virtually a quantum leap in insight and perhaps will even be mutational when it occurs.

The technologies that have allowed us to link all spaces,

the scholarship that has enabled us to investigate so many other times, the psychic probes that make us capable of intimacy with the depths of ourselves—these are the organs and sensory systems of an evolutionary body become conscious of itself, causing us to quicken into becoming members of a larger order of being.

But with so enormous a vision and possibility, the message is currently larger than the medium; the needed activation of powers and capacities is too great to be woven into a loom of meaning and application that was meant to express a much more limited fabric of being and behavior. The mind-body vehicle that most of us have, and which most of our education currently develops, is inadequate to fulfill the prescriptions of the time.

Consider that in the last sixty years we have moved from an economy of scarcity to one of plenty, to one of relative scarcity again. The global village with its worldwide instantaneous communication systems and its range of striking power makes political frontiers foolish and the rise of the planetary human a necessity. At the same time, however, the growing self-consciousness of peoples and nations, especially in underdeveloped countries, persists in using the nineteenth-century form of nation-states as the vehicle through which identity and self-expression can be found. The recent political seizures in Eastern Europe show the extent to which peoples will go to preserve their ethnic identities and ancient hatreds. Thus we have an implicit global village and an all-too-explicit proliferation of separate and separating nations. In America the desperate need to forge a coherent international policy is constantly vitiated by the growing balkanization of federal, state, and local governments.

In religion we see, on the one hand, a growing understanding and appreciation of other systems of devotion and, on the other, the rise of naive and narrowing fundamentalisms or of simplistic esotericisms that give the illusion of "being right" at the expense of the real complexity and interdependence of things. Psychologically, the unfolding of levels and capacities of brain and consciousness gives us less attachment to ego and personality; but, as of this writing, there is a popular and insidious movement toward willful self-aggrandizement and the intimidation of others as a justifiable and successful way of life. This dangerous streak has little in common with the so-called rugged individualism of the psychology of the pioneer. It is a much more contemptuous and calculating form that rips the individual from the moral flow of the universe and is symptomatic of the inadequacy of pop psychologies and values.

If we are to survive, we cannot continue to cling to the atavisms and anachronisms that could give us a few years of Band-Aid solutions, but end in a millennium of darkness. For the problem of human survival, when you come right down to it, is no longer that of discovering new economic or political solutions, but rather one of the deepening and growth of the qualities of mind and body of the human race. We are still raised to have the faculties of a much more limited and bounded culture. We have not educated our conscious receptors to take in the amount of information and the multiple levels of knowing and feeling that we need for modern decision making and for the intricate subtleties of the present emotional cosmos. We are being educated for about the year 1925, not for the world of the twenty-first century.

The either/ors that loom are both chilling and challenging. As Gerald Heard has noted, we are precariously unbalanced in our present existence, tragically aware "of our persistent and ever-increasing production of power and our inadequacy of purpose; of our critical analytic ability and our creative paucity; of our triumphantly efficient technical education and our ineffective, irrelevant education for values, for meaning, for the training of the will, the lifting of the heart, and the illumination of the mind; of the boredom that haunts our extending leisure and the futility of our recreation."[2]

Part of our task is that of challenging the now defunct political imagination, which hitherto has organized around stratified bureaucracies, empires, and nation-states, and within which people only intermittently communicated with each other. Now that we are in an age of frightening interdependence, the old territorial imperatives must give way to the necessities of a mutually shared planet. The knowledge that we have entered into planetary community with its binding together of peoples compels an organic vision of what must be done to achieve an ecology of cultures. For it is now clear that neither America, nor any other country in the world can ever again look forward to a specific national character or identity. With the opening of borders and the legal or illegal tides of immigration, countries are becoming multicultural, and never again, or not for a long long time, will know an ethnic and linguistically homogeneous population.

Before this convergence, a culture like America served as a melting pot, where everyone melted into a mucilaginous whole. Everything became very moderate. All extremes, all interesting edges of individual or ethnic personality, were melted off, giving a kind of blandness to the American persona and an immoderate moderation to the American sensibility. Now, the coming of global interdependence demands a far richer acculturation—one might almost call it a polymorphous acculturation. This is not to be confused with the current but transient era of the hodgepodge, wherein the rampant availability of cross-cultural and cross-historical styles, fashions, religions, and philosophies combines into zany kaleidoscopes, surreal syntheses, doubtful mergers. Be it Marxist macrobiotics, tantric capitalism, or the proliferating combos of "early awful" or "late worse," these are but the burgeoning grotesques, the lowest common denominator of something that is about to happen.

That something, I believe, is the availability of the planetary person. It involves a new vision based on perspectives of global interdependence and cross-cultural learning of what it means to be human—a kind of global Dromenon. It involves the discovery of ways of making noninvidious comparisons of culture, so that different societies and their perceptual-cultural bases can be seen as complementary to each other. As Alberto Krygier, president of the World Management Council says, "I am thoroughly convinced that the most important phenomenon in this period of history is neither the collapse of Communist ideology nor the emergence of a global economy nor the presence of Japan as a decisive world force, but the degree of cultural connectivity in the world today."[3] No longer can a single society try to overwhelm all others with the presumed "rightness" of its religious, economic, or political ideology. We need the full complement of known and unknown human capacities if we are to respond to the problems and complexities of our time. And it is only in the tapestry of cultures that we begin to gain any notion of the range and variety of these capacities.[4]

The threads of the new tapestry will be woven upon the loom of a renewed and deepened partnership between men and women. For there is no question but that the larger spiral includes the hidden Dromenon of *herstory*.[5] Now on the eve of the post-individual, we stand attendant at a phenomenon that is too deep to be denied, too necessary to be negated. Fifty-two percent of the human race is about to join as full partners in the business of human affairs. And at this point we begin to understand one reason why women were kept out of the fuller domain of life's enterprises—their necessary preoccupation with child-bearing and -rearing. This cycle has now reached its completion as the earth quickly approaches the saturation point in human density.

If the earth is indeed a living organism, whose nervous system is nearly all in place with the spread of human "neurons," then women's roles must necessarily be expanded in all fields of endeavor, as they were in the old partnership societies. Such expansion both allays population growth and makes women available for the complex requirements of the emerging planetary culture. The "noosphere" of Teilhard de Chardin may be more real than mythic. The global mind-field may be closer than we think, and essential to its happening is the rich mind-style of women, now ready to emerge after centuries of gestation in the preparatory womb of time. Inanna has ascended; *herstory*—rich and fecund—is coming up into the light. This development is perhaps the most important event of the last five thousand years, and its consequences may well have an unimaginable effect on planetary cultural evolution. The coming to the fore in our time of the genius and dimensionality of female sensibility is as critical to the issue of human survival as it is confusing to the traditional styles and standards of most cultures. It is especially confusing to those who still follow in the footsteps of Midas.

There is no turning back from the fact that women are now joining men in full partnership in the entire human agenda. As this new relationship develops, it spirals back and gathers in the achievements of the earlier partnership cultures of the late neolithic age. Thus, not only will men be released from the old polarities of gender that force them into limited and limiting roles, but qualities of intelligence will be added to the human mind-pool that will render most previous problem-solving methodologies obsolete. Linear, sequential solutions will yield to the knowing that comes from seeing things in whole gestalts—in constellations, rather than as discrete facts. With women involved, the emphasis will probably be more on affirming solutions that are true but not accurate, rather than on ratifying answers that are accurate but not true in a deeper sense. The appreciation of process will be celebrated along with the seeking of end goals.

Cultures in which the feminine archetype is powerful tend to emphasize being rather than doing, deepening rather than producing and achieving. Such cultures, as we have seen, are nonheroic; they make things work, cohere, grow. If, for a hundred thousand years or so, you've been stirring the soup with one hand and holding a child with the other, kicking off the woolly mastodon with one foot and rocking a cradle with the other, watching out for the return of the hunters with one eye and determining with the other on which cave wall you will paint a magical bison, you are going to develop a very complex consciousness. Such a consciousness is extraordinarily well adapted to orchestrating the multiple variables of the modern world and to knowing how to get along with its multicultural realities.

Philosophically, in the reality structure of the feminine archetype, great Nature is just as important within as it is without. The principle of *unus mundus*—the unified reality stream, the integrated universe with its many strata and dimensions—is operative here; the realm of inwardness has as much ontological status as the external world. The feminine principle expresses itself as an unfolding of levels of existence, not as a conquest of facts.

In the supreme dialectic between logos and eros, the feminine consciousness reveals a movement towards eros. Logos, the principle of ordering and mastery—traditionally a more masculine principle—is essential to the creation and sustenance of civilization. (As I use the term here, *logos* is a social principle, having to do with the manipulation and orchestration of social forms. This is in contrast to *Logos*, as used theologically to denote the energy, coding, and incarnation of the creative spirit of God.)

But unlike logos, eros is concerned with the interrelationship of psyche and nature. Under the principle of eros, we become not *systematic* (often the goal of Individual man) but *systemic*, the province of the Post-individual human, orchestrating our lives to mesh creatively with the finely balanced systems of nature. We become aware of ourselves not as an encapsulated bag of skin dragging around a dreary and demanding ego, but rather as an organism-environment, engaged in fields of life—from the subtle awareness of the psychic weave between ourselves and others to the networking of ourselves within the larger social organism.

Today, as we advance to the stage of the post-individual and the planetary society, it is essential to avoid the domination of one principle over the other. If eros is rising, it is as a necessary corrective to the tyranny of logos. Dominated by logos, eros becomes stalemated in obsessive sexuality and desire. Conversely, dominated by eros, logos is stalemated in dogmatic, habituated patterns of social order and ritual. The creation of a new reality, in both its social and personal forms, must manifest a new blending and rich interplay of eros and logos. Then eros can become a deepening, unifying principle, granting us resonance with larger fields of life, leading us to become planetary persons, and bringing true global and psychic interdependence. Logos can then grow in kind and become a more sensitive regulating principle, subtly guiding the interchange of psyche and social order toward the flowering of a world civilization that preserves human differences and wide variations in cultures. A balance of these principles partners the planet and engenders the soul.

For the past several decades, many of us in research and clinical psychology have witnessed a remarkable activation of

LIFE FORCE

images of female principles, archetypes, and goddesses in our
research subjects and clients. In my present role of working
with cultures all over the world, I can testify to the rise of these
female archetypes on a global basis. This, along with the proliferation of books, articles, and conferences on the role of the
Goddess, is a phenomenon that has great implications for
culture and consciousness. The women's movement may be
the outward manifestation of something that is happening on
depth levels in mythic and archetypal space-time. Whether
the movement has evolved because the current world crisis
necessitates the rise of the Goddess to restore the balance of
nature, or because the release of women into full partnership
demands a similar release of the female archetypal principle,
or even because, in the cosmic cycle of things, the time of the
Goddess has again come around, we cannot say. But all the
evidence indicates that the feminine archetype is returning.
The renaming of the earth by scientists with the ancient name
of the Earth Goddess Gaia is the signal that Earth Herself and
herstory are at last regaining their former glory.

Denied and suppressed for thousands of years, or, what
is almost as bad, sanitized and given only mercy jobs by wary
male theologians, the Goddess archetype returns at a time
when the breakdown of the old story leaves us desperate for
love, for security, for protection, for wisdom, for meaning. It
finds us yearning for a nurturing and cultivation of our whole
being, that we might be adequate stewards of the planetary
culture.[6]

Now, because of the technological cords that link us to
other nations, because of our need to join with these nations
to preserve the earth's remaining resources, and because the
worldwide communication network facilitates a sharing of
culture and a depth of awareness never possible before, we
are on the brink of opportunities for human and cultural
development hitherto unknown. We are on the brink of the

planetary person, who, I believe, is very different in his or her hopes and possibilities from the regional or cosmopolitan person of earlier eras. Just as the cosmopolitan person represents a leap in concerns and in consciousness over the regional person, so too the planetary person is part of a wholly different modality of knowing and being. Planetary consciousness involves a profound awareness of the earth, a potentiating recovery of one's historical as well as herstorical self, and a deep willingness to learn from the genius of other cultures. This person is both the consummation of where we have been and the next stage of the upward spiral. As such, she is our hope, our dream, our beckoning evolutionary vision, a point of contact with that which never was but is always happening.

The vision of the planetary person is confluent with the vision of the possible human. Never before has the vision of what human beings can be been more remarkable. We are living at what promises to be the beginning of the golden age of brain, mind, and body research. Where we stand with regard to these may well compare to where Einstein stood in 1904 with his discovery of the special theory of relativity, which helped accomplish the great revolution in physics. The new explorations and current advances in brain, mind, and body research are increasingly allowing us to view and probe the vast and subtle range of human capacities and gradually to learn to use these capacities more productively and more humanely. As I have said, we are still being educated for the demands of the early twentieth century, and so we use but a fraction of our capacities—perhaps 10 percent of our physical capacity and no more than 5 percent of our mental potential. We live as crippled, limited versions of who and what we really are, and in this era of grow or die, we can no longer get away with such tragic and eroding disuse.

What would happen to human beings and to society in general if we were to increase by even a few percentage points the use of our untapped potential? Much in the new scientific research and the vision of the possible human is predictive of this increase and its consequences. Even more surprising, the research confirms many of the capacities described in those myths of new ways of being discussed in the Preface. We discover that the myths are not outlandish fantasies of the pursuit of the unreal by the implausible. They tell of capacities all humans have, virtually every one of which can be demonstrated in the laboratory with many hundreds of subjects. These capacities can be learned, integrated into daily life, and applied constructively to the solution of many social problems—enhancing education, teaching "nonlearners," rehabilitating ex-prisoners, as well as greatly restoring and extending the physical and mental capacities of the elderly.

As I discussed briefly in the Preface, I have been involved with the creation and implementation of such programs for some time now and, with my associates, have found that human potential is a vast and inexhaustible resource. We have discovered, for example, that most people, given opportunity and education, can realize more of their potential in varying degrees. Their bodies can be psychophysically reeducated so that a much better physical functioning is achieved. As the body's capacities are extended, so are its capacities for awareness, its abilities to move and to sense. Cognitive and feeling functions improve because of changes in the brain's motor cortex, which precede changes in the muscular system and affect adjacent brain areas. Because brain tissue processes tend to diffuse and spread to neighboring tissues, changes in the motor cortex have a parallel effect on tissues that have to do with thought and feeling.

In our applications of these methods to education and the rehabilitation of the elderly, we have found that certain movement exercises frequently result in enhanced capacities for learning, remembering, and problem solving. We find throughout our work that if you wish to extend the capacities of the mind, you must at the same time extend the capacities of the body which is the instrument of that mind. This is why talking therapies don't work as well as they might. They often treat the patient as a purely mental construct, neglecting the deeper cultural disorder that sanctions a dualism of mind and body, a dualism that the therapist tacitly accepts.

In other aspects of our research and in my training workshops, people learn to think in images as well as in words, to practice in subjective time the rehearsal of skills, and to experience the acceleration of thought processes. They learn to think kinesthetically with the whole body, to experience cross-sensing, the self-regulation of pleasure and pain, and to acquire voluntary control over some of the autonomic functions by means of biofeedback and autogenic training. As an exciting extension to this kind of research, we find that research subjects can be taught to speak to their own brains directly, so entering into conscious orchestration of mood, attitude, learning, and creativity.

In our research with mental capacities, however, we have found that to explore these processes it is often necessary to break through the surface crust of consciousness—to *penetrate the cultural trance*—and to disinhibit blocked capacities. When we want to enable a potential experience to become manifest, we can sometimes alter attention on the spectrum of consciousness, going beyond the limits within which the inhibitions operate. Throughout history human beings have invented or discovered many ways to alter consciousness as a gateway to subjective realities, heightened sensitivity, and aesthetic, creative, and religious apperceptions. Ritual drumming, dancing, chanting, fasting, ingesting mind-altering plant substances, yogas, and meditative states—such means have helped to suspend the structural givens and cultural expectations of a certain reality construct—the conditioned mindscape—so that alternative realities and solutions can be perceived.

In our own laboratory we have worked with many of these enabling procedures, employing contemporary counterparts and methodologies, occasionally marrying ancient techniques to modern technology. We have invented or borrowed new instrumentation by which depth probings of the psyche can be accomplished and capacities that have been blocked can, to an extent, be unfettered and guided experimentally. Still, in some sense, there really is no such thing as an altered state of consciousness, for by its very nature consciousness is always altering. The term is used only to lend clarity to different phasings along the spectrum of consciousness. Most of us exist with regard to the spectrum and dimensions of consciousness as if we were inhabiting only the attic of ourselves, with the first, second, third, and fourth floors and the basement going uninhabited and remaining unconscious.

As we begin to extend the domain of consciousness and take up residence in these other realms of ourselves, the pragmatic effects are remarkable. People can learn how to work with dream content, how to concentrate and to remember better, how to think along several tracks at the same time. There is a tapping of the creative process and an experiencing of those levels of the self where the images are archetypal, mythological, and possibly transpersonal.

To evoke and work with these capacities is to gain access to some perspectives on the ecology of one's own inner space, affording an inner eye and ear attuned to the patterns that maintain the dynamics of existence. One begins to perceive in one's own psychic depths the realm of the Dromenon. And with this is occasioned a sense of restoring the ecological balance between inner and outer worlds. A deepening occurs that is, at the same time, a larger use of the self, a more complete self-knowing. To realize these is to bring individuals into very different relationships to their world.

Our discussion could pursue many different kinds of potentials, and what will be presented here will only be the tip of the iceberg of thirty years of research into the possible human. Many of my other books deal with the range of human potentials and their development.[7] But here, let us take a closer look at those techniques that awaken human sensibility to the coherence of the ecologies of inner and outer space. Let us look, then, at modes of enhancing the senses and extending the uses of imagery and time.

By the time we reach maturity, for most of us our sensorium is a shrunken, crippled version of what it could be. As people grow older in our culture, they undergo a progressive diminishment of sensory acuity and sensory knowing. They become progressively less able to see, to touch, and otherwise to utilize their senses. This loss would seem to be attributable in part to our verbalizing, conceptualizing mental processes and not just to impairment by age. In many hunting and tribal societies, for example, it is the adult and not the child who evinces the most acute and orchestral balance of senses. In our culture we have the evidence of professionals who have to keep up a certain sensory acuity for the sake of their art—the musician's ear, the artist's eye, the perfumer's nose. The blunting of perception has led me to formulate Houston's law: *Concept louses up percept.*

Conceptualization, of course, is essential to the continuance of culture—it sustains the very fabric of civilization. But civilization, as the patriarch Sigmund Freud has warned us, has its profound discontents. In societies where sensory experience is depreciated as a cultural norm (so that one can put most of one's energies into mastering the environment), the body itself suffers attendant harpies—the neuroses, obesities, aggressions, and even the widespread death wish that seems to characterize much of psyche and history in the twentieth century. Is it worth seeing as through a glass darkly, or touching as if one were wearing gloves, or hearing as if through wads of conceptual cotton wool? Such simple matters may be the stuff of which historical catastrophes are made. Such simple matters may also be the stuff of which is made the agnostic reflex that paralyzes and encapsulates so much of Western sensibility. Primed by the sensory removal from the immediacy of the world, conceptualization isolates consciousness from its object—thought from being—the local consensual reality from the larger Reality. An experience of some kind of *ecstasis*, be it sensory or psychological, seems to be the best way out of this reflex and its implacable self-righteousness. Otherwise, we are conditioned to allow it to act so continuously and automatically that many of our best insights and intuitions, our clearest percepts and glimpses of the wider realms, are shut down by the insistent immediacy of the reflex. Worse, it keeps us from the complexity of things, leaving us in a state of puerile innocence not unlike the dogs and cats that William James speaks of as occupying our living rooms without any idea of the intricate and absolutely fascinating goings-on around the house.

In our laboratory we have discovered that it is quite possible to prevent perceptual impairment in the young and, to varying degrees, to restore to older people some of the sensory acuity they have lost. An initial exercise might involve the use of deep relaxation and active imagination to clean the rooms of perception, those five rooms where the senses make their homes, where the debris and general messiness represents a state of sensory laziness and constraint. By working intensely to clean these rooms, the subject is accomplishing an electrochemical event in his or her sensory centers and discovers that the metaphors of active imagination are *real* occurrences and do *real* work. Thus it is not surprising that after the exercise, most subjects find their depth perception enhanced and their relationship to the sensory world much more vital and interesting. Opening the person to a wider spectrum of patterns and ideas from the perceptual world then acts to inform and extend the horizons of the conceptual world.

Another exercise increases the intensity and experiential duration of pleasure. Interestingly enough, pleasure proves easier to work with than pain, possibly because the potentials of pleasure seem less familiar in our culture and thus are more open to the laboratory experience. In one simple experiment, a subject is told to experience a velvet fabric in three ways: first, by touching it in the ordinary ways; second, by touching it while in trance and with suggestions of heightened sensitivity; and third, by touching the fabric while in a very relaxed and receptive state, thinking of it as a source of pleasure. In most every case the greatest pleasure is had when the fabric is regarded as the source of pleasure. The fabric then seems to be alive, and touching is like interaction with some other living thing. Furthermore, almost the entire awareness of the subject is occupied by the experience of touching and by the pleasure sensations it affords. The fabric becomes personal and no longer an object. It acquires a quality of "thou," which in the sensory world is always more pleasurable than "it" because it is more attended to by the observer. To increase sensory acuity, we often have to suspend that mode of consciousness which insists on objectifying the world.

In other states of consciousness—be they meditative states, hyperalert states, trance states, or states of contemplative attention—a percept will be received quite differently by the perceiver. Alter attention on the spectrum of consciousness and a flower might become a breathing star, a sympathetic friend, a mandala of light and enlightenment, or just some old purple petunia. Alter attention on the spectrum of consciousness and virtually any percept becomes a multivalent reality.

What are the overall effects on someone who begins to make use of the extended sensorium? Apart from more creative and sensitive use of the body-mind, there is also deepened personal sensitivity concerning ecological and symbiotic relationships, with nature perceived as a thou, in all parts personal and sentient. To students of psychology and anthropology, this emphasis on the personal quality of things may appear regressive, animistic, even primitive. Yet modern ecological and scientific studies would appear to confirm the basic reliability of this "primitive" tendency. For example, to treat the particulars of existence as thous implies a degree of participation not usually extended to those particulars. But the ecological perspective respects a much larger arena of participation and interpenetration than we "civilized" folk permit ourselves. The personalizing, participatory ambience of the "primitive" world-view and cosmology—the world of Castaneda's Don Juan, for example—may be closer to the facts of things than the acausal randomness and separateness of official speculation.

The truth and wisdom of highly developed and creative minds, cross-fertilizing realities within and without, further assure us that radical selfhood and objectification run counter to the ecological flow of things. We are as much the informed as we are the informer. We are resonance phenomena. Heisenberg's theory of the indivisibility of the phenomenon from the observer affirms this. There is no innocence on either side. Thus Kant's notion of the mind-brain imposing its innate categorical imperatives on the outer environment, or current neurological dicta that see reality as the brain in a feedback loop with itself, can only be partially responsible for our perceptions. If we are part of a wider universe, as the Dromenon of our time suggests, then we have a wider body and a wider spectrum of receivership. If we are part of the cosmic ecology, then somewhere in our being we have the organs to perceive and relate to that ecology.

The excesses of externalizing, objectifying consciousness necessitate finding new ways of utilizing one's humanness—not the anti-ecological manipulation and exploitation of one's environment, but the developing, exploring, and integrating of our inner capacities. To restore the balance of nature, to extend the ecological continuum between inner and outer worlds, culture must now go inward to cultivate the vast untapped resources of the psyche.

In exploring the psychodynamics of inner space, one discovers again and again what humanity has always known: that the key to the depths lies in the development and understanding of imagery. We know that the human being has a natural capacity to think in images as well as in words. This capacity is very widespread and perhaps universal in young children. An emphasis on verbal processes, in education and elsewhere, inhibits this capacity, but it can be reactivated. In some artists, scientists, and mathematicians, and in certain others, the inhibition has been less effective. By his own statement, Einstein's most important thought was accomplished with visual and kinesthetic images, not with words or numbers. He described himself in an important letter to the mathematician Jacques Hadamard as someone in whom visual and muscular or kinesthetic thinking was predominant. Similar statements have been forthcoming from other highly creative people. When one thinks in images, solutions and ideas can emerge that were impossible when the thinking was purely verbal. The present state of brain research suggests that thinking in images may involve areas of the brain where the thought process is more passive and receptive and also more susceptible to patterns, to symbolic processes, to constellational constructs.

More information is therefore likely to be condensed in the dynamics inherent in the coded symbolic breakthrough. The so-called creative breakthrough might then be seen as the manipulation of these larger patterns of information which are part of the imaginal, symbolic process.

Many children are natural visualizers, but often become cut off from their visualizing capacity by the verbal-linear processes that the educational system imposes on them. Such children may subsequently suffer a sense of inferiority as well as do poorly in school. Bright and talented as they may naturally be, they quickly lose a sense of their own capacities and intelligence, not only in school and among their peers, but throughout their lives.

The one fairly large-scale effort to preserve the imaging capacity of children was the experiment of the Jaensch brothers in special schools in Marburg, Germany, in the 1920s, and the results were most encouraging. Children taught to use the image-thought process were, by the time they reached their teens, more creative and better able to draw. Also, they scored higher on intelligence tests than comparable children whose imagery was allowed to meet the usual fate of atrophy and inhibition imposed by educational processes too oriented to the verbal. In our own programs with participating schools, we are able to prevent the inhibition of this faculty in children by allowing education to be a training in images as well as in words. We are able to effect a disinhibition in adults so that they have access alternatively to both verbal and visual thought process. This results in the ability to consider more alternatives, more solutions, and, in general, to think more creatively. Depth levels of patterning and information become available, since imagistic thinking leads inevitably to dimensions of the imaginal and archetypal realms.

In our laboratory we have been able to facilitate access to the imagery process through a variety of means, such as the use of instrumentation and the use of induced or self-induced altered states of consciousness. When ideoretinal patterns are stimulated with stroboscopic light, subjects experience imagery. Sensory deprivation chambers or subtle audiovisual overload also stimulate imagery centers in the brain. The subject enters into an unconscious partnership with the forms and colors flowing in front of him or her and begins to project onto the screen previously internal imagery. At this point, the subject might shut his or her eyes and discover that the "show" is continuing in the form of eidetic imagery seen with the eyes closed. Most of our work now relies on the induction of states of consciousness that evoke imagery, such as hyperalert states, trance states, and states employing what are essentially active imagination processes.

Let me now indicate a few of our findings resulting from our imagery studies with hundreds of subjects.

First, the visual imagery process appears to be essentially creative, tending to gather meanings and seek out solutions. For example, images observed long enough will cease to be random or disconnected and will organize into symbolic drama, narrative, or problem-solving processes. Fiction and drama could be manifestations of this inherent tendency. Tantric Buddhist and Sufi spiritual disciplines as well as some of the proliferating image therapies may be indebted to it for their efficacy.

Second, prolonged, vivid, narrative imagery, especially if it is experienced repeatedly, increases motivation to do creative work, and also sometimes breaks through creative blocks, which may exist within the imagery process. The old chestnut suggests that genius is composed of 98 percent perspiration and only 2 percent inspiration, a conundrum that still leaves us with the question: Where did all those geniuses get the wherewithal to perspire so much? Could it be that imagistic thinking (a frequent occurrence among geniuses and highly creative persons) is bonded in neurophysiological terms with psychic and hormonal energizers? The state of brain research is still too primitive to be sure, but the phenomenological evidence points in that direction.

Third, our early studies with LSD, and later our nondrug investigations, suggest a four-stage typology of imagery corresponding to a descent into four major levels of the psyche. We termed these levels the *sensory*, the *recollective-analytic*, the *symbolic*, and the *integral*.

On the shallowest or sensory level, imagery is initially perceived as random color patterns, checkerboards, vortices, and other ideoretinal form constructs. Imagery may then become more specific, with pictures, scenes, faces, but remains disconnected and without any particular meaning.

On the second, recollective-analytic level of imagery, the subject begins to explore his or her own psychological inner space. At this stage imagery tends to be more reflective or analytic. One studies one's past, one's problems, and one's potentialities, somewhat as in psychoanalysis. Memories, both verbal and visual, are more than ordinarily accessible, providing a greater quantity of materials with which to work. Visual thought on this level seems to be more concrete and also to demonstrate a more than usually free flow of imagination and fantasy. Further, the combination of visual thought and its symbolic codings of patterns of information provides considerably more data, as well as variant views of this data, for subjects to use for personal reflection or for problem-solving of any kind.

On the third and symbolic level, which is deeper than the second and may require experience of the second level, a rich mythopoetic symbolism develops, in which one's own life may be seen in terms of guiding patterns or goals, symbolized, as in a myth-making process, so that a concrete symbol can stand for one's personal life and its context. The movement here is beyond the personal-particular of the second level and toward the personal-universal, with its broadening contexts and more universal formulations. Here the symbolic images are predominantly historical, legendary, mythical, ritualistic, and archetypal. The subject may experience a profound and rewarding sense of continuity with evolutionary and historic process. Or one may image rituals in which one participates with all five senses and with profound emotion, so that a rite of passage can have the same effect as an actual rite, significantly advancing one toward maturity.

Another subject may image the archetypal figures of fairy tales, legends, or myths, and perhaps discover the broad patterns of his or her own life as the subject identifies with Prometheus, Parsifal, Psyche, Oedipus, Inanna, Faust, Isis, Don Juan, or some other figure. Lately, the Wise Old Woman has been emerging with astonishing frequency in the imaginal levels of both male and female subjects, suggesting a profound change in the psychodynamics of the present historical situation. In these mythic and symbolic dramas, too, the sense of participation may be strong, as the images emerge in a meaningful and purposive sequence, and the symbols appear in undisguised relevance to the person's life and problems.

The granting of reality to a geophysical realm perceived in an altered state of consciousness has an ancient and honorable tradition. The Sufi mystics, for example, speak of the *alam al-mithal* or *mundus imaginalis*, an intermediate universe thought to be as ontologically real as the sensory empirical world and the noetic world of abstract intellect. It exists in a meta-geography that possesses extension and dimension as well as figure, color, and other features perceived by the senses. But this world can be experienced only by those who are exercising their psychospiritual senses, and through this special form of imaginal knowing, gain access to a visionary world not unlike the *mundus archetypus* of Carl Jung. There dreamers and visionaries return again and again, extending consciousness and reality at the source level of gnosis and creative process, a place where the self moves freely amid archetypes and universals, listening to the pulse and dynamic coding of the transforming patterns of the Dromenon.

Finally, there is the integral level of the experience, in which the subject feels a kind of subjective "descent" to a level of awareness apprehended as Essence, Ground of Being, or even God. When experienced, it is felt as an *entelechy*—a kind of structuring, dynamic energy rising up from the depths and informing and energizing the other three levels. This four-stage typology suggests that the energizing fundamental reality (the entelechy) rises first to the third level and there assumes its universal paradigms, reinforcing and invigorating the mythic structures. Then, moving upward, it energizes the personal, historical, and psychological structures at the second level and, finally, intensifies the sensory levels by cleaning the doors of perception both within and without. The tendency throughout, as in the religious experience, is a flooding into the world at large of this experience, giving the person a sense of new communion and commitment to the social and ecological orders. Thus does the imaginal descent into the ecology of the inner world remythologize and energize the ecology of the outer world.

Our many cases of religious and creative exploration of the imaginal world by subjects tell us much about the relationship between the inner cosmos of the human psyche and the outer cosmos of the universe as a whole. They tell us about the resonance and sustenance of patterns within and without. If the personality is in some sense the universe in miniature, then the generic images of the depths are as much a part of nature as wind, sand, and stars. Great Nature is contained within and without, the planes of life demanding differing frequencies for its manifest forms, but offering perhaps equal ontological reality. Our studies of imagery suggest that the individual psyche opens up to the Psyche of Nature, and images and archetypes in our consciousness, perhaps, reflect that wider reality. Thus, what we perceive in the imaginal mythopoesis of our interior world may be the reflections of not only the movements of the innerverse but those of the outer reality as well. If imaginal archetypes reflect myths, they also reflect the movements of outer Nature. Again, the ecology of the wider life affirms that all is resonance, but also that we can do much to become conscious participants in this resonance.

The question of resonance brings us to the untapped potential of our time world. It may be that we are flow patterns through time. In the process metaphysics of Henri Bergson and Teilhard de Chardin, time can be seen as a dynamic matrix, a near-ultimate superstructure that gives us our codings for quantum jumps of evolutionary change. And yet we know and explore so little of the time world, caught as we are in the tyranny of clock time—which, truth to tell, is closer to Euclidean space than it is to time. Therefore, one of the major research programs of our foundation has had to do with the expanded uses of time.

Our studies indicate that it is possible to increase greatly the rate of thought or amount of subjective experience beyond what is ordinarily possible within a unit of clock-measured time. Under certain conditions of altered consciousness, a person might experience within a few minutes as measured by the clock such a wealth of ideas or images that it will seem that hours, days, or even longer periods must have passed to have experienced so much. Only a few minutes of objective (clock) time have elapsed; the change has been on the level of subjective experiential time, and the explanation lies in the phenomenon of accelerated mental process (AMP).

It has long been known that AMP occurs spontaneously under conditions of dreaming sleep (the "hours long" dream that takes only a few seconds or minutes of clock time). Then there are the cases related to great emotional stress. A man falling from a bridge and expecting to die, who by some chance is saved from death, may later recount that during the fall, his whole lifetime appeared before his eyes, or that he relived all significant events without any haste—events seemed to happen at the normal, everyday rate. The Swiss Mountain Club has recorded hundreds of such experiences as reported by climbers who have fallen, expecting to die, but have survived. My own experience when I was nineteen and given to parachuting confirms this. Once, after a jump, I had an experience of falling for an exceptionally long time after pulling the jump cord. Before the emergency chute opened a few seconds later, it seemed to me that most of the significant events of my life—not every little pork chop and Hershey bar, but the main events up to the age of nineteen—went by as images at their own natural pace.

We used to think that such experiences were mere crisis hallucinations with no validity at all. Now we take them more seriously, since we realize that the brain can process millions of images in microseconds. Perhaps in near-death situations, these images are patterned in a life-review cycle.

Imagery is crucial in experiences of AMP, because imagistic thinking does not seem to be bound by the time-inhibited mechanisms that retard the flow of verbal thought. Most thinking is geared to speech and to the movements of the body in work or play—an additional cause of the slowness of most thinking. But thinking need not be limited by the slow pace of our physiological being or by the linear inhibitions of our verbal thought. In the phenomenology of high-level creativity, the mind races over many alternatives, picking, choosing, discarding, synthesizing, sometimes doing the work of several months in a few minutes.

In teaching subjects the potential of AMP, we begin by

telling them that their normal rate of thought or subjective experiencing is very much slower than need be. Some previous experiments are described to them so that they clearly understand that subjective events are not bound by any laws of time or motion that may apply in the objective world. Then the subject might be enabled to experience a fairly elaborate adventure or fantasy story within a brief unit of clock-measured time. At the end of a minute most subjects feel that much more subjective experience has occurred than could ever be confined within the given minute. Thus the subject is becoming conditioned from his or her usual temporal referents in the objective world by going beneath the surface crust of consciousness to discover the more fluid categories of space and time that operate in the depths of the psyche.

When accelerated mental process has been practiced sufficiently, one can learn very quickly and dramatically, or perhaps apply learnings that were previously ineffective, all within the context of a subjective reality. A subject might rehearse musical or athletic skills with suggestions of accelerated mental process, so that, for example, a Beethoven sonata that might ordinarily require hours of practice can be practiced in the AMP state in five minutes, with the subject emerging from trance feeling as if he or she has been practicing for hours and showing considerable improvement in playing. The applications of this process are very wide—to almost any skill that a person needs to improve.

Many subjects who have become proficient in the process begin creating their own works of art, music, or poetry. Subjective time is critically related to the creative process. In accelerated mental process there is simply not the "time" to mobilize the usual creative blocks, and so subjects who previously showed little creativity find themselves engaged in the automatisms of the creative process, with self-creating works of art emerging from their minds and demanding expression.

LIFE FORCE

The most difficult self-creative works to obtain have been poems, whether or not the research subject had ever written poetry. In one instance, however, a male Jungian analyst, age forty-four, was engaged in a conversation about the famous case of Coleridge writing "Kubla Khan." Coleridge had taken some opium and fallen into a kind of sleep in which images rose up before him as things, with a parallel production of the correspondent expressions, without any sensation or consciousness of effort. The subject, who was in trance during this discussion, delivered himself of a rambling and rather long psychological analysis of what he felt might be an explanation of Coleridge's experience. He then was asked whether he did not find the economy of poetic language admirable when compared to that of most psychologists. He laughingly agreed, adding that economy of language was very difficult for him to achieve. He had occasionally tried to write poetry, but tended to become abstract as well as too verbose.

The subject was next given the usual discussion of the phenomenon of AMP and invited to make a creative application. It was suggested that he would have an experience somewhat like that of Coleridge, although only one minute of clock time was to be allowed; images and associated words would come into consciousness effortlessly, and all he had to do was remember them and tell us afterward. Before he could protest that this was impossible, he was firmly ordered to begin. At the end of the minute, he related an amusing imagery sequence described in very concentrated—but nonetheless poetic—language. Later he added the title:

Tantric Vision

Seated just under a symbol-studded
Mandala of Light

Was an Avatar with long white hair and a
    graceful youth's body.
To his left was an archetypal serpent.
To his right, a numinous lion.
Not knowing the hierarchy Here, or which
    Phenomenon
    to venerate first,
I made love to the beautiful goddess
    stretched out
    on the soft lotus petals.
Then, from the Heavens, a Voice like a
    thunder clap said:
    WELL CHOSEN, MY SON!

Subsequent experiments and practice enabled the subject
to write many poems, rich in imagery and vivid in expression.
The subject later noted an important change in his prose style
and speech patterns as well. Everything became more concise, and his work contained many more concrete images, making it seem more vital. Evidently, a creative block had been
broken through unintentionally during the course of the
experiments.

One could speculate on the relationship between creativity
and the metaphysics of time. Clock-conditioned knowing
inevitably impedes the flow of creative thought because it
habituates that thought to the serial beat, which for the most
part, leads to routines or banal probabilities. When one enters
into a durative time field beyond the militant beat of past-
present-future, one enters into a field continuum that contains
all answers. Seen under the rubric of Time, the creative process becomes a participation in realms of synchronicity. In the
creative act the world becomes selectively illumined by remarkable and remarkably creative correspondences that one did not

LIFE FORCE

see before. The automatisms of the creative process—the self-creative works of art that seem to rise under conditions of altered consciousness, altered time, and the vital use of imagery—testify, perhaps, that these conditions provide entry into the synchronous time zone wherein meanings and patterns of information that would normally take years to pursue become linked in a resonance pattern that provides the creative breakthrough.

The furthest reaches of synchronicity (and, for that matter, creativity) are probably mystical experiences of universal correspondence. "That Art Thou" is the deepest knowing. The uniqueness of the self is the final resolution. One is extended and multiplied throughout time and space, through inner and outer worlds. Nothing is unfamiliar or unrelated. All ecologies are centered in one's self, and one is ecologically interdependent with all that is. The knower, the knowledge, and the known become part of an undifferentiated unity that is the *unus mundus*, the eternal dance between the One and the Many, the Dromenon.

It is my belief that these changes herald the coming of the post-individual and the era of the planetary person, and that this age can find its correspondence in the time of second maturity.

For the first time in human history many, many people are continuing to live for a long time. While the population of the United States is more than three times what it was in 1900, the number of older people is almost nine times as large. By the year 2000 we will have over thirty million people over sixty-five years of age. If you look at a graph of the last two hundred years, you see a steady rise in life expectancy, as if the Life Force itself was asserting its own expansion in an amplitude of years. At the time the American Constitution was written, a normal life span was in the thirties; a hundred years ago, it was in the forties. Then the span took an exponential leap, so that today, it is in the seventies. Projecting from this, life expectancy will be in the nineties by the Tricentennial; and by the time of the four hundredth anniversary of the United States (2176), we might reach the biologically natural life span of one hundred and twenty. I say "biologically natural" because the human being is one of the few members of the animal kingdom that does not live ten to twelve times the age of puberty. Further, recent mitotic and cellular studies of human tissue have been taken by some gerontologists to indicate that we could have one hundred good years—which we certainly do need in order to deal with the growing complexity of life and the necessity for both long-term and constantly renewed education and deepening.

When they were few, the elderly were revered, cherished, acknowledged. Now that they are many, we don't know what to do with them and have instituted, even legislated, procedures that have turned the potentially greatest among us into vegetables. Gerontophobia—the fear that arbitrarily alienates, segregates, stereotypes, and discriminates against people on the basis of advanced age—is one of the worst and most debilitating diseases of modern society. It raises lies and distortions to the level of fatuous platitudes, declaring old age to be an affliction that renders one increasingly sexless, useless, and powerless. It sanctions the isolation of the "afflicted" from the rest of society, building glorified playpens for the well-to-do; and for those who are less well-off, it creates "homes" that are limbos of sensory and existential deprivation. Recently a study was made of a group of healthy young college students who took up residence in one of these homes, requesting to be treated exactly like the elderly inmates. After several days they began to display symptoms of senility.

Another aspect of the disease of our society in regarding the elderly as afflicted is that we demand that they stay in a state of arrested animation. Still feeling their life whole within them, they are forced to remain as ignorant of their potentials as are their juniors. Thus, like our era, they often fluctuate between a nervous elation and a chilling despair—the involutional melancholy that haunts those people and times whose potentials are ready to emerge, but are disacknowledged or actively repressed instead. In older age the distractability that had been the great placebo of our earlier years has vanished. At the same time there is an intensity that comes with age that few have suspected or explored.

The American poet John Hall Wheelock reflected this deeply when he said on his ninetieth birthday, ''I've always wanted to live long. I had a lot of work I wanted to do. In old age, things become more intense rather than less so. Things get more poignant—so many associations—everything reverberating with everything else.''

It may be that finally the holocaust of the elders is ending. We are gradually coming to see that the years beyond sixty, the years of our second maturity, may be evolution's greatest gift to humanity. Relieved of the armoring of authority of one's first maturity, as well as its accompanying narrowing of vision, one gains in these years the liberty to inquire rather than order, to question rather than reply. No longer encapsulated by ends and goals, delivered from specialized commitments, the old are free to explore the fullness of their psychophysical powers, the latencies of their human potentials. This statement may seem strange to those familiar with the current studies and literature indicating that aging is accompanied by many factors involving cellular and structural decay. Other theories offer information suggesting that soon there will be ways in which we can reset the cellular aging clock and thus send senescence on its way to obsolescence. At the Foundation for Mind Research, Robert Masters is conducting ongoing research into ways in which substantial rehabilitation could be accomplished, in part through a functional rejuvenation that is within the capacities of many elderly people. He writes:

> The reduced movement, blunted sensing, impaired mental processes, etc., of the elderly person are to a large extent the products of habitual modes of behaving—faulty use— which gradually inhibits brain cells, distorts the kinesthetic sense and muscle feedback, keeps some muscles chronically over-contracted while others, at the same time, remain hypotonic, and thus deforms the skeletal alignment, inhibiting movement of the joints, impairing breathing, reducing flow of blood to the brain, and so on—a constellation of effects that produces the appearance as well as the feeling of old age. The cause is not really "old age," however, since the brain cells can be disinhibited, the sensing improved, the muscle patterns reorganized, the joints freed, and movement, including breathing, enhanced to an extent that must be seen, or, better, felt for oneself, if it is to be believed. [8]

The sociopolitical realities of aging are also being reconsidered from a fresh point of view. Maggie Kuhn, founder of the national activist group the Gray Panthers, says:

> I am very glad I have achieved my seniority. I count myself fortunate. I wish all my peers could enjoy their wrinkles as much as I enjoy mine. I regard them as badges of distinction that I have worked hard for. . . . This is a new age of liberation, self-determination and freedom. This is an age when it is appropriate to form new coalitions of the people whom society has cruelly separated. . . . Older women, for example, have the most to gain from the women's movement. . . . Older women have a great deal

to teach younger women. Too long have old and young been kept apart. This separation is artificial because, really, life is a continuum. . . .

I like to think that age is a great universalizing force, something we all have in common. Aging puts us in the same life experience as animals, plants, flowers, and rocks. As we face the universal experience of aging, we can be part of the whole created order. That concept can refurbish our spirits, empower our bodies, and help us talk about age and deal with its terrors and fears. . . . Aging is, in fact, a triumph, a result of strength and survivorship. Old age is the time to take risks and initiate social change. Old people are free to take risks. They have nothing to lose.[9]

In this spirit, Maggie Kuhn and her intergenerational Panthers prowl watchfully in the field of social consciousness keeping a vigilant eye on policies and services that affect the lives of those elder citizens who have been deprived of their own political voice. The group's activism addresses an array of issues from housing, economics, and health to compulsory retirement, always with concern for age discrimination.

Part of the success of the Gray Panthers and similar organizations is that they have proved that the elderly, with their multiple skills and breadth of perspective, are also living repositories of change, and thus are the people able to give the most practical counsel and offer the most far-seeing visions on making society work. That's why grandpersons should be educators, and why the great chain of being between generations must be restored if we are to survive our time. Again, Maggie Kuhn says it beautifully:

Our goal is responsible adulthood. We who are old are the elders of the tribe and the elders are charged with the tribe's survival and well-being. When we consider how much there is to do in this democracy, we see how crucial it is for all of us to join together. We need to pool the energy and get on with the building of community. [10]

One considers Virgile Barel, born in 1890 and the oldest deputy in the French National Assembly, who said some years ago, "I am assaulted by a need for action. My intellectual curiosity has in fact increased. Ideas come to me at every moment." One thinks of the late Buckminster Fuller, born in 1895, whose mind was a teeming cornucopia of ideas and projects, and who continued to race round and round the planet until practically the day he died, while holding the hand of his dying wife and partner of many years, offering to all who heard him an operating manual for spaceship Earth. One thinks of so many elders, known and unknown, who—by virtue of having kept their lives and minds active—have reached a stage of insight into the nature of things that raises problem solving to the level of a metaphysical art form.

For me this phenomenon was crystallized in watching my good friend Margaret Mead in her seventies develop what is virtually a new human aesthetic joined to the scientific process—what she called a *macroscope*—to create a different way of understanding and dealing with the world. In Margaret Mead's macroscopic view of the planet, the human lens is placed over global problems in such a way that the world is seen both as a whole and as a dynamic flux of countless concrete instances. I once asked her to apply this concept to the effects of modernization. First she focused her lens on planetary problems, then on the village of Peri in New Guinea, where she had done extensive field research. She recalled that when the next village moved in, the weight of its presence put too much pressure on the edge of the sand, and Peri became flooded. She then moved back and forth between clear memories of specific events and thinking about the whole globe. She drew analogies for me between molecular biology and massive ecosystems. Everything became interconnected and relevant to everything else. As she moved to greater and greater clarity, I observed her define needs, make plans, become strengthened in her resolve, and begin to take practical steps to ameliorate some of the problems she had seen. This was the genius of the elder in action. This was the wise feminine raised to its rich potential.

One of the most important potentials of second maturity is the capacity for spiritual development. From my own experience of working with elderly people, I find that many, having known the breadth of existence, have the capacity for knowing the subtleties of the depths as well, in ways that they could not have known before. No longer needing to compete, to be acceptable, to be likeable, and all those other things considered respectable in society, they are finally uncaged in their elder years—free to release energies and capacities that the culture restrained in them when they were younger. The new energies that people sometimes release after sixty-five or seventy are not really new at all. They were always there, present at any stage of human development; but now in their elder years, people do not have to spend a great deal of their energy holding back who they are, leashing the hound of heaven.

With this freedom they also gain both the time and the abilities to join the ecology of their external existence to that of their internal existence. Thus can we become in later years living exemplars of the fact that Reality is a continuum in which subjective experience is as real and important as objective experience. Our depths open up to a larger universe and a richer knowing, one in which a more complete ''use-full-ness'' can be attained. The spiritual growth that follows is therefore grounded in one's biological, everyday existence. For the elderly person, daily life can become a spiritual exercise, whereas for the younger, the pursuit of spiritual realities is too often divorced from common experience.

A capacity for all-embracing kinship is what shapes the elder's spirit. Carl Jung, in his final retrospective remarks, saw this keenly when he wrote, ''Yet there is so much that fills me: plants, animals, clouds, day and night, and the eternal in man. The more uncertain I have felt about myself, the more there has grown up in me a feeling of kinship with all things.''[11] Or as Petag, a Yuha Mani, an old Sioux shaman, said, ''As I get older, I burrow more and more into the hills. The Great Spirit made them for us, for me, I want to blend with them, shrink into them, and, finally, disappear in them. As my brother Lame Deer has said, all of nature is in us, all of us is in nature. This is as it should be.''[12]

In becoming an elder, one moves finally beyond the dualisms and divisiveness that inhibit the natural developmental process of spiritual growth. One is able to assume the attributes and potentials of both sexes without fear of recrimination. This adds greatly to one's capacity for spiritual knowing. In many societies, therefore, one needs an abundance of years in the world before it is considered appropriate to begin one's deep inner training. Among the Navahos, for example, the healer or medicine man or woman does not begin his or her most critical training until around the age of fifty, after families have been raised and characters have been tempered and refined by a great deal of life experience. In the classical Jewish tradition, similar proscriptions apply to those who wish to begin a study of the mystical Kabbalah.

I once asked Dr. Gay Gaer Luce, the cofounder of SAGE, a growth center for older people that employs methods and techniques similar to those described earlier in this chapter, what she found men and women in their seventies and eighties learning that they could not have learned in earlier years. She replied:

Well, I could list things such as teaching, counseling younger people, helping very ill peers, writing retrospectively. I'm working with a group of people at SAGE, for example, who, I believe, are going to become remarkable healers. It has taken them a year to realize that what and who they are is actually of value for people in crisis. They didn't sense that what they were doing was annealing and needed, and they have no sense of authority about it. After all, there's been no tradition of a "healing" role in their lives. They are simply the kinds of people who will be able to come and sit next to a patient in the hospital and silently, without having to say anything, make that person feel better, give that person hope, allow that person to have the security to relax. Their presence and energy can allow healing to happen. They generate solace out of their person, their beingness. That same energy in a younger person is more personalized, is more attached and shows itself in sympathy, identification, passion. . . . When I have been in the presence of a group of older people who are beginning to realize themselves more deeply, I sense a transmission that has nothing to do with words or philosophy. It has to do with something about the wisdom of living, now transmitted through a way of being, through a kind of energy and beingness that is direct. It's like someone opening their eyes on you; none of that can be expressed in words. The luminousness an older person has to offer is sometimes almost overwhelming.

I recommend Dr. Luce's books highly, for they are among the finest explorations of the capacities and genius of second maturity ever written. [13]

Without the same needs for personalized ego satisfaction that they had when they were younger, elder persons are capable of expressions of unconditional love, perhaps the most healing and empowering force in the world today. Witness, for example, eighty-three-year-old Mother Teresa's extraordinary activities of unconditional love among the destitute and dying of India. The expression of this love among elders is rooted in some sense in the return on a deeper level to the generalized awareness that we had known as children. As post-individual, one no longer has the specialized commitments that dictate so many of the concerns and obligations of one's first maturity. Now one is free to express a generalized affection and good will, to explore many more choices and options, and, in one's relationships with others, to express an anxiety-free concern and dispassionate approbation. With so broad a view and so expansive a feeling, it is no wonder that the elderly become seers and visionaries, detecting the deeper levels of events and wider fields of life.

A beautiful friend of mine, Mavis Moore, an elder and sage in the highest sense, sent me a letter recently describing the clear seeing that occurs when one ripens into second maturity:

> If I listen, I can have what aging means rather than how it appears to others. The labels of the world find no identity in me. This clear seeing is not a trying to change something but is like taking wrappers off a statue so that its form may be more factually defined by the eye. It is not creating the form; it is unveiling the form whether the form be the potentiality of an acorn to be an oak or of age to bestow more wisdom by deepening experience. One might, from the many versions of reality of which age is the culminating one, come at last to the nature of things, looking out upon an ever new, unrepeatable freshness and firstness.

In our ends are our beginnings, and what we find among elders is the reacquisition of childhood on higher levels. This is *neoteny*—the principle of increased capacity to comprehend experience through an ever-fresh and childlike approach. Seen from the perspective of an entire lifetime, the neotenic process moves from a high degree of unspecialization (in infancy and childhood), to a high degree of specialization (in adolescence and first maturity), to a high degree of unspecialization that comprehends specialization (in second maturity). [14] This principle of neoteny assigned to the condition of our second maturity may be the aim of life and the way into the second spiral. The first spiralings of culture and consciousness might be seen as the developing fetus of our emerging selves. With the post-individual and the capacities of our elder years, we are potentially able to be born at last, a birth that will take us into a larger reality and a richer and more complex humanity, one that includes the highest partnership between male and female both in society and within ourselves. This birth is symbolized by the second spiral, which includes and comprehends all the previous fetal developments of history and human behavior.

I once met a man, an old man, who was on intimate terms with the second spiral. Let me tell you what he was like. Let me tell you about walking the dog with Mr. Tayer.

When I was about thirteen, I used to run down Park Avenue in New York City, late for school. I was a great big overgrown girl, and one day I ran right into a rather frail old gentleman in his seventies and knocked the wind out of him. He laughed as I helped him to his feet and asked me in French-accented speech, "Are you planning to run like that for the rest of your life?"

"Yes, sir," I replied. "It looks that way."

"Well, bon voyage!" he said.

"Bon voyage!" I answered and sped on my way.

About a week later I was walking down Park Avenue with my fox terrier, Champ, and again I met the old gentleman.

"Ah," he greeted me, "my friend the runner, and with a fox terrier. I knew one like that many years ago in France. Where are you going?"

"Well, sir," I replied, "I'm taking Champ to Central Park."

"I will go with you," he informed me. "I will take my constitutional."

And thereafter, for about a year, the old gentleman and I would meet and walk together in Central Park. His name, as far as I could make out, was Mr. Thayer or Mr. Tayer.

The walks were magical and full of delight. Mr. Tayer had absolutely no self-consciousness and would suddenly fall on his knees and exclaim to me, "Jeanne, look at the caterpillar! What does the caterpillar think? Does he know what he is going to become? Eh, Jeanne—feel yourself to be a caterpillar. What will you be when you become a butterfly? The next stage, Jeanne. The next stage! Metamorphosis! It is so exciting."

His long, gothic, comic-tragic face would nod with wonder.

"Eh, Jeanne, look at the clouds! God's calligraphy in the sky! All that transformation—moving, changing, dissolving, becoming. Eh, Jeanne—are you a cloud? Be a cloud."

Or there was the time that Mr. Tayer and I leaned into the strong wind that suddenly whipped through Central Park, and he told me, "Jeanne, sniff the wind. The same wind may have once been sniffed by Jesu Christ, by Alexander, by Jeanne d'Arc. Sniff the wind once sniffed by Jeanne d'Arc. Sniff the tides of history!"

It was wonderful. People of all ages followed us around, laughing—not at us, but with us. Occasionally Mr. Tayer would give short comical addresses on the history of the Central Park rocks. More often he would speak of the rocks directly. "Ah my friend the mica schist layer, do you remember when. . . ?" He seemed to know an awful lot about old bones and rocks.

He seemed to know a great deal about spirals, too. Once I brought him the shell of a snail, and he waxed ecstatic for the better part of an hour. Snail shells and galaxies and the meanderings of rivers were taken up into a great hymn to the spiraling evolution of spirit and matter. When he had finished, his voice dropped, and he whispered almost in prayer, "Omega . . . omega . . . omega. . . ."

But mostly Mr. Tayer was so full of vital sap and juice that he seemed to flow with everything. Always he saw the interconnections between things—the way that everything in the universe, from fox terriers to mica schist to the mind of God, was related to everything else and was very, very good.

I remember coming home once and telling my mother, "Mother, I met my old man again, and when I am with him, I leave my littleness behind." For Mr. Tayer looked at you as if you were God-in-hiding, and the love with which you were regarded was unconditional. In his presence one felt empowered to be who one really was.

And then one day I didn't see him anymore. I would frequently go and stand outside of the Church of St. Ignatius Loyola on Eighty-fourth Street and Park Avenue, where I often met him, but he never came again.

In 1961 someone lent me a copy of a book titled *The Phenomenon of Man*. The book, from which the jacket had been removed, was strangely familiar in its concepts. Occasional words and expressions loomed up as echoes from my past. When, later in the book, I came across the concept of the "omega point," I was certain. I asked to see the jacket of the book, looked at the author's picture, and, of course, recognized him immediately. There was no forgetting or mistaking that face. Mr. Tayer was Teilhard de Chardin, the great priest-scientist, poet, and mystic, and during that lovely and luminous year I had been meeting him outside the Jesuit rectory of St. Ignatius, where he was living at the time.

THE DROMENON FOR
THE POST-INDIVIDUAL:

The Fields of Life

The therapeutic mystery of this stage is that of the fields of life. Neither earth, air, fire, or water, these fields, like the second spiral, include them all, sustaining and supporting them as well as assuring the continuity and evolution of all the forms of life. Unspecialized, they comprehend all specialization, and provide the dynamic continuum within which growth and deepening are possible. They have been thought to be composed of electromagnetic or bioplasmic energies, or even of those substances that sustain the cosmos. But whatever they may be, in human terms love is the core of this vitality of the fields of life, and so love will be the principle and final force used in this mystery, which is both the conclusion and the new beginning of the long journey we have taken together.

STAGE ONE
Fielding the Other

Each of the participants chooses a partner and sits opposite him or her, preferably cross-legged on the floor. Closing their eyes, the partners touch fingertips and listen closely as the Guide speaks to them:

"Put your entire consciousness into the points of contact between you and your partner, feeling the flow of life passing back and forth through your hands. Let your awareness be com-

257

pletely absorbed by this flow of life. You may be feeling heat, the pulsing of the blood through the veins, muscular sensations, and even perhaps a flow of energy like an electrical current passing from your partner to you and from you to your partner. Keep your consciousness focused on the contact between your hands. Let the awareness of the currents of life flowing between you grow even stronger until, after a while, you may not even know where your hands leave off and where your partner's begin and whether it makes any difference" (five minutes).

"Now, very slowly, move your hands apart, so that there is only about a half-inch distance between them. Continue, however, to feel the flow of life passing across the space between the hands. Begin to detect the field of life between your hands and those of your partner. Let this energy field grow stronger, and as it does so, begin to feel a flow of energy from heart to heart, and let it, too, grow slowly stronger.

"Gradually, begin to explore your capacities to mutually sense the fields between your hands. Feeling the links between your fields like subtle adhesions, let one partner move his or her hands slightly, and let the other partner's hands be 'pulled along' by the power of the linked fields. To make this connection even more sensitive, let the partner who is following close his or her eyes and see if the hands can be led simply by the awareness of the movement of the field. Switch back and forth several times between leading and following within the hand fields.

"Now place your hands about a half-inch above each other's heads, and begin to bring your hands down the entire sides of each other's bodies, always keeping them about a half-inch away from the surface. Do this as a mutual blessing, an empowering of the field of life of the other.

"As you continue in this, let your heart centers open even more to each other, and be aware of the flow of a kind of grace and deep acknowledgment from one heart to the other. Some of you at this point may even begin to feel a rising in you and a sending forth of a kind of impersonal but unconditional love. Whether you feel this or not, let the flow of grace between you and the deep acknowledgment and blessing of the fields of life continue.''

STAGE TWO
The Spiraling of the Life Fields

The Guide will say:

"Put your hands down now and rest for a moment, listening all the while to my words. And know that there are many traditions that speak of a system of *chakras,* centers of power within the body. Placing your right hand about a half-inch from the surface of the heart chakra area, take a few moments to sense the fields emanating from this region.[15]

"Moving your hand in a clockwise spiraling fashion now, proceed to 'connect' the fields between these major centers or chakras in the following manner: beginning at the heart; circling down to solar plexus; circling up to the throat; circling down to the sexual chakra, located around the area of the pubic bone; circling up to the third eye, the chakra of the pineal gland area; circling down to the root chakra located at the base of the spine; circling up to the crown chakra; circling down the area of the knees; circling upward to the transpersonal chakra, located about a foot above the head; and, finally, circling down to the grounding chakra located in the feet.[16]

"In this state of impersonal love and blessing continue to make these spiraling fields, always returning to the heart chakra to begin the spiral anew" (five minutes).

"As you continue to do this, be aware now of adding another dimension to this fielding that you are doing. Be aware that you are not only connecting the vital fields and centers of life of the other, thus perhaps helping to accomplish a deeper integration of the other's whole body-being, but that also, in some way, you are activating that spiral of life that can help bring the other into the new spiral of human evolution, the first turning of which incorporates the spirals of the previous four stages of psycho-historical development. Act now in your fielding of the other as if you are indeed evoking not just a physical and mental integration of the other, but are bringing that person at the same time into the larger order of being" (five minutes).

STAGE THREE
The Therapeia *of the Heart*

The Guide now says:
"Placing your right hands on each other's heart region, and reaching around with your left hand to hold the back of that heart region, become aware of the fact that each of you is now holding the heart of the other between your hands. Without speaking, sit quietly for a few moments, eyes closed, in this position, becoming ever more conscious of the life core of the other whose heart you are holding. Feel the fields between your two hands, passing and repassing life and energy through the body frame of the other, to heal the heart if it needs to be healed, but in any case to evoke and deepen its potential. And let your own heart be likewise healed and evoked" (five minutes).
"Let your arms rest for a minute now. We are now about

to perform the *therapeia* of the heart, reminding you that the Greek word *therapeia*, from which the word *therapy* is derived, has as its root meaning 'support or caring,' and, as a secondary meaning, 'the doing of the work of the god.' In a moment we will again hold each other's hearts in our hands, continuing to send energy and blessings; but this time, linked by the communion of fields and hearts, we will enter together into a deep and beautiful mystery of listening and guidance.

"Let one of you be the Speaker, let the other be the One Who Listens. Speaker, you will speak your concern for your next development in life. It might be some plan or project that you wish to enter upon, or even some past or present concern that troubles or challenges you and that you need to work out in a different way. Whatever it is, tell it simply and succinctly to the other.

"One Who Listens, you will listen with your entire being.

"And as you are listening, try to do so in a state of unconditional love and nonjudgment, allowing perhaps the larger reality of which you are a part, with all its wisdom and knowings, to inform your heart as you attend to the need of the other. Let High Being prevail in you; and when you finally speak, speak from the place of High Being after you have listened carefully to the need of the other, giving advice and direction as it seems appropriate, but always from the higher place and not just from the knowings of your local self.

"Hold each other's hearts between your hands again, and perform the *therapeia* of the heart. You have fifteen minutes to speak, listen, and respond before the One Who Listens becomes the Speaker and the Speaker becomes the One Who Listens."

After about fifteen minutes the Guide will tell the participants to take a minute to stretch and relax, in silence, and then again to hold each other's hearts in their hands, resuming the therapeia of the heart, exchanging roles. She will say again, "One Who Listens, do so with the most complete attention, sitting in the place of High Being, allowing the flowing of unconditional love, and not speaking until wisdom prevails in your soul."

After about fifteen minutes the Guide will ask the partners to sit quietly for several minutes, holding each other's hearts between their hands and allowing deep blessing, healing and acknowledgment to flow between them. At the end of this time the Guide will ask the partners simply to hold each other's hands, while she plays some quiet, reflective music to allow time and ambience for deeper understanding and integration to occur. When the music ends, the Guide will ask the participants to reflect on what has happened.

Many will feel that they have received advice and clarification of great subtlety and wisdom. Others will note how during this process they became open to depths of understanding within themselves that they did not even know they had. Most will feel, to some extent, healed and filled with grace, as if they had engaged in a sacrament of integration.

At the conclusion of this process, the participants should celebrate and welcome each other into full personhood.

Instructions for Going Solo

You can't go solo in the Dromenon for the post-individual. As it is about empathy, communication, and communion it really is essential that you call upon a good friend, or someone you trust very much to join you for this final process. Put the Guide's instructions on tape and together enjoy the experience. With your friend accompanying you, it becomes a celebration, a wonderful finale to your journey through the psycho-historical recovery of the self. And when you finish, have a party, or do something wonderful to honor and commemorate the occasion.

EPILOGUE

And so, having recovered ourselves in the first spiral of psyche and history, we come to the end of the journey, which is the beginning. And as we stand at the threshold of the next spiral, we need a deeper, more comprehensive apparatus of knowing, a richer use of psychic energy, a new and extended ecology of being.

In this journey we have come to know ways of seeing as earlier cultures saw and have joined their ways to ours, to regain the greater complexity of reality. No longer seeing life in neatly separated planes, with discrete and exclusive modes of explanation, we now see the spiraling circles and begin to understand the mazes inscribed on floors of early dancing grounds, the spiral labyrinths of Egypt, Greece, and ancient Britain, the intricate circlings set in the pavement of medieval chathedrals. We see them now—profound and activating Dromenons, carrying one through all spheres and planes of influence, and giving a principle of correspondence to everything and everyone. In the words of Jill Purce, we know that to dance these ancient Dromenons is to enter at once into "the cosmos, the world, the stages of individual life, the temple, the town, the man, the woman, the womb, the intestines, the convolutions of the brain, the consciousness, the heart, the pilgrimage, the Journey, and the Way." Now, looking at the labyrinth on the floor of Chartres, we remember the searching language of modern physicists, who speak of the "curvature of space and time, and describe the structure of our universe as a vortex ring."[17]

Now it is time to create the new dance. To discover it will demand attention, awareness, and dedication of considerable intensity. To demand new ways of being is a constant movement of mind and body and spirit, which is simultaneously dance and work and prayer. It is the discovery and development of one's potential for the creative rebuilding of self and earth. It is the Dromenon, in which one becomes as conscious of one's soul as one is of one's body, and as conscious of the other as one is of the earth. But in the Dromenon the boundaries between body and soul, other and earth, are effaced. One is the field of life. The body moves itself spiritually, and the spirit bodily. In the Dromenon of new being, one is in a state of rhythm and resonance between inner and outer worlds; and being in a state of rhythm, one finds oneself in a state of grace. The boundaries of body and soul open, boundary after boundary falls away, until we reach the final and ultimate knowledge, which tells us that God is love, which is movement in creative form—or as Dante declared in his moment of final revelation in the closing lines of *The Divine Comedy:*

> *L'amore che muove il sol*
> *e l'altre stelle.*
> (The love that moves the sun
> and the other stars.)

Notes

1. See, for example, Fritjof Capra's excellent analysis of this stage in his book, *The Turning Point* (New York: Bantam Books, 1983).
2. Heard, p. 91.

3. Quoted in Brian Stanfield, "Alberto Krygier's Hyper-Connections," in *Edges*, Vol. 5, no.1, p. 33.

4. For an excellent and suggestive treatment of the shifts toward the planetary person, see Willis Harman, *Global Mind Change* (Indianapolis: Knowledge Systems, 1988).

5. The annals of herstory are finally surfacing. A splendid pioneer study was Elise Boulding's comprehensive *The Underside of History: A View of Women Through Time* (Boulder, CO: Westview Press, 1976). For a wide scale accounting of women's activities in many countries and the place of herstory in each, see *Sisterhood is Global*, ed. Robin Morgan (Garden City, NY: Anchor Books, 1984). A fascinating study of the internal dynamics of the more hidden aspects of women's culture and psyche is found in Clarissa Pinkola Estés, *Women Who Run With the Wolves: Myths and Stories of the Wild Woman Archetype* (New York: Ballantine Books, 1992).

6. I have adapted this discussion of the rise of the feminine from my words on the same subject in *The Search for the Beloved*, pp. 15-16.

7. See for example Robert Masters and Jean Houston, *Mind Games* (New York: Delta, 1972); Robert Masters and Jean Houston, *Listening to the Body* (New York: Delta, 1978); Jean Houston, *The Possible Human* (Los Angeles: J. P. Tarcher, 1982); Jean Houston, *The Search for the Beloved: Journeys in Sacred Psychology* (Los Angeles: J. P. Tarcher, 1987); Jean Houston, *Godseed: The Journey of Christ* (Wheaton, IL: Quest Books, 1992); Jean Houston, *The Hero and the Goddess: The Odyssey as Mystery and Initiation* (New York: Ballantine Books, 1992). See also Jay Earley, *Inner Journeys: A Guide to Personal and Social Transformation Based on the Work of Jean Houston* (York Beach, ME: Samuel Weiser, 1990).

8. Robert Masters, "Psychophysical Re-education: The Aging Revolution," *Dromenon*, Vol. II, No. 1 (June, 1979).

9. Maggie Kuhn, "The Gray Panthers: Networking for New Community," *Dromenon*, Vol. II, (June, 1979), pp. 24-25.

10. Kuhn, p. 24.

11. Carl Jung, *Memories, Dreams, Reflections* (New York: Vintage, 1963), p. 359.

12. Quoted in Joan Halifax, *Shamanic Voices* (New York: E. P. Dutton, 1979), pp. 174-175.

13. For an excellent presentation of the experience of the SAGE program and dozens of clearly presented exercises that have contributed to the growth of the SAGE participants, see Gay Gaer Luce, *Your Second Life* (New York: Delacorte Press/Seymour Lawrence, 1979). A rewritten and updated version of this book is to be found in Gay Gaer Luce, *Longer Life, More Joy: Techniques for Enhancing Happiness*

and Inner Vision (North Hollywood, CA: Newcastle Publishing Co., 1992).

14. Some studies suggest that in many cases, the initial stages of "second childhood" may be owing to a tendency of the brain to activate and recapitulate earlier stages of its experiences. The child that one was rises neurologically in the elder one has become. (Is this elder version of neoteny the preparation for a new birth?) Instead of mocking and decrying the phenomenon and plying our elders with opiates to inhibit their rising child, perhaps we should encourage this phase with some of the same opportunity and delight that we give to growing and exploring children. In pursuing this thesis I have taught a number of gerontologists to work with the elderly in ways that get them to move, dance, and recover their coordination, as well as providing them with arts-enriched environments and many opportunities for learning and exploration. They have reported back that as the result of these activities, they have seen many cases of the symptoms of senility departing, and their clients entering into a new process of psychological, cognitive, and emotional growth. They learn new skills and deepen and refine old ones. It is a kind of childhood revisited, but on a higher and deeper level. For tapes and news of programs to enhance the psychophysical functioning of the elder, contact Dr. Robert Masters, Box 3300, Pomona, NY 10970.

15. I owe the development of this stage of the experience to some suggestions given me by Gay Luce, who had in turn received instruction in the spiraling of the chakras from the students of W. Brugh Joy, M.D. Dr. Joy's version of the spiraling is more complex than the one offered here and can be found in his book *Joy's Way* (Los Angeles: J. P. Tarcher, 1979).

16. This is a simple grounding exercise. Those who feel uncomfortable about meditating on the chakras can continue to focus on the heart area.

17. Jill Purce, *The Mystic Spiral* (New York: Crossroads Books, 1981).

AFTERWORD: GERALD HEARD, POSTMODERN "MAGIC MYTHMAKER"

by John V. Cody, Ph.D.

Life Force & the New Dromenon: Passing on the Heardian Torch

> *Over the years I found in my own work continuous echoes of the ideas of Gerald Heard.*　　　　　Jean Houston[1]

> *Gerald Heard is one of the very few who can properly be called philosophers, a man of brilliantly daring theory and devoted practice. I believe he has influenced the thought of our time, directly and indirectly, to an extent which will hardly be appreciated for another 50 years.*　　　　Christopher Isherwood[2]

Historically speaking, if we late twentieth-century seekers are able to see farther into the mysteries of man, nature, and cosmos than earlier generations, it may be because we stand on the shoulders of giants. Again and again, the flame of our creative vision has been fanned to renewed life by that living chain of inspiring men and women who have linked their hands as "relay runners" of the spirit, passing on to us precious torches of human and spiritual possibilities.

One of these luminous torch bearers, who for three

John Cody is an Assistant Professor in the Department of Interdisciplinary Studies at the University of San Francisco. He is completing several studies related to Gerald Heard.

267

decades has played the role of a "global midwife" to the new age of the human potential, is American psychologist Jean Houston, the author of *Life Force*. Houston's credentials as a leader in transformational and spiritual psychologies are impressive.[3] By devising contemporary uses of myth, ritual, and mind-body exercises, she has tapped into our profound capacities to realize self-empowerment and a life of continuous growth. During the past three decades she and her husband Robert Masters have conducted pioneering research and theory-building to liberate our physical, mental, and creative abilities. Through her internationally renowned, life-changing workshops and pathbreaking books,[4] she continues to nurture and disseminate sparks from several torches of wisdom that she has personally inherited from her own favorite "relay runners." Houston's forerunners in the spirit include Margaret Mead, Buckminster Fuller, Teilhard de Chardin and, perhaps most noteworthy, the remarkable philosopher-historian, Gerald Heard, whose inspiration is apparent on every page of *Life Force*.

Jean Houston's *Life Force*, first published in 1980 and now republished by Quest Books, is one of her most important studies, a book that relays to a new generation of readers the torch and "continuous echoes of the ideas of Gerald Heard." On the occasion of this new edition of *Life Force*, it seems appropriate to sketch the scope of Heard's influence on twentieth-century thinkers and cultural movements. Heard's contributions, we will see, are potent, time-released seeds that continue to give birth to vitalizing works like Houston's *Life Force*. In addition, Heard ranks as a major prophet and "magic mythmaker" of the emerging "postmodern" paradigm, our ongoing "Psychological Revolution" that affirms the creative role of psyche in constructing reality.[5]

Jean Houston acknowledges Gerald Heard's pervasive

influence on the structure, ideas, and mind-body healing rituals (or *dromena*) of *Life Force*. For example, Houston's brilliant repertoire of her own psycho-historical exercises in *Life Force*, techniques designed to recover the missing dimensions of our deep self, are creative extensions of the therapeutic techniques found in Heard's magnum opus, *The Five Ages of Man*.[6] Houston's underlying theme in *Life Force* also echoes Heard's psycho-spiritual thesis in *The Five Ages of Man*: the key to history's meaning is the evolution of consciousness, which is tending toward a utopian transformation of the human mind-body:

> In brief, the really possible Utopia would be this world experienced by a psychophysique at full aperture.[7]

Houston's *Life Force* creatively adapts the core ideas and fivefold structure of Heard's *The Five Ages of Man*. In that book, Heard draws daring correlations between the five developmental stages of consciousness in the human individual's life cycle (beginning with birth/infancy and ending in ''second maturity'') and the postulated five ages of the human race's cultural history (from pre-individual society to a future post-individual mutated society). Heard also advances a parallel third quintet of five therapies—modern counterparts of the ancient initiation rites and mysteries—designed to help us humans make successful transitions between each of our five life-cycle stages. Inspired by Heard, Houston in the pages of *Life Force*, creates her own mind-body transformative rituals. Houston's rites of passages are powerful new versions of what Heard—following Cambridge anthropologist Jane Harrison—terms the ''Dromenon,''[8] the spiral, unfolding labyrinthine dance, whose rhythms of awakening stir our deeper nature and reconnect us to our body, society, and universe.

AFTERWORD

The "Magic Mythmaker"

> He [Gerald Heard] tried to show the Pattern That Connects; and, in his vision of what humanity could be, he provided the seedlings of what subsequently led to the development of the best in the human potential movement as well as the psycho-spiritual and psychophysical growth movements of the next decades. There is little doubt in my mind that Gerald Heard was a key figure in the genesis of these movements and deserves far more attention than he has received.   Jean Houston[9]

Who was Heard, and what is his legacy to our transitional age that now is posed with expectancy on the brink of a new millennium and a new postmodern global civilization?

Gerald Heard (1889-1971) has got to be one of the best-kept secrets of the twentieth century. Few today, two decades after his death, would recognize his name. Of Heard's thirty-plus books dealing with philosophy, religion, science, history, and literature, not one today is in print, and his last printed volume, the brilliant novel of ideas, *AE: The Open Persuader* (1969), is not even officially attributed to him.[10]

An Anglo-Irish historian, BBC science journalist, novelist and mystic seer, Heard authored over thirty books in the fields of science, history, religion, philosophy, and fiction. What unifies Heard's thought is his postmodern consciousness. A learned advocate of exploring taboo areas of nonconsensus reality (including psychic research, mysticism, psychedelics, pacifism, UFOs, synchronicity, homosexuality, terror, madness and criminality), he saw these offbeat topics as sharing a common link to the mysterious role played by consciousness in molding our bewildering variety of reality maps—a world view that may be termed "postmodern."[11] For Heard, postmodern trends were rooted in an epistemological or "Psychological Revolution." In effect, we are the first generation conscious of the non-selfconscious, the first era to have explored the psyche through the consciousness movement and through human potential psychologies.

Heard was one of the first twentieth-century thinkers to detect harbingers of this postmodern New Age or psyche-oriented cultural breakthrough. He interpreted the New Physics—along with psychic research, ecology, holistic field theory, Gestalt psychology, consciousness-changing drugs, semantics, and the sociology of knowledge—as part of a vaster cultural mutation of the collective psyche. Heard believed that the goal of earthly existence, dramatized in his last, anonymously published work *AE*, is to employ a variety of creative means to realize a transformed body-mind, capable of childlike, generalized awareness or what he called "panaesthesia." Through these means, humanity, the still "unfinished" evolutionary species and the "growing edge of the Life Force," would ascend in a spiral path to ever-higher levels of awareness. He hints at this mutational goal in the closing words of *The Five Ages of Man* (1963):

> But in that vision the human mind, made for ecstasy and infinitude, experiences a reverence which alone can give purpose to every experience and meaningful delight to every act. [12]

Heard was, in a nutshell, a scientifically informed postmodern "mythmaker" and "meaning-maker" with strong mystical leanings. A hybrid scientific-shaman and fascinating Hermetic figure, he aimed at bringing to birth a new postmodern, psychologically-aware mythos, an up-to-date world view that could heal the split soul of humans by balancing means with meaning, power with purpose, body and matter with mind and spirit. This myth would empower the human potential to realize new ways of being, knowing, and acting.

Like Carl Jung, Heard sought to heal humanity's divided psyche, the modern split whereby our overdeveloped rationalist ego separates us from our submerged integral consciousness, intuition, and body-mind. If we could heal our fissured soul, Heard believed, we might avert individual neurotic self-destruction and our civilization's collapse through war, violence, ecocide, and the waning of social cohesion. His efforts to create a counter-paradigm to the alienating myth of mechanistic rationalism would lead him to explore mind-body techniques, the "perennial philosophy" of mysticism, psychedelics, and what he was fond of calling the "growing edge" of advanced research and knowledge. Heard was busy mapping out the cultural-scientific contours of this new, emerging paradigm a full generation before Fritjof Capra or Marilyn Ferguson popularized the dawning of a post-mechanist era in the mid-1970s and early 1980s. Heard was an advanced scout of the "Aquarian frontier," helping to fashion "the evolutionary image of human potentiality" along with Sri Aurobindo, Ouspensky, Jean Gebser, Buckminster Fuller, and Pierre Teilhard de Chardin. [13]

Heard's independent mind and spirit were evident early on when he rebelled against both his conservative family upbringing and his culture's outdated world view. In his twenties, after weathering a stormy crisis of faith, conscience, and health, he abandoned plans to become an Anglican priest (the profession of his grandfather, father, and brother). [14] For the rest of his life, he played the role of an unorthodox seer-visionary, who explored practical techniques of "training for a life of growth" and transforming human nature. To achieve humanity's mutation, he bridged theory and praxis by creating a paradigm based on the most current scientific cosmology and its deduced ethic of an expanding spirial of love, consciousness, and lifelong growth of the total person. This Heardian postmodern paradigm transcends the dichotomy of naturalism vs. supernaturalism by wedding post-mechanistic science to post-anthropomorphic, ecstasy-oriented, Life-accepting religion.

Heard began his paradigm-shifting explorations of post-modern reality as early as his student days at Cambridge University (1909-1913) during the exciting era of the birth of the New Physics and the revival of interest in psychical research. In his view, a new epoch began around 1912 when the New Physics created a new cosmology resembling "metaphysics," a world view that required a corresponding change in the way we think: a shift from analytic to integral, transpersonal consciousness. At Cambridge, he won undergraduate honors in history and pursued postgraduate work in the philosophy of religion, but, in truth, he "specialized in unspecialization,"[15] and throughout his life he embodied "neoteny," a youthful, open spirit of creative versatility as BBC science commentator (1930-1934), pacifist crusader, philosopher, novelist, mystic, historian of civilization, inspiring lecturer, and visionary.

As a young man, Heard served as secretary, first to Lord Robson of Jesmond (1852-1918), who had been Liberal Attorney General in the government of Prime Minister Asquith; and next to Sir Horace Plunkett (1854-1932), the founder of the agricultural cooperative movement in Ireland and a champion of the Irish cultural renaissance. Plunkett's friends and house guests included a literary-political *Who's Who* of celebrities, including Bernard Shaw, Lady Gregory, William Butler Yeats, Lennox Robinson, and poet George Russell, the last known also by his Gnostic pen name, "Æ." Heard's Cambridge connections and his contacts as Oxford (where he taught for a time as a lecturer), together with his front row seat in Plunkett's circle, allowed him to rub shoulders with the Irish, English, and American cultural-political luminaries of the 1920s and 1930s. He also served as literary editor of the prestigious, though short-lived, journal, the London *Realist* (1929-1930), whose contributing editors included H. G. Wells, Arnold Bennett, Herbert Read, and Aldous and Julian Huxley.

With World War II looming on the horizon, in the spring of 1937 Heard (then 47) emigrated to America with his friend and fellow pacifist Aldous Huxley. They settled, appropriately, in Los Angeles, California, a frontier land resembling the ancient Levant or Hellenistic Alexandria in its youth, exploratory freedom, and creative tensions. California provided the two British expatriates a multicultural cauldron in which to stir up new dreams and experiment in bringing to birth a transformational paradigm and civilization.

Heard was to spend the last thirty-four of his eighty-two years in America, though because of their pacifist convictions, neither he nor Huxley were permitted to become American citizens. Together, during the next quarter century, these two free spirits were voyagers on an intellectual-spiritual odyssey exploring Eastern and Western mysticism (including Vedanta and Buddhism),[16] psychedelics, and mind-body transformative techniques.

To counter the destructive currents of mechanism and rationalism, Heard and Huxley pioneered in establishing some of the foundations of what became known as the American human potential movement. Heard's human-potential legacy for consciousness studies and mind-body-soul transformative exercises would be independently carried on by (among others) psychologist Jean Houston, Esalen Institute cofounder Michael Murphy,[17] and that remarkable "Wayfarer," James C. Ingebretsen.[18] Heard also made important, though often overlooked, contributions to major cultural trends, including the early days of both the psychedelic revolution and the gay liberation movement. Under the pen name of D. B. Vest, Heard wrote several pathbreaking articles on the evolutionary and spiritual significance of homosexuals.

Heard's versatility, scintillating conversation, and mind-boggling syntheses of science and religion made him an influential, enormously admired thinker. His prolific outpouring of nonfiction writings (books on science, philosophy, architecture, history, spirituality, and UFOs) as well as his critically acclaimed fiction (the Holmesian "Mr. Mycroft" detective novels, science fiction, horror tales, and a fairy-tale parable about evolution) brought him to the public's attention. He was befriended by a distinguished roll call of authors, artists, musicians, academics, Hollywood celebrities, comedians, business executives, wild animal trainers, and clerics: Aldous Huxley, E. M. Forster, Roger Fry, John Betjeman, W. H. Auden, Stephen Spender, Christopher Isherwood, Mrs. G. B. Shaw, Henry and Clare Booth Luce, Igor Stravinsky, Fritz Kunkel, Professor Huston Smith, Professor Evelyn Hooker, Jean Houston, Ray Bradbury, John Huston, Dave Brubeck, Jennifer Jones, Ivan Tors, Steve Allen, James. C. Ingebretsen, Michael Murphy, the Jesuit Father John Courtney Murray, and Bill Wilson (cofounder of Alcoholics Anonymous)—to name just a few of those he influenced. Heard reached thousands more through his books, articles, lectures, TV and radio broadcasts.

Unfortunately, I cannot communicate the living charm, humor, or wit that Heard conveyed with his dramatically modulated BBC voice. Heard has to be heard, as well as read, in order for his genial spirit to come fully alive.[19] Listening to him speak on recordings and film, one recaptures the flair of his extraordinary mind: its exuberant dance of ideas, the rainbow shower of provocative insights that combine profundity with vivacity. This "Wellsian supermind" was tempered by Irish whimsy and more than touch of the saint, radiating to his audiences a "contagion of hope," the deep conviction that the cosmos and our human lives are possessed of meaning, direction, and vast reservoirs of untapped potential to meet with "initiative" the choices, ordeals, and initiation challenges of unlimited growth.

Heard sustained his creative spirit in full vigor until his eightieth year with his possible publication of *AE: The Open Persuader* (1969), and, one suspects, this youthful, "neotenic" spirit of "interest-wonder" (*AE,* p. 170) lasted even to the drawing of the final curtain (August 14, 1971). Heard's death ended a five-year ordeal of repeated strokes that imprisoned his brilliant mind—still possessed of all its volcanic, imaginative awareness—in a frail, finally bed-ridden body. His close friend, the author Christopher Isherwood, commented movingly on Heard's confrontation with the "terminal mystery" and the artistic, open curiosity and wonder with which the "magic mythmaker" met his next adventure:

> On August 14, early in the afternoon, Gerald Heard quietly stopped breathing. . . .
>
> Gerald's life had always seemed to me to have the aspect of an artistic performance, expressed in a language of metaphors and analogies. I now asked myself the question: Did his performance still seem valid, as true art must, in relation to the terminal mystery? I felt that it did—that our glimpses of him, undergoing this searching five-year test, had been powerfully reassuring. I believed that he had indeed been able to see his temporary state of dying in the context of what is both now and always "the real situation," and that therefore one of his favorite metaphors, "taking a look around the corner," had now become a description of his actual experience.
>
> That day, I wrote in my diary:

I am only just beginning to realize that it has happened, at last. My chief feeling at this moment is that I would like to get on the air and tell the brute stodgy thick-skinned world that it has lost one of its few great magic mythmakers and revealers of life's wonder. [20]

Conclusion: Heard's Postmodern Dromenon of Metacomedy

In sum, Heard—wearing the Hermetic masks of "magic mythmaker," prophet of postmodern consciousness, and psychopomp (soul-guide) to modernized mystery rituals of mind-body transformation and ecstasy—was an influential explorer of "the growing edge of the Life Force."

Heard's final masterpiece of liberation literature—or what he calls "metacomedy"—is *AE: The Open Persuader* (1969). *AE* embodies metacomedy, his philosophic-esthetic notion of the emancipatory role of art and literature, viewed as a ritual (*dromenon*) intended to heal "the whole sundered nature of man, psyche and physique" [21] and to create for humans a "metacomic" sense of life that enables us to experience purposeful communion on three levels: (1) integration with our inner selves, (2) cohesive "association" with our society, and (3) meaningful "orientation" or a profound feeling of oneness with the cosmos.

As a "magic mythmaker" and "revealer of life's wonder," Heard's entire life purpose was directed to raising the curtain on humanity's "Fifth Age" or what he elsewhere calls the "Third Act": the new postmodern, post-individualist epoch of "Metacomedy," which transcends the two previous historical Acts of "Comedy" (pre-individualism) and "Tragedy" (individualism) to give us the "God's-eye view" of the communion of all being, beyond all of our laughter and all of our tears.[22]

> The Third Act is due. And the writer must face it. . . .
> Beyond Tragedy lies Meta-comedy. The central figure of that play is known in Asiatic drama. There is no tragic goal in the Indian Theatre. The very world Play they call Lila, the weaving dance that displays and resumes the universe. The central figure who dances out of the cosmos, Shiva, consummates laughter and tears in an ecstasis that goes beyond pleasure and pain.

The spiral dance of the New Dromenon, with its stirring rhythms of vision and its global awakening of mankind in body, mind, and soul, has been accelerated by seminal works such as Heard's *The Five Ages of Man, Training for a Life of Growth,* and *AE: The Open Persuader.* Jean Houston's *Life Force,* together with her other writings and the choreography of her mind-body *dromena,* carries forward the torch of Heard's inspiration. Creative works such as these make more likely the chances that the curtain of the Third Act of "Metacomedy" will continue to rise and usher in the metamorphosis of postmodern, integral consciousness. As Houston exhorts us: "Now it is time to create the new dance."

Notes

1. Jean Houston, from the first edition of *Life Force* (New York: Delacorte Press, 1980), p. 27.
2. This Isherwood quote is found in a journal Heard edited for a short while: *Growing Edge* (Winter 1958) 1, no.1 p. 8.

3. For an assessment of Houston's contributions to the consciousness and human potential movements, see David Toolan, *Facing West from California's Shores: A Jesuit's Journey into New Age Consciousness* (New York: Crossroad, 1987), Chapter 11, "Jean Houston's Ritual Theater." See also Jay Earley, *Inner Journeys: A Guide to Personal and Social Transformation Based on the Work of Jean Houston* (York Beach, Maine: Samuel Weiser, 1990).

4. See, for example, Houston's volumes: *The Possible Human: A Course in Extending Your Physical, Mental, and Creative Abilities* (Los Angeles: J. P. Tarcher, Inc., 1982), *The Search for the Beloved: Journeys in Sacred Psychology* (Los Angeles: J. P. Tarcher, Inc., 1987), *Godseed: The Journey of Christ* (Wheaton: Quest, 1992), and *The Hero and the Goddess* (New York: Ballantine, 1992).

5. I use this slippery term "postmodern" to describe Heard for want of a better word. Heard, was *sui generis,* a pioneering maverick— even what Colin Wilson calls an "Outsider," and so he eludes all faddish academic categories. A good introduction to postmodern currents is Walter Truett Anderson's *Reality Isn't What It Used To Be: Theatrical Politics, Ready-to-Wear Religion, Global Myths, Primitive Chic, and Other Wonders of the Postmodern World* (San Francisco: Harper & Row, 1990). Our following section will help clarify the meaning of this term.

6. Gerald Heard, *The Five Ages of Man: The Psychology of Human History* (New York: The Julian Press, © 1963, published in January 1964).

7. Gerald Heard, *The Five Ages of Man,* p. 332.

8. Houston has been deeply influenced by Heard's short story, "Dromenon." This is an archetypal tale about a modern architectural scholar who, assisted by an Orphic-Hermetic soul-guide, gains enlightenment (*gnosis*) after being initiated by a variety of mind-body techniques, especially by dancing through a labyrinthine maze (dromenon) that lies concealed beneath an antique British church. "Dromenon" is one of the stories found in H. F. Heard's *The Great Fog* (New York: Vanguard, 1944).

9. Jean Houston, from the first edition of *Life Force* (New York: Delacorte Press, 1980), p. xiii.

10. I am completing two book-length studies of Heard: (1) *Gerald Heard: The Postmodern Magic Mythmaker,* which surveys and analyzes Heard's life, times, ideas, and influence; and (2) *Bibliography of Works by or Related to Gerald Heard,* a comprehensive 300-page annotated bibliography on Heard works and related secondary literature. See the Winter, 1992 issue of *Gnosis* magazine for my essay, "Gerald Heard: Postmodern Soul Guide to the Beyond Within," for Heard's role in the early days of the American psychedelic movement.

AFTERWORD

I will also soon publish my monograph study "Gerald Heard's Postmodern Metacomedy: An Introduction to *AE: The Open Persuader*." *AE* was published anonymously in 1969 by One, Inc., of Los Angeles. *AE*, as I interpret it, is a veritable *summa* of Heard's mature thought (his most advanced, integrated, imaginative, candid —and sometimes ironic—summing up of his lifetime quest for meaning), an awesomely brilliant philosophic novel of ideas, structured by a subtle, artistic design that embodies Heard's vision for a courageous, contemporary science fiction, one unified around his two life-affirming principles ("metacomedy" and "neoteny") and integrated by his provocative master theme of the literal mutation of the human mind-body. *AE* is, I am convinced, Gerald Heard's crowning achievement of his life's intellectual, philosophic, artistic, and spiritual odyssey to achieve free self-expression, psychological wholeness, and ecstatic integration of body, mind, and spirit.

11. Heard's postmodern mindstyle "fits" best in the field of "consciousness studies" together with its related cultural trends (for example, human-potential, growth-oriented, transformational, and transpersonal psychologies; perennial philosophy spiritualities; and the amorphous "New Age" movements). Heard's postmodern sensibility anticipates the consciousness movement's theme of the social construction of reality by consciousness (along with altered states of consciousness). The human psyche constructs our multiple reality grids or "reality maps." These consciousness-created maps are our "reality tunnels," or more simply our conflicting beliefs, values, assumptions, and world views. See representative studies about the creative interplay between consciousness and reality by authors Charles T. Tart, Stanislav Grof, John Lilly, Andrew Weil, Alan Watts, and Robert Anton Wilson.

12. Heard, *The Five Ages of Man*, p. 382.

13. See Theodore Roszak's *Unfinished Animal: The Aquarian Frontier of the Evolution of Consciousness* (New York: Harper Colophon Books/ Harper & Row Publishers, © 1975, 1977), p. 80.

14. Heard's first name reveals his rebellious, independent spirit. Born Henry FitzGerald Heard (being named after his father, the Rev. Henry James Heard), Heard later threw off the "Henry" (because of his dislike of his father's ultra-conservative values) and adopted the name "Gerald." In his fiction writings, he generally signed himself "H. F. Heard."

15. This is a phrase frequently used by Heard of humanity's characteristic method of "neoteny" or "neotenic" (youth-extending) evolution. See, for example, Heard's *Pain, Sex and Time: A New Outlook on Evolution and the Future of Man* (New York: Harper & Brothers Publishers,

1939), p. 298. Neoteny ("retention of youthful traits") is a key concept that runs throughout Heard's system of thought.

16. See David Robb, "Brahmins from Abroad: English Expatriates and Spiritual Consciousness in Modern America." *America Studies* 26, no. 2 (Fall 1985): 45-60; and Hal Bridges, *American Mysticism: From William James to Zen.* New York: Harper & Row Publishers, 1970, especially pp. 82-86 for a discussion of Heard, mainly in the context of Vedanta in America.

   Although always independent, both Heard and Huxley were active in the Vedanta Society of Southern California and frequently wrote for *Vedanta for the Western World* (Los Angeles: The Vedanta Society of Southern California, 1945; New York: The Viking Press, 1960); and *Vedanta for Modern Man* (New York: Harper, 1951; paperback editions: New York: Collier Books, 1962; and New York: Mentor Book/New American Library, 1972).

17. Heard's influence (the example of his 1940s Trabuco College experimental research center, his books, and a four-hour conversation in the summer of 1961) was a major catalyst in motivating Michael Murphy and Richard Price to co-found Esalen Institute in Big Sur, California, the "world's premiere human potential center." For Heard's contributions to Esalen and the American human potential movement, see Walter Truett Anderson, *The Upstart Spring: Esalen and the American Awakening* (Reading, Mass. & Menlo Park, CA: Addison-Wesley Publishing Company, 1983), pp. 12-13.

18. James C. Ingebretsen, J.D., a Los Angeles lawyer and one-time President of Spiritual Mobilization, was dramatically influenced by Heard, beginning in the middle 1950s. For the following 37 years, Ingebretsen has been a seminally important force in promoting not only Heard's ideas but those of many others in the human-potential, Jungian, Gnostic, and consciousness-studies fields (for example, Ira Progoff, Dane Rudhyar, Pir Vilayat Inayat Khan, and William Bridges). Ingebretsen published Heard's *Training for a Life of Growth* (1959) and *Growing Edge* journal (1958-1959), and sponsored numerous lectures, "Wayfarer" conferences, and educational projects undertaken by Heard.

19. A good audio-tape introduction to Heard's ideas and vocal style is the 3-part 1966 lecture series, "The Current View of Man in His Society." These tapes may be obtained from Pacifica Radio Archive, 3729 Cahuenga Blvd. West, North Hollywood, CA 91604.

20. Christopher Isherwood, *My Guru and His Disciple* (New York: Penguin Books, 1981), pp. 303-304. See also Isherwood's other comments on Gerald Heard during this five-year period of Heard's stroke-induced incapacity: *My Guru and His Disciple*, pp. 293 and 296.

21. Quoted from Heard's 53-page unpublished typescript essay, "Meta-comedy," p. 37, in the UCLA Heard Archives, Box 38.
22. Heard, "Waiting for the Third Act." [London] *Times Literary Supplement* (June 3, 1960): 355 ff. We are citing the reprint of this article which appears in Stephen Spender, ed., *The Writers' Dilemma* (London, New York, Toronto: Oxford, 1961), pp. 25-34.

SELECTED BIBLIOGRAPHY

Allen, J.W. *History of Political Thought in the Sixteenth Century.* New York: Barnes & Noble, 1960.

Argüelles, José and Miriam. *Mandala.* Boulder: Shambhala, 1972.

Atchity, Kenneth and E. J. Barber. "Greek Princes and Aegean Princesses: The Role of Women in the Homeric Poems." *Critical Essays on Homer.* Boston: G. K. Hall & Co., 1987.

Bacon, Francis. "Sphinx, or Science." *The Works of Francis Bacon,* Vol. VI. London: Longmans, 1870.

Bhagavad Gita, trans. by S. Radhakrishnan. New York: Harper and Brothers, 1948.

Benedict, Ruth. *Patterns of Culture.* Boston: Houghton Mifflin, 1961.

Bergson, Henri. *Creative Evolution,* trans. by Arthur Mitchell. New York: Henry Holt, 1911.

Berry, Thomas. *The Historical Theory of Giambattista Vico.* Washington, D.C.: Catholic University of America Press, 1949.

———. "The New Story." *Dromenon,* Vol. I, No. 4, December 1978. First published in *Teilhard Studies,* No. 1, *Anima,* Winter, 1978.

Boulding, Elise. *The Underside of History: A View of Women Through Time.* Boulder, CO: Westview Press, 1976.

Burtt, E. A. *The Metaphysical Foundations of Modern Science.* New York: Anchor Books, 1954.

BIBLIOGRAPHY

Campbell, Joseph. *The Masks of God: Creative Mythology*. New York: The Viking Press, 1968.

Capra, Fritjof. *The Turning Point*. New York: Bantam Books, 1983.

Castaneda, Carlos. *A Separate Reality*. New York: Simon & Schuster, 1971.

———. *Journey to Ixtlan*. New York: Simon & Schuster, 1972.

———. *Teachings of Don Juan*. Berkeley: University of California Press, 1968.

Dante. *Paradiso*, trans. by Louis Biancolli. New York: Washington Square Press, 1966.

Dodd, E. R. *The Greeks and the Irrational*. Berkeley and Los Angeles: University of California Press, 1963.

Donne, John. "An Anatomie of the World: The First Anniversary." *The Complete Poetry and Selected Prose of John Donne*, Charles M. Coffin, ed. New York: Modern Library, 1952.

Early, Jay. *Inner Journeys: A Guide to Personal and Social Transformation Based on the Work of Jean Houston*. York Beach, ME: Samuel Weiser, 1990.

Einstein, Albert. *Side Lights on Relativity*, trans. by Perret, W., and G. Jeffrey. London: Methuen, 1922.

Eisler, Riane. *The Chalice and the Blade*. New York: Harper & Row, 1987.

Eliot, T. S. *Four Quartets*. New York: Harcourt Brace Jovanovich, 1971, a Harvest/HBJ Book.

———. *The Wasteland and Other Poems*. New York: Harcourt Brace Jovanovich, 1971, a Harvest/HBJ Book.

Ellis-Fermor, Una. *The Jacobean Drama*. New York: Vintage Books, 1964.

Emerson, William. *Infant and Childbirth Re-facilitation*. Guilford: University of Surrey Press, 1984.

Erikson, Erik H. *Childhood and Society*. New York: Norton, 1963.

_____. "Identity and the Life Cycle: Selected Papers." *Psychological Issues*, Vol. I, No. 1. New York: International University Press, 1959.

Estes, Clarissa Pinkola. *Women Who Run with the Wolves: Myths and Stories of the Wild Woman Archetype*. New York: Ballantine Books, 1991.

Feuerstein, Georg. *Structure of Consciousness: The Genius of Jean Gebser, An Introduction and Critique*. Lower Lake, CA: Integral Publishing, 1987.

Freud, Sigmund. *The Complete Psychological Works of Sigmund Freud*, trans. by James Strachey. London: Hogarth Press; The Institute of Psycho-Analysis, 1966.

Frost, Robert. "The White-tailed Hornet." *Robert Frost's Poems*, introduction and commentary by Louis Untermeyer. New York: Pocketbooks, 1971.

Fry, Christopher. *A Sleep of Prisoners*. New York: Oxford University Press, 1951.

Gadon, Elinore W. *The Once and Future Goddess*. New York: Harper & Row, 1989.

Gebser, Jean. *The Ever-Present Origin*, trans. by Noel Barstad with Algis Mickunas. Athens, OH: Ohio University Press, 1986.

Gesell, Arnold, Frances L. Ilg, and Louise Ames. *Youth: The Years from 10 to 16*. New York: Harper & Row, 1956.

Gesell, Arnold, and Frances L. Ilg in collaboration with Louise B. Ames and Glenna E. Bullis. *The Child from Five to Ten*. New York: Harper and Row, 1946.

Gimbutas, Marija. *The Early Civilization of Europe*. Monograph for Indo-European Studies 131, University of California at Los Angeles, 1980.

Grene, David, and Richmond Lattimore, eds. *The Complete Greek Tragedies*, 4 vols. Chicago: The University of Chicago Press, 1959.

BIBLIOGRAPHY

Hadamard, Jacques. *The Psychology of Invention in the Mathematical Field.* New York: Dover, 1954.

Halifax, Joan. *Shamanic Voices.* New York: E. P. Dutton, 1979.

Harmon, Willis. *Global Mind Change.* Indianapolis: Knowledge Systems, 1988.

Harrison, Jane E. *Ancient Art and Ritual.* New York and London: Home University Library, Williams and Norgate, 1913.

_____. *Themis.* London: Cambridge University Press, 1927.

Heard, Gerald. *The Five Ages of Man.* New York: Julian Press, 1963.

Heard, H. F. (Gerald Heard). *The Great Fog.* New York: The Vanguard Press, 1944.

Hegel, Georg Friedrich. *The Phenomenology of Mind,* trans. by J. B. Baillie. London: Allen and Unwin, 1931.

_____. *The Philosophy of History,* trans. by J. Sibree. New York: Wiley, 1944.

Heinlein, Robert. *Stranger in a Strange Land.* New York: Putnam, 1961.

Heisenberg, W. *Physics and Beyond.* New York: Harper & Row, 1971.

Hesiod. *Works and Days, Theogony, The Shield of Herakles,* trans. by Richmond Lattimore. Ann Arbor, Michigan: University of Michigan Press, 1959.

Hillman, James. *Loose Ends.* Zurich: Spring Publications, 1975.

Homer. *The Iliad,* trans. by Richmond Lattimore. Chicago: University of Chicago Press, Phoenix paperback, 1951.

_____. *The Odyssey,* trans. by W.H.D. Rouse. New York: The New American Library, 1937.

Hooker, Richard. *The Laws of Ecclesiastical Polity.* London: Everyman's Library, 1907.

Houston, Jean. "Consider the Stradivarius." *Dromenon,* Vol. I, No. 5-6, February 1979.

Houston, Jean. *Godseed: The Journey of Christ.* Wheaton, IL: Quest Books, 1992.

_____. "Myth, Consciousness, and Psychic Research," in E. Mitchell, ed., *Psychic Exploration: A Challenge to Science.* New York: G. P. Putnam's Sons, 1974.

_____. "Prometheus Rebound: An Inquiry into Technological Growth and Psychological Change," in D. Meadows, ed., *Alternatives to Growth I.* Cambridge: Ballinger, 1977. Also published in *Forum,* University of Houston, Vol. 13, Nos. 1 and 2, Spring and Summer-Fall, 1975.

_____. "Putting the First Man on Earth." *Saturday Review,* February 22, 1975. Also published in A. Rosenfeld, ed., *Mind and Supermind.* New York: Holt, Rinehart & Winston, 1977.

_____. "Re-Seeding America: The American Psyche as a Garden of Delights." *Journal of Humanistic Psychology,* Vol. 18, No. 1, Winter, 1978.

_____. "Rhythms of Awakening." *Dromenon,* Vol. I, No. 2, 1978.

_____. "The Coming of Age of Aging: Gay Luce in dialogue with Jean Houston." *Dromenon,* Vol. II, No. 1, June 1979.

_____. "The Ecology of Inner Space." *Dromenon,* Vol. I, No. 1, 1978.

Houston, Jean. *The Hero and the Goddess: The Odyssey as Mystery and Initiation.* New York: Ballantine Books, 1992.

_____. "The Mind of Margaret Mead." *Quest,* July/August 1977.

Houston, Jean. *The Possible Human.* Los Angeles: J. P. Tarcher, Inc., 1982.

_____. "The Psychenaut Program." *The Journal of Creative Behavior,* Vol. 7, No. 4, 4th quarter, 1973.

_____. "The Quickening." *Dromenon,* Vol. II, No.2, August-September 1979.

BIBLIOGRAPHY

Houston, Jean. *The Search for the Beloved: Journeys in Sacred Psychology.* Los Angeles: J. P. Tarcher, Inc., 1987.

———. "Through the Looking Glass: The World of Imagery." *Dromenon,* Vol. II, No. 3-4, Winter, 1979.

Huxley, Aldous.*The Doors of Perception.* New York: Harper & Row, 1963.

Jaensch, E. R. *Eidetic Imagery.* London: Routledge & Kegan Paul, 1930.

Jaspers, Karl. *Way to Wisdom: An Introduction to Philosophy.* New Haven: Yale University Press, 1966.

Jaynes, Julian. *The Origin of Consciousness in the Breakdown of the Bicameral Mind.* Boston: Houghton Mifflin, 1977, 1990.

Jonas, Hans. *The Gnostic Religion.* Boston: Beacon Press, 1958.

Joy, W. Brugh. *Joy's Way.* Los Angeles: J. P. Tarcher, 1979.

Jung, Carl G. *The Collected Works of Carl G. Jung,* Vols. IX, XI, XII, and XIII, trans. by R. F. C. Hull, Bollingen Series XX. New York: Pantheon Books, 1959.

———. *Memories, Dreams, Reflections.* New York: Vintage Books, 1963.

Kohlberg, Lawrence. "Moral Development." *International Encyclopedia of the Social Sciences,* Vol. 10. New York: The Free Press and Macmillan Co., 1968.

Kohlberg, Lawrence. "Moral Development and Identification." *Child Development.* Sixty-second Yearbook of the National Society for the Study of Education, ed. by Harold W. Stevenson. Chicago: University of Chicago Press, 1963.

Kuhn, Maggie. "The Gray Panthers: Networking for New Community." *Dromenon,* Vol. II, No. 1, June 1979.

Kuhn, Thomas. *The Structure of Scientific Revolutions.* Chicago: The University of Chicago Press, 1968.

Leboyer, Frederick. *Birth Without Violence.* New York: Alfred A. Knopf, 1975.

Levy-Bruhl. *How Natives Think*. London & New York: George Allen and Unwin, 1926.

Liedloff, Jean. *The Continuum Concept*. New York: Alfred A. Knopf, 1977.

Lowith, Karl. *Meaning in History*. Chicago: University of Chicago Press, 1949.

Luce, Gay Gaer. *Longer Life, More Joy: Techniques for Enhancing Happiness and Inner Vision*. North Hollywood, CA: Newcastle Publishing Co., 1992.

Luce, Gay Gaer. *Your Second Life*. New York: Delacorte Press/ Seymour Lawrence, 1979.

Machiavelli, Niccolò. *Discourses on the First Decade of Titus Livy*, trans. by N. H. Thompson, Book 1, Ch. XII. London: 1883.

_____. *The Prince*, trans. by L. Ricci. New York: Modern Library, 1940.

Markley, O. W. *Changing Images of Man*. A Report of the Center for the Study of Social Policy, Stanford Research Institution, Menlo Park, 1973.

Marx, Karl. *Early Writings*. T. B. Bottomore, ed. New York: McGraw-Hill, 1964.

Masters, Robert. "Psychophysical Re-education: The Aging Revolution." *Dromenon*, Vol. II, No. 1, June, 1979.

Masters, Robert, and Jean Houston. *The Varieties of Psychedelic Experience*. New York: Holt, Rinehart & Winston, 1966. Later published as a Delta paperback.

_____. *Mind Games*. New York: Viking Press, 1972. Later published as a Delta paperback.

_____. *Listening to the Body*. New York: Delacorte Press, 1978. Later published as a Delta paperback.

Mead, Margaret. *Continuities in Cultural Evolution*. New Haven and London: Yale University Press, 1964.

_____. *World Enough: Re-Thinking the Future*. Boston-Toronto: Little, Brown and Co., 1975.

BIBLIOGRAPHY

Montaigne, Michel. *The Complete Essays of Montaigne,* Vol. II, trans. by Donald M. Frame. New York: St. Martin's Press, 1960.

Morgan, Robin, ed. *Sisterhood is Global.* Garden City, NY: Anchor Books, 1984.

Plato. *The Republic,* trans. by F. M. Cornford. London and New York: Oxford University Press, 1945.

———. *The Symposium,* trans. by Benjamin Jowett. New York: The Liberal Arts Press, 1957.

Platon, Nicolas. *Crete.* Geneva: Nagel Publishers, 1966.

Purce, Jill. *The Mystic Spiral.* New York: Crossroads Books, 1981.

Reichard, Gladys A. *Navaho Religion: A Study in Symbolism.* New York: Bollingen, 1963.

Saint Augustine. *The City of God.* London: Everyman Edition, 1945.

Schneewind, J. B. *Values and the Future,* Kurt Baier and Nicholas Rescher, eds. New York: The Free Press, 1971.

Schumacher, E. F. *Small Is Beautiful: Economics As If People Mattered.* New York: Harper and Row, 1975.

Smith, Adam. *Wealth of Nations.* New York: Modern Library, 1937.

Soleri, Paolo. *The Omega Seed: An Eschatological Hypothesis.* Garden City: Anchor Press/Doubleday, 1981.

Sorokin, Pitirim. *Modern Historical and Social Philosophies.* New York: Dover Publications, 1963.

———. *Social and Cultural Dynamics.* 2 vols. New York: American Book Co., 1937.

Spencer, Theodore. *Shakespeare and the Nature of Man.* New York: Macmillan, 1951.

Spengler, Oswald. *The Decline of the West,* trans. by Charles Francis Atkinson. New York: Knopf, 1934.

Stanfield, Brian. ''Alberto Krygier's Hyper-Connections.'' *Edges*, Vol. 5, No. 1, 1992.

Steiner, George. *In Bluebeard's Castle*. New Haven: Yale University Press, 1971.

Teilhard de Chardin, Pierre. *The Phenomenon of Man*. New York: Harper & Row, 1959.

Thompson, William Irwin. *At the Edge of History*. New York: Harper & Row, 1971.

Thucydides. *The Peloponnesian War*, trans. by R. Crawley. New York: The Modern Library, 1951.

Toynbee, Arnold. *A Study of History*, Vols. 1-10. London and New York: Oxford University Press, 1955.

Vico, Giambattista. *The New Science*, trans. by Thomas Goddard Bergin and Max Herald Fisch. Garden City: Anchor Doubleday, 1961.

Villasenor, David. *Tapestries in Sand: The Spirit of Indian Sand Painting*. Heldsberg: Naturegraph Press, 1966.

Waley, Arthur. *The Analects of Confucius*. London: Allen and Unwin, 1938.

_____. *The Way and Its Power*. New York: Grove Press, Inc., 1958.

Walker, D. P. *Spiritual and Demonic Magic from Ficino to Campanella*. London: Warburg Institute, 1958.

Weber, Max. *The Protestant Ethic and the Rise of Capitalism*, trans. by Talcott Parsons. New York: Charles Scribner's Sons, 1958.

Wheelwright, Mary C. *Beautyway: A Navaho Ceremonial*. New York: Pantheon Books, 1957.

White, Lynn Jr. *Medieval Technology and Social Change*. London: Oxford University Press, 1967.

Whitehead, Alfred North. *Process and Reality*. New York: Macmillan, 1929.

BIBLIOGRAPHY

Wilber, Ken. *The Atman Project: A Transpersonal View of Human Development.* Wheaton, IL: Quest Books, 1980.

Wilber, Ken. *Up from Eden: A Transpersonal View of Human Evolution.* Boston: Shambhala Publications, 1986.

Wilhelm, Richard. *Secret of the Golden Flower.* New York: Harcourt Brace Jovanovich, 1931.

Wolkstein, Diane and Samuel Noah Kramer. *Inanna: Queen of Heaven and Earth: Her Stories and Hymns from Sumer.* New York: Harper & Row, 1983.

Yates, Francis. *Giordano Bruno and the Hermetic Tradition.* London: Routledge & Kegan Paul, 1964.

Audio tapes of related lectures and seminars given by Jean Houston, as well as tapes of the Mystery School, are available through:

Wind Over the Earth, Inc.
1980 Eighth Street, Ste. F
Boulder, CO 80302
1 (800) 726-0847

Psychophysical exercise tapes are available through:

KontraKundabuffer Corporation
P.O. Box 3300
Pomona, NY 10970

If you are interested in receiving information about seminars given by Jean Houston, please write to:

Jean Houston
P.O. Box 3300
Pomona, NY 10970

INDEX

293

INDEX

INDEX

INDEX

Houston (*Con't.*)
 on Odysseus, 87
Human developmental stages
 adolescent stage, 137–142
 childhood stage, 88–89,
  95–96
 infancy stage, 52, 54–55
 maturity stage, 188–189
 second maturity stage, 211,
  244–256, 266
Human developmental
 stages, theories of. *See
 also* Ages of Man,
 viewpoints of the
 Erikson, 22–24
 Freud, 22
 Gebser, 28–35
 Heard, 35–38, 39
 Jung, 26–28
 Kohlberg, 25–26
 Piaget, 24–25
 Wilber, 28–35
Human potential
 current research on,
  226–232
 and the ecological crisis,
  11–12, 50–51
 and materialism, 10, 20
 in post-individualistic
  societies, 216–217,
  224–226
 in present-day myths, 8–10
Human potential,
 development of. *See also*
 Ages of Man, viewpoints
 of the; Human
 developmental stages
 in children, 94–95, 96–97
 Dromenon for, 147–155
 use of myth in, *xxii–xxiii*
 theoretical next stages of,
  216–217, 224–226
Human potential movement

Heard's role in, *xviii–xix*,
  274
 Houston's role in, 267–279
Humans, comparison of to
 animals, 169–170, 173–174
Hunter-gatherer societies. *See*
 Pre-individualistic
 societies
Huxley, Aldous, 274

Iliad, The, xiv–xv, 79, 81, 83,
  84
Illumination, Dromenon for,
  150–155
Imagery process
 and accelerated mental
  process (AMP), 240
 effect of on consciousness,
  233–239
In Bluebeard's Castle (Steiner),
  177–178
Inanna, myth of, 119–123
*Inanna, Queen of Heaven and
 Earth* (Wolkstein/Kramer),
  121
India, view of individualism
 in, 159–160
Individualistic societies
 use of allegory in, 163–165
 ascetic views of, 159–160
 consciousness in, *xii*,
  160–190
 Dromenon for, 191–205
 ecological crisis and, 187,
  188–190
 hierarchical order in,
  163–175
 materialism in, 176–177
 relationship of to maturity
  stage, 188–189
 religion in, 175–177
 technology in, 178–187

INDEX

INDEX

INDEX

Also Available From Quest Books

Life Force Audio Tapes

Narrated by Jean Houston as a companion to this book
Experience Jean Houston's voice as she guides the listener through processes for groups or individuals. Journey with her through the stages of human development.

Godseed: The Journey of Christ

Jean Houston revitalizes the story of Christ by presenting to readers the possibility of "being Christs." Dr. Houston draws from philosophy, mythology, Jungian psychology, mysticism, anthropology, new science, and just plain creativity to present the familiar gospel stories in a new light.

Godseed Audio Tapes

Narrated by Jean Houston as a companion to the book
Jean Houston's voice guides the listener through most of the exercises in her book. These exercises—covering major events in the life of Christ, including birth, baptism, healing ministry, death, and resurrection—help listeners realize the story of the Christ happening right now in the heart.

FORTHCOMING QUEST BOOKS FROM JEAN HOUSTON

The Mystery School Series: American Archetypes

A three-book series based on Jean Houston's Mystery School seminars.

Book I is *Public Like A Frog: Entering the Lives of Three Great Americans.* Through lectures and processes drawn from the lives of Emily Dickinson, Thomas Jefferson, and Helen Keller, Jean Houston encourages readers to discover their public self as well as their private spiritual identity. **Available Fall, 1993.**

Books II and III continue Jean Houston's exploration of the archetypes which shape and inform the American experience. **Available Fall, 1994 and Fall, 1995.**

For more information or for a free catalog please write to:
Quest Books
The Theosophical Publishing House
P.O. Box 270, Wheaton, Illinois 60189-0270

QUEST BOOKS
are published by
The Theosophical Society in America,
Wheaton, Illinois 60189-0270,
a branch of a world organization
dedicated to the promotion of the unity of
humanity and the encouragement of the study of
religion, philosophy, and science, to the end that
we may better understand ourselves and our place in
the universe. The Society stands for complete
freedom of individual search and belief.